Deterring America

Faced with America's military superiority, many countries are
turning to weapons of mass destruction (WMD) as a means to deter
United States intervention. However, the events of 11 September
awakened America to a degree of vulnerability it had never
experienced before, making it increasingly unwilling to tolerate
such weapons in the hands of unstable and unpredictable regimes.
Through theoretical, historical, and prescriptive lenses, this book
explores the modern security dilemma created by the twin fears of
American encroachment and vulnerability which form a vicious
cycle of insecurity that challenges traditional notions of deterrence.
Using Iraq and North Korea as case studies, Derek Smith argues
that the United States may need to reevaluate its foreign policy
strategies against WMD proliferation, giving renewed attention to
defensive measures, negotiated disarmament, interdiction, and
perhaps preemption.

DEREK D. SMITH is currently studying at Yale Law School. He
received an AB in Government from Harvard University and a
D.Phil. in International Relations from Oxford University as a
Keasbey Scholar. He has written articles on nonproliferation issues
for *Security Studies, National Security Studies Quarterly*, and *The
Korean Journal of Defense Analysis* and has taught international
security courses at Oxford and Yale.

Deterring America

Rogue States and the Proliferation
of Weapons of Mass Destruction

DEREK D. SMITH

CAMBRIDGE
UNIVERSITY PRESS

CAMBRIDGE UNIVERSITY PRESS
Cambridge, New York, Melbourne, Madrid, Cape Town, Singapore, São Paulo

Cambridge University Press
The Edinburgh Building, Cambridge CB2 2RU, UK

Published in the United States of America by Cambridge University Press, New York

www.cambridge.org
Information on this title: www.cambridge.org/9780521683135

First published 2006

Printed in the United Kingdom at the University Press, Cambridge

A catalogue record for this publication is available from the British Library

ISBN-13 978-0-521-86465-7   hardback
ISBN-10 0-521-86465-8   hardback

ISBN-13 978-0-521-68313-5   paperback
ISBN-10 0-521-68313-0   paperback

For my family

Contents

Acknowledgments

Thanks to Yuen Foong Khong for his guidance and encouragement when this book was a rough idea for a Master's thesis. Rick Cupitt, Christopher Ford, John Gaddis, Colin Gray, Oona Hathaway, Daniel Joyner, Rob McAnnally, Mitchell Reiss, Ashley Roach, Delbert Smith, Hew Strachan, and Ruth Wedgwood were extremely helpful in talking through ideas and reviewing parts of the manuscript. I am also indebted to numerous individuals who were willing to give of their time and participate in interviews. For their much-appreciated assistance and advice during the publication process, I thank John Haslam, Jackie Warren, Carol Fellingham Webb, and Maria Angelaki of Cambridge University Press. Finally, I am grateful to my family for their support and love throughout.

Earlier versions of some of the material in this book appeared in articles published in the journals *Security Studies* and *The Korean Journal of Defense Analysis*, and are included here with their permission.

Abbreviations

BW	biological weapons
CB	chemical-biological weapons
CW	chemical weapons
DMZ	de-militarized zone
DPRK	Democratic People's Republic of Korea
IAEA	International Atomic Energy Agency
IMO	International Maritime Organization
MAD	mutual assured destruction
NMD	National Missile Defense
NPT	Nonproliferation Treaty
NSS	National Security Strategy
PSI	Proliferation Security Initiative
SUA	Convention on the Suppression of Unlawful Acts against the Safety of Maritime Navigation
UN	United Nations
UNCLOS	United Nations Convention on the Law of the Sea
WMD	weapons of mass destruction

Part I   Deterrence in a modern era

I Introduction

The tragic events of 11 September 2001 challenged traditional conceptions of deterrence. Notwithstanding the immense retaliatory capabilities of the United States, an adversary was willing to attack and face the consequences. This was likely because an organization such as Al Qaeda is decentralized, and so is relatively insulated against US reprisals. As President Bush remarked in a speech at West Point in June 2002, "Deterrence – the promise of massive retaliation against nations – means nothing against shadowy terrorist networks with no nation or citizens to defend."[1] It may seem somewhat puzzling, then, to broaden the crisis of confidence in deterrence to include so-called "rogue"[2] states that do have a nation and citizens to defend. Justification for such an extension would generally only arise if leaders of rogue states were extreme risk-takers or confident that they could assist terrorists without being discovered.[3] Bush continued, "Containment is not possible when unbalanced dictators with weapons of mass destruction can deliver those weapons on missiles

[1] George W. Bush, Graduation Speech, West Point, New York, 1 June 2002.

[2] Many authors take issue with the fairly widespread practice of grouping worrisome states together with the descriptive but depreciatory adjective "rogue." Unfortunately, alternatives such as "states of concern" have failed to make their way into common usage, and a collective term is necessary. See "Defining terms" on p. 12 for further detail. See also Eric Herring, "Rogue Rage: Can We Prevent Mass Destruction?" *Journal of Strategic Studies* vol. 23, no. 1 (March 2000): 188–212.

[3] This is a very contentious issue, particularly because alleged ties to Al Qaeda were part of the justification for the 2003 US invasion of Iraq, but were later explicitly rejected by a July 2004 Senate Intelligence Committee Report. See US Senate, Select Committee on Intelligence, *Report on the US Intelligence Community's Prewar Intelligence Assessments on Iraq* (Washington DC: 7 July 2004). Available at http://www.gpoaccess.gov/serialset/creports/iraq.html. See also Dana Priest, "Al Qaeda–Iraq Link Recanted," *Washington Post*, 1 August 2004. For an opposing viewpoint, see Bill Gertz, "British Report Links Al Qaeda, Baghdad," *Washington Times*, 15 July 2004.

or secretly provide them to terrorist allies."[4] In such circumstances, according to the September 2002 *National Security Strategy* (NSS), the United States should consider pursuing offensive means to defeat the threat:

> We must be prepared to stop rogue states and their terrorist clients before they are able to threaten or use weapons of mass destruction against the United States and our allies and friends . . . Given the goals of rogue states and terrorists, the United States can no longer solely rely on a reactive posture as we have in the past.[5]

The trouble is that the United States does not have a clear sense of the goals of most rogue states. It may be that their leaders seek weapons of mass destruction (WMD)[6] for largely protective purposes, intending only to threaten their use. Unlike suicide bombers, such states may seek to portray themselves as defensively suicidal, like a national land mine primed to detonate and injure the trespasser as well as destroy itself. This was effectively Iraq's strategy prior to the 2003 US invasion (Operation Iraqi Freedom), when Saddam Hussein obliquely threatened to employ WMD in the event of war.[7] Although the United States decided to proceed anyway, there was intense concern at the time over the likelihood and consequences of Iraqi WMD use,[8] which hardly inspires confidence for a similar resolution of such conflicts in the future.

---

[4] George Bush, Graduation Speech, 1 June 2002.

[5] US Government, *The National Security Strategy of the United States of America* (Washington DC: September 2002), 14, 15.

[6] While use of the collective term "WMD" is commonly understood and analytically practical, it carries the risk of overlooking important distinctions between nuclear, biological, and chemical weapons. I discuss such differences in greater detail in "Defining terms" on p. 12.

[7] Inspections after Iraqi Freedom, of course, have failed to reveal WMD stockpiles in Iraq. See Special Advisor to the Director of Central Intelligence, *Comprehensive Report on Iraq's Weapons of Mass Destruction* (30 September 2004). Available at http://www.cia.gov/cia/reports/iraq_wmd_2004/index.html.

[8] See James Dao, "Pentagon's Worry: Iraqi Chemical Arms," *New York Times*, 19 May 2002; Milton Viorst, "Imagining the Worst-Case Scenario in Iraq,"

Since the goals of rogue states are not static, US actions (such as Iraqi Freedom) and policies (such as the NSS) may alter calculations as to whether WMD acquisition is a wise choice. Although some states may moderate their policies and renounce WMD – as Libya has done – it appears just as likely that others will seek more robustly to deter interference in their affairs by threatening and potentially initiating WMD attacks, either against troops on the battlefield, US allies, or the American homeland itself. If rogue states choose the latter course, despite the outcome of Iraqi Freedom, the growing destructiveness of their capabilities may lead US officials eventually to back down from similar confrontations given the inherent risks posed by a less ambiguously WMD-armed adversary. This has become a particularly salient point in the ongoing disarmament impasse with North Korea and Iran, as it appears that the United States has all but ruled out military strikes and is reluctant to impose harsh economic penalties in response to likely advances in their respective nuclear programs. In this way, the current US strategy could be both self-defeating and counterproductive, leading to greater proliferation and consequently more chances for WMD transfers to terrorist organizations.

Without a strong understanding of the varying motivations behind rogue state development of WMD, a standardized response to proliferation runs the risk of not disarming the most dangerous states, or attempting to disarm those better left alone. This book aims to provide a framework for a more nuanced US response to WMD proliferation. It will consider US action in regional crises and conflicts involving important interests, ranging from the reversal of local

New York Times, 12 September 2002; Bradley Graham, " 'Scorched Earth' Plans in Iraq Cited," Washington Post, 19 December 2002; Philip Smucker, "Iraq Flexes its Military Trump Card," Christian Science Monitor, 19 March 2003; Greg Jaffe, "Intelligence Suggests Hussein Allowed Chemical-Weapon Use," Wall Street Journal, 20 March 2003; David E. Sanger, "US Officials Fear Iraqis Plan to Use Gas on GIs," New York Times, 25 March 2003; Jessica Guynn, "As Coalition Nears Baghdad, Chemical Arms a Question Mark," The Mercury News, 3 April 2003; Thomas Fuller, "Iraq Vows 'Unconventional' Tactics to Defend Capital," New York Times, 4 April 2003; Bill Gertz, "Coalition Still Wary of Chemical Weapons," Washington Times, 5 April 2003.

aggression to the destruction of terrorist camps and WMD facilities, or even the removal of an adversary's regime. A major premise is that deterrence is in a state of flux as regional powers attempt to employ WMD to deter the United States and neutralize its conventional weapon superiority, while the United States tries to avoid being deterred and to maintain leverage over potential adversaries. Resolution of these conflicting ambitions will depend on a combination of interests, military capability, and resolve. In remote conflicts, the United States will become ever more reluctant to fight for non-vital matters under the shadow of catastrophic damage, and its adversaries will thereby become more willing to run the risk of severe counterattack. This book will also evaluate various foreign policy options for responding to these strategic changes, including a preventive war doctrine and the potential for a global quarantine against WMD.

REASSESSING DETERRENCE

A threshold issue is whether deterrence alone can suffice to provide for US security. According to traditional deterrence theory – developed during the bipolar era of mutual assured destruction (MAD) between the superpowers – the sheer terrifying potential of weapons of mass destruction ought to make them suitable only for defensive purposes.[9] Speaking of nuclear weapons, Kenneth Waltz claims, "[N]othing can be done with them other than to use them for deterrence."[10] In an imaginative illustration, Robert Sandoval muses, "With the defense of its borders entrusted to forces structured around the firepower of nuclear weapons, any nation not now a nuclear power, and not harboring ambitions for territorial aggrandizement, could walk like a porcupine through the forests of international affairs: no threat to its neighbors, too prickly for predators to

---

[9] A.J.C. Edwards, *Nuclear Weapons, the Balance of Terror, the Quest for Peace* (London: Macmillan, 1986), 3.

[10] Kenneth N. Waltz, "Waltz Responds to Sagan," in Scott D. Sagan and Kenneth N. Waltz, *The Spread of Nuclear Weapons: A Debate* (New York: W.W. Norton, 1995), 98.

swallow."[11] Seemingly confirmed by the nearly half-century of peace during the Cold War, this formulation runs into two fundamental dilemmas in the post-Cold War era.

First, there may be, or could be in the future, WMD "porcupines" in the world that do have ambitions for territorial aggrandizement; some states may use a mutual deterrent relationship to provide strategic cover for local aggression, a phenomenon referred to as the "stability–instability paradox."[12] A rogue state need not ever carry out an actual WMD attack, or even threaten it, as long as it is enough of a possibility to make the expected costs of military action unacceptable to the United States. For example, in 1990 Saddam Hussein "saw his extensive arsenal of mass destruction weapons, especially Iraq's known chemical weapon capacity, as a strategic umbrella to dissuade any foreign interference in his plans" for Kuwait.[13] As with Iraqi Freedom, although Hussein miscalculated in his assessment,[14] it is not difficult to envision similar scenarios where less substantial aggression coupled with more robust WMD capabilities could lead the United States to think twice about risking that a war would remain conventional.

Second, while a state may not be overtly expansionist, the 11 September attacks sharpened the world's awareness of the danger of allowing unstable or revolutionary regimes to harbor terrorist elements within their borders, providing them with cover as they plot for the perfect opportunity to strike. Beyond providing sanctuary, some antagonistic leaders may develop symbiotic relationships with terrorist organizations, employing them as proxies to carry out an attack which they can then disavow as the handiwork of unknown extremists. Even if a state does not have direct links to terrorist networks, it

---

[11] Robert R. Sandoval, "Consider the Porcupine: Another View of Nuclear Proliferation," *The Bulletin of the Atomic Scientists* vol. 32, no. 5 (May 1976): 19.

[12] Robert Jervis, *The Illogic of American Nuclear Strategy* (Ithaca, NY: Cornell University Press, 1984), 29–34. Deterrence theorists often cite the Soviet invasion of Afghanistan in 1979 as a classic example of this concept.

[13] Avigdor Haselkorn, *The Continuing Storm: Iraq, Poisonous Weapons, and Deterrence* (New Haven, CT: Yale University Press, 1999), 19.   [14] See chapter 3.

might sell on the black market WMD that could eventually end up in the wrong hands.[15] In these scenarios, traditional deterrence theory is far from conclusive. By enabling offensive activity, WMD may strain mutual deterrence to the limits. How to approach these dangerous situations, when the world community may simply not be able to leave the porcupines of the forest alone, is the main challenge this book seeks to address.

Uncertainty regarding the concept of deterrence is not in any way a result of its suffering from academic neglect. There is an extensive literature on the bipolar dynamics of the Cold War,[16] the history and strategy of rogue states,[17] the effects of asymmetries of power and

---

[15] North Korea has not been a model of restraint in its proliferation activities; see David E. Sanger and William J. Broad, "Evidence is Cited Linking Koreans to Libya Uranium," *New York Times*, 23 May 2004; Donald Kirk, "N. Korea Flirts with 'Red Line,'" *Christian Science Monitor*, 28 May 2004.

[16] See Bernard Brodie, *The Absolute Weapon: Atomic Power and World Order* (New York: Harcourt, 1946); Henry Kissinger, *Nuclear Weapons and Foreign Policy* (New York: Harper & Brothers, 1957); Robert Osgood, *Limited War: The Challenge to American Security* (Chicago: University of Chicago Press, 1957); Albert Wohlstetter, "The Delicate Balance of Terror," *Foreign Affairs* vol. 37, no. 2 (January 1959): 211–34; Morton Halperin, *Limited War in the Nuclear Age* (Westport, CT: Greenwood Press, 1963); Wolfgang K.H. Panofsky, "The Mutual-Hostage Relationship between America and Russia," *Foreign Affairs* vol. 52, no. 1 (October 1973): 109–18; Paul H. Nitze, "Deterring our Deterrent," *Foreign Policy* no. 25 (winter 1976–77): 195–210.

[17] See Adel Darwish and Gregory Alexander, *Unholy Babylon: The Secret History of Saddam's War* (London: Victor Gollancz, 1991); Kenneth Katzman, *The Warriors of Islam: Iran's Revolutionary Guard* (Oxford: Westview Press, 1993); Rick Atkinson, *Crusade: The Untold Story of the Gulf War* (London: HarperCollins, 1994); Michael J. Mazarr, *North Korea and the Bomb: A Case Study in Nonproliferation* (London: Macmillan, 1995); Michael R. Gordon and Bernard E. Trainor, *The General's War* (New York: Little, Brown and Company, 1995); Don Oberdorfer, *The Two Koreas: A Contemporary History* (London: Warner Books, 1997); Leon V. Sigal, *Disarming Strangers: Nuclear Diplomacy with North Korea* (Princeton, NJ: Princeton University Press, 1998); Anthony H. Cordesman, *Iran's Military Forces in Transition: Conventional Threats and Weapons of Mass Destruction* (Westport, CT: Praeger, 1999); Kongdan Oh and Ralph C. Hassig, *North Korea: Through the Looking Glass* (Washington DC: Brookings Institution Press, 2000); Said K. Aburish, *Saddam Hussein: The Politics of Revenge* (London: Bloomsbury, 2000); Andrew Cockburn and Patrick Cockburn, *Out of the Ashes: The Resurrection of Saddam Hussein* (London: Verso, 2000); Timothy V. McCarthy, "Saddam's Toxic Arsenal: Chemical and Biological Weapons in the Gulf Wars," in *Planning the Unthinkable: How New Powers will use Nuclear, Biological, and Chemical Weapons*, edited by Peter R. Lavoy, Scott D. Sagan, and James J. Wirtz (Ithaca, NY: Cornell University Press, 2000);

interest,[18] WMD proliferation,[19] the psychological aspects of crisis situations,[20] the specter of terrorism,[21] prospects for missile defense and counterproliferation,[22] and more general theoretical analyses of

Joseph S. Bermudez Jr., *The Armed Forces of North Korea* (New York: I.B. Tauris, 2001); Victor D. Cha, "Making Sense of the Black Box: Hypotheses on Strategic Doctrine and the DPRK Threat," in *The North Korean System in the Post-Cold War Era*, edited by Samuel S. Kim (New York: Palgrave, 2001); Kori N. Schake and Judith S. Yaphe, *The Strategic Implications of a Nuclear-Armed Iran*, McNair Paper No. 64 (Washington DC: Institute for National Strategic Studies, National Defense University, 2001); Anthony C. Cain, *Iran's Strategic Culture and Weapons of Mass Destruction*, Maxwell Paper No. 26 (Maxwell Air Force Base, AL: Air War College, April 2002); Shahram Chubin, *Whither Iran? Reform, Domestic Politics and National Security*, Adelphi Paper No. 342 (Oxford: Oxford University Press, International Institute for Strategic Studies, 2002).

[18] See Andrew Mack, "Why Big Nations Lose Small Wars: The Politics of Asymmetric Conflict," *World Politics* vol. 27, no. 2 (January 1975): 175–200; Yohanan Cohen, *Small Nations in Times of Crisis and Confrontation* (Albany, NY: State University of New York Press, 1989); Barry Wolf, *When the Weak Attack the Strong: Failures of Deterrence*, RAND Note (Santa Monica, CA: RAND, 1991); T.V. Paul, *Asymmetric Conflicts: War Initiation by Weaker Powers* (Cambridge: Cambridge University Press, 1994).

[19] See Leonard S. Spector, with Jacqueline R. Smith, *Nuclear Ambitions: The Spread of Nuclear Weapons 1989–1990* (Boulder, CO: Westview Press, 1990); Kathleen C. Bailey, *Doomsday Weapons in the Hands of Many: The Arms Control Challenge of the 90s* (Chicago: University of Illinois Press, 1991); Martin van Creveld, *Nuclear Proliferation and the Future of Conflict* (New York: The Free Press, 1993); William E. Burrows and Robert Windrem, *Critical Mass: The Dangerous Race for Superweapons in a Fragmenting World* (London: Simon & Schuster, 1994).

[20] See Robert Jervis, *Perception and Misperception in International Politics* (Princeton, NJ: Princeton University Press, 1976); Irving L. Janis and Leon Mann, *Decision Making: A Psychological Analysis of Conflict* (New York: The Free Press, 1977).

[21] See Marvin E. Wolfgang, *International Terrorism* (Beverly Hills, CA: Sage, 1982); Jessica Stern, *The Ultimate Terrorists* (Cambridge, MA: Harvard University Press, 1999); Gary Ackerman and Laura Snyder, "Would They if They Could?" *Bulletin of the Atomic Scientists* vol. 58, no. 3 (May/June 2002): 41–47; Jessica Stern, *Terror in the Name of God: Why Religious Militants Kill* (New York: Ecco, 2003); Graham Allison, *Nuclear Terrorism: The Ultimate Preventable Catastrophe* (New York: Times Books, 2004).

[22] See Barry R. Schneider, *Future War and Counterproliferation: US Military Responses to NBC Proliferation Threats* (Westport, CT: Praeger, 1999); Bernard I. Finel, "The Role of Aerospace Power in US Counterproliferation Strategy," *Air & Space Power Journal* vol. 13, no. 4 (winter 1999): 77–89; *Biological Weapons: Limiting the Threat*, edited by Joshua Lederberg (Cambridge, MA: The MIT Press, 1999); *Prevailing in a Well-Armed World: Devising Competitive Strategies against Weapons Proliferation*, edited by Henry D. Sokolski (Carlisle, PA: Strategic Studies Institute, 2000); Dean Wilkening, *Ballistic-Missile Defence and Strategic Stability*, Adelphi Paper No. 334 (Oxford: Oxford University Press, International Institute for Strategic Studies, 2000); James J. Wirtz and Jeffrey A. Larsen, *Rockets Red Glare: Missile Defense and the*

deterrence.[23] Its rich scholarly heritage notwithstanding, the collapse of the Soviet Union and the accelerating proliferation of WMD necessitate a new look into how deterrence theory should inform foreign policy decisions. The world is no longer a stand-off of the titans; rather, it can be described as "a strange hybrid, a *uni-multipolar* system with one superpower and several major powers."[24] In this strategic environment, conflict is much more likely to be between mismatched nations, as the United States confronts various weaker regional opponents. While each side can certainly harm the other, potentially severely, assured destruction is no longer mutual in quite the same way.[25] Because of this, deterrence interactions will probably be unlike those in the past, and thus require fresh examination.

The Bush administration has correctly identified deterrence as an area of strategic uncertainty, but has put the cart before the horse

Footnote 22 (*cont.*)

> *Future of World Politics* (Boulder, CO: Westview Press, 2001); James M. Lindsay and Michael E. O'Hanlon, *Defending America: The Case for Limited National Missile Defense* (Washington DC: Brookings Institution Press, 2001); *The Gathering Biological Warfare Storm*, edited by Jim A. Davis and Barry R. Schneider (Maxwell Air Force Base, AL: USAF Counterproliferation Center, 2002); Michael A. Levi, *Fire in the Hole: Nuclear and Non-Nuclear Options for Counterproliferation*, Working Paper No. 31 (Washington DC: Carnegie Endowment for International Peace, November 2002); Robert S. Litwak, "The New Calculus of Pre-emption," *Survival* vol. 44, no. 4 (winter 2002–03): 53–80; Jason D. Ellis, "The Best Defense: Counterproliferation and US National Security," *The Washington Quarterly* vol. 26, no. 2 (spring 2003): 115–33.

[23] See Thomas C. Schelling, *Arms and Influence* (New Haven, CT: Yale University Press, 1966); Patrick M. Morgan, *Deterrence: A Conceptual Analysis* (Beverly Hills, CA: Sage, 1977); Kenneth N. Waltz, *The Spread of Nuclear Weapons: More May Be Better*, Adelphi Paper No. 171 (London: International Institute for Strategic Studies, 1981); Edward Rhodes, *Power and MADness: The Logic of Nuclear Coercion* (New York: Columbia University Press, 1989); Keith B. Payne, *The Fallacies of Cold War Deterrence and a New Direction* (Lexington, KY: The University Press of Kentucky, 2001); Patrick M. Morgan, *Deterrence Now* (Cambridge: Cambridge University Press, 2003); Lawrence Freedman, *Deterrence* (Cambridge: Polity Press, 2004).

[24] Samuel P. Huntington, "The Lonely Superpower," *Foreign Affairs* vol. 78, no. 2 (March/April 1999): 36 (italics in the original).

[25] Beyond an asymmetrical ability to cause harm, the United States has also developed incredibly sophisticated defensive technologies that may allow its military to fight and win even on a battlefield contaminated by chemical and biological weapons, potentially undermining an adversary's deterrent threat. Advances in missile defense systems, although far more controversial, may have a similar effect. See chapter 5.

by not developing a framework for determining when it is most likely to succeed or fail. Without a more fine-tuned approach, the international community is likely to label the US strategy a blunt tool of veiled aggression, potentially inviting resistance from US allies and retaliation from its adversaries. This subject thus not only has immediate relevance in crafting more practical counterproliferation options against rogue states, but has considerable import for international order more generally. Of course, there will unavoidably be great disagreement over how free a hand the United States ought to have in intervening abroad, much of it depending on one's perspective. Limiting America's freedom of action might seem like a welcome development to those discontented with a perceived trend toward US unilateralism.[26] Some Chinese officials, in particular, are worried that US efforts to protect itself against coercion and blackmail, such as through missile defenses, "will make the American military too brave, and that will be very, very dangerous for everyone."[27] Given the mixed record of US foreign policy, including instances when America probably overstepped its bounds, this is an understandable concern.[28]

On the other side are those who rely on the United States for their security, or believe that only America has the military strength capable of providing the backbone for international order and peace.[29] The United States may not have an impeccable nation-building record, and may at times be neglectful when it comes to humanitarian intervention, but it still plays a major role in many peacekeeping operations and helps to keep some regional hotspots from flaring into war through mediation and security guarantees. To some, the prospect of the United States being deterred from responding to rogue

[26] Stephen M. Walt, "Beyond Bin Laden: Reshaping US Foreign Policy," *International Security* vol. 26, no. 3 (winter 2001–02): 60.

[27] Quoted in Erik Eckholm, "Experts Try to Make Missile Shield Plan Palatable to China," *New York Times*, 28 January 2001.

[28] For a slightly charged account of America's past sins, see William Blum, *Rogue State: A Guide to the World's Only Superpower* (London: Zed Books, 2001).

[29] See, e.g., Charles Krauthammer, "The Unipolar Moment," *Foreign Affairs* vol. 70, no. 1 (1990–91): 25; Samuel Huntington, "Why International Primacy Matters," *International Security* vol. 17, no. 4 (spring 1993): 82.

state provocations would mean a much more dangerous world, one in which regimes like the Taliban would remain in control of Afghanistan, providing a safe haven for Al Qaeda to continue master-minding terrorist plots around the globe. Moreover, small, weak states are likely to be the most vulnerable if the United States is forced to retreat into a "Fortress America" mentality.[30] Kuwait might not be a country today if the United States had not led the United Nations (UN) coalition to confront Iraq in 1990–91. Victor Utgoff notes, "the world needs at least one state, preferably several, willing and able to play the role of sheriff, or to be members of a sheriff's posse, even in the face of nuclear threats."[31]

As one might imagine, neither side is entirely convincing on its own. Richard Betts makes the astute observation that "American activism to guarantee international stability is, paradoxically, the prime source of American vulnerability."[32] If the United States over-reaches itself and gains a reputation as a unilateral bully, it is likely to find much needed international cooperation in peacekeeping and nation-building missions lacking as well as growing resistance to its policies. In sum, it is far from apparent what kind of strategic doctrine will serve US interests, and this book attempts to shed light on how best to make an educated guess.

DEFINING TERMS

Given that Cold War deterrence theory was so heavily dominated by considerations of the nuclear balance, it is worth remembering that other weapons are likely to take center stage during conflicts in the post-Cold War era. For instance, biological weapons (BW), chemical

---

[30] James R. Schlesinger, "The Strategic Consequences of Nuclear Proliferation," in *Arms Control for the Late Sixties*, edited by James E. Dougherty and J.F. Lehman Jr. (Princeton: D. Van Nostrand, 1967), 175.

[31] Victor A. Utgoff, "Proliferation, Missile Defence and American Ambitions," *Survival* vol. 44, no. 2 (summer 2002): 90. See also Colin Gray, *The Sheriff: America's Defense of the New World Order* (Lexington, KY: University Press of Kentucky, 2004).

[32] Richard K. Betts, "The New Threat of Mass Destruction," *Foreign Affairs* vol. 77, no. 1 (January/February 1998): 28.

weapons (CW), and radiological weapons are all capable of causing extreme damage, and may be more readily accessible to rogue states and terrorists than a complete nuclear device. Even certain conventional weapons, with exotic names like "fuel air explosives" and "thermobaric bombs," are beginning to have yields that rival nuclear blasts.[33] At the same time, these military technologies have significant differences that are important to note, especially regarding the ease with which they are weaponized and employed in wartime. Analysts often single out smallpox, for example, as an incredibly infectious biological agent that would be quite difficult to contain if released among a civilian population.[34] As dangerous as this virus would be in the hands of a terrorist, it would be fairly difficult to use effectively in a tactical operation on the battlefield given the possibility of inoculation, the delayed manifestation of symptoms, and the technical challenges involved in engineering a warhead that would not destroy its contents upon impact. Conversely, CW such as sarin and mustard gas are more readily employed in wartime situations given their immediate effect, but would be difficult to spread among a civilian population unless delivered efficiently in a crowded environment. Overall, despite the important distinctions between different types of weapons, which I will note when relevant, for the purposes of this book a collective term is needed and WMD offers a simple, commonly used, and analytically helpful shorthand.[35]

An even more contentious debate over terminology persists owing to the lack of a useful and widely accepted alternative to the somewhat pejorative term of "rogue states." Such an adjective is likely to conjure up negative connotations, leading to the implicit assumption that these states are aggressively inclined and rarely adhere to the norms and rules of international relations. This is problematic not least because the list of "rogues" seems to be rather fluid,

---

[33] See Andre C. Revkin, "Advanced Armaments," *New York Times*, 3 December 2001.

[34] William J. Broad, Stephen Engelberg, and James Glanz, "Assessing Risks, Chemical, Biological, Even Nuclear," *New York Times*, 1 November 2001.

[35] Although the proliferation of missile technology is also a major security threat, I do not include missiles within the definition of "weapons of mass destruction."

with today's friend quite easily becoming tomorrow's enemy, and vice versa. As one commentator put it: "The reality is that whether a country is perceived as a threat or a rogue state or a member of the 'axis of evil' is more closely linked to whether countries are perceived to be friendly toward the United States than it is to a state's actual behavior or the actual threat it poses to international order."[36] Moreover, states such as Pakistan seem to straddle the boundary of the term, and others like Syria and Iran are clearly in a transitional phase that makes placing them in a collective category without differentiation somewhat problematic.

Yet, as with the acronym WMD, a more general term is necessary for discussions of proliferation issues with a broad and theoretical perspective, and no substitute has taken hold in the literature. This does not mean that I agree with the current US classification, though it does include several states that have had a troubling track record in recent international conflicts from any perspective. I use "rogue state" more as an analytic tool to describe states, and will rely upon the working definition provided by Elaine Bunn: "those who brutalize their own people, display no regard for international law, threaten their neighbors, are determined to acquire weapons of mass destruction, sponsor terrorism around the globe, and reject basic human values."[37] To balance objectives I will mention specific states whenever possible, but use the term "rogue states" when appropriate, keeping in mind that this is an elastic grouping with a disputed membership.

ORGANIZATION

This book aims to analyze WMD proliferation through theoretical, historical, and prescriptive lenses. Chapter 2 employs the first, establishing a theoretical foundation from which to analyze case studies and extract policy recommendations. It will introduce some of the

---

[36] Pascal Boniface, "What Justifies Regime Change?" *The Washington Quarterly* vol. 26, no. 3 (summer 2003): 67.

[37] M. Elaine Bunn, "Preemptive Action: When, How, and to What Effect?" *Strategic Forum*, no. 200 (July 2003): 3.

elementary concepts of deterrence theory, outlining several of its basic assumptions and briefly reviewing the history of nuclear strategy. It will also reveal some potential flaws in the theoretical construct of deterrence, cataloguing examples of extreme risk-taking, explaining the influence of asymmetries of interest and psychological effects, and analyzing the special challenges posed by last resort threats and millenarian regimes.

Then, in Part II, chapters 3 and 4 will apply this theoretical construct to the real world, examining the US deterrence relationship with Iraq and North Korea, the two most significant contemporary examples of asymmetrical WMD deterrence. Each case study will draw upon chapter 2 to explain how deterrence operated in these intensely dangerous situations.

Part III of the book will be forward-looking, considering how to craft US foreign policy in light of the changing nature of deterrence. Chapter 5 will begin by introducing various options available to US policymakers besides deterrence, including export controls, defenses, and preemptive strikes. Faced with the possibility that these traditional tools may be inadequate to cope with new threats, chapter 6 will delve more deeply into the dilemmas posed by preventive war, exploring its historical, legal, and strategic ramifications. Finally, chapter 7 will propose a novel approach to WMD proliferation: establishing a global quarantine against all forms of WMD transfer.

2 Deterrence theory and its flaws

Deterrence as a concept is hardly new, dating back even to the Babylonian Code of Hammurabi in the seventeenth century BC, when virtually any serious crime was punishable by death.[1] In fact, threats of retaliation and punishment are a feature of everyday life, from parents attempting to discipline their children to statesmen haggling over the details of a treaty. In the words of Thomas Schelling, "Nations, like people, are continually engaged in demonstrations of resolve, tests of nerve, and explorations for understandings and misunderstandings."[2] Given its ubiquitous presence, it is not surprising to discover that deterrence has attracted the attention of scholars and policymakers alike.

Yet, despite this interest, deterrence is still often misunderstood and remains an elusive concept. Leaders are dumbfounded when their threats are ignored, and equally struggle to discern whether the threats of their adversaries are genuine. Largely this is because deterrence is at root a psychological phenomenon, and it will never be possible to be certain of another person's state of mind. Even though some ambiguity will persist, however, it does not follow that the United States should categorically accept or reject the functioning of deterrence. Pursuing the former could invite the limited aggression and sanctuaries for terrorists mentioned in chapter 1. Adopting the latter is a recipe for global conflict and perhaps greater insecurity. A better understanding of the principles behind deterrence is the first

---

[1] Jean-Louis Gergorin, "Deterrence in the Post-Cold War Era," in *The Use of Force: Military Power and International Relations*, edited by Robert J. Art and Kenneth N. Waltz, 4th edition (Lanham, MD: University Press of America, 1993), 447.

[2] Thomas C. Schelling, *Arms and Influence* (New Haven, CT: Yale University Press, 1966), 93.

step toward striking a middle ground between these extremes and crafting a sensible US policy against WMD proliferation. This chapter will present the classic formulation of deterrence theory, its historical context, and its potential shortcomings.

BASIC CONCEPTS

Deterrence traditionally means persuading an opponent that the costs of a particular action will outweigh any potential benefits.[3] The aspect of persuading an opponent alludes to the psychological nature of deterrence, often an interplay of uncertain promises and threats that may be bluffs or firm commitments. Also, the reference to potential benefits highlights the future-oriented nature of any deterrent threat, promising a certain reaction only in response to the undesired choice of another actor. If, on the other hand, a form of punishment is threatened to spur action, or administered until the other side acts, scholars typically label the strategy as compellence.[4] This difference is significant because while an adversary facing a deterrent threat can pretend that it never intended to act, compliance with a compellent threat often involves open submission to specific demands of the compeller, and thus may inflict greater reputational costs on the opponent for giving in.[5]

Another important distinction concerns the nature of the response to an adversary's action. Glenn Snyder explains that, "Essentially, deterrence means discouraging the enemy from taking military action by posing for him a prospect of cost and risk outweighing his prospective gain. Defense means reducing our own prospective costs and risks in the event that deterrence fails."[6] Obviously the two can be combined, and a robust defense is likely

---

[3] Alexander L. George and Richard Smoke, *Deterrence in American Foreign Policy: Theory and Practice* (New York: Columbia University Press, 1974), 11.

[4] Schelling, *Arms and Influence*, 70.

[5] Dean Wilkening and Kenneth Watman, *Nuclear Deterrence in a Regional Context* (Santa Monica, CA: RAND, 1995), 68.

[6] Glenn Snyder, "Deterrence and Defense," in *The Use of Force*, edited by Art and Waltz, 350.

to make a deterrent threat especially menacing. Similarly, theorists distinguish between deterrence based on denial (attempting to convince an adversary that he is unlikely to achieve his objective) and that based on punishment (threatening to destroy something the opponent values greatly). Deterrence can also be based on positive inducements rather than merely negative consequences: reassurance is a tactic where one seeks to convince an adversary of one's benign intentions, hoping to forestall aggressive action; conciliation involves offering rewards to an opponent in order to achieve the same result.[7]

Finally, deterrence theory draws important distinctions between general and immediate deterrence, and direct and extended deterrence.[8] General deterrence refers to a rivalry between states that may lead one side to anticipate potential enemies and seek to change the overall balance of power, but rarely includes overt military threats. By contrast, immediate deterrence consists of a challenger making an explicit threat to use military force and the defender attempting to dissuade the opponent from attacking by threatening some form of reprisal. Direct deterrence describes the familiar Cold War relationship where each superpower seeks to prevent nuclear attacks on its homeland, whereas extended deterrence involves attempts to protect regional allies from war. Again, any real-world cases will likely involve a mixture of all of these categories. During the 1990–91 Gulf War, for instance, the United States was concerned about direct attacks on American cities, as well as missile strikes against Israel and Saudi Arabia. Though the lack of functioning long-range missiles limits most rogue states to threatening regional targets, their capacity for state-

---

[7] David Garnham, *Deterrence Essentials: Keys to Controlling an Adversary's Behavior* (Abu Dhabi: Emirates Center for Strategic Studies and Research, 1995), 8.

[8] This section is drawn from Herman Kahn, *On Thermonuclear War* (Princeton, NJ: Princeton University Press, 1969), 126–44; Patrick M. Morgan, *Deterrence: A Conceptual Analysis* (Beverly Hills, CA: Sage, 1977), ch. 2; Kenneth Watman and Dean Wilkening, with John Arquilla and Brian Nichiporuk, *US Regional Deterrence Strategies* (Santa Monica, CA: RAND, 1995), 13–15; Patrick M. Morgan, *Deterrence Now* (Cambridge: Cambridge University Press, 2003), 80–115.

sponsored international terrorism involving WMD requires a consideration of both direct and extended deterrence.

DETERRENCE STRATEGIES

Underlying any deterrent threat are the closely intertwined concepts of capability and credibility. While capability is generally straightforward and quantifiable, based on the military force that a state can bring to bear in a conflict, credibility is a much more fluid and qualitative variable, stemming from the probability that such force will be used. For instance, a state may have very formidable armed forces, but if it is bound by domestic opinion to use them only in defense of the homeland, any strategy of extended deterrence will lack credibility. According to Scott Sagan, credibility is based on a wide range of components including the perceived interests at stake, one's reputation for following through on threats, the legitimacy of the conflict, and the so-called "audience costs" of backing down.[9] As this list makes clear, indeterminate factors such as value judgments and subjective assessments are at the heart of credibility, underscoring its protean nature. For instance, Kenneth Watman and Dean Wilkening point out that a state's reputation will decay quickly and tends to be specific to a given leader, a particular type of interest, and a particular type of warfare.[10] As a result, one can never be sure that a deterrent threat is adequate, even if there is one hundred percent certainty in the mind of the deterrer; it is always possible that the opposing side will misperceive the credibility of a threat. Despite these inherent limitations, theorists have tried to develop strategies that are most likely to foster credibility, and a few significant aspects are discussed below.

To reinforce the perception of one's resolve, a common tactic is to employ commitment techniques that increase the costs of failing

[9] Scott D. Sagan, "The Commitment Trap: Why the United States Should not Use Nuclear Threats to Deter Biological and Chemical Weapons Attacks," *International Security* vol. 24, no. 4 (spring 2000): 98. For a further explanation of audience costs, see the following paragraph.

[10] Watman and Wilkening, *US Regional Deterrence Strategies*, xi.

to act. This is akin to announcing publicly that one is about to go on a diet so that friends will act as a constant source of pressure to maintain the obligation. In the jargon of deterrence theory, making such a pledge imposes "audience costs" on oneself in the event of reneging on the promise. In a more dramatic illustration, the military image of "burning bridges" to make retreat impossible is the classic example of cementing one's resolve. As Thomas Schelling put it, "What we have to do is get ourselves into a position where we cannot fail to react as we said we would – where we just cannot help it – or where we would be obliged by some overwhelming cost of not reacting in the manner we had declared."[11] The American decision to post troops in Western Europe as a "tripwire" against Soviet aggression was one instance of bolstering resolve, with the United States making the defense of Europe a more certain prospect by effectively denying itself the opportunity of retreat and abandonment.

The idea that denying oneself options can actually be beneficial may seem counterintuitive at first. Schelling describes this phenomenon as a "paradox that the power to constrain an adversary may depend on the power to bind oneself."[12] Considering the game of "chicken" may help to clarify this concept. If two drivers are about to start accelerating toward one another, it would send a powerful message if one driver chose to throw his steering wheel out the window. The other driver would then have no choice but to concede the contest or suffer catastrophe. Of course, while this technique can be a very effective way of enhancing resolve where interests or capability are lacking, the hidden danger is that it is always possible that both drivers will make the same decision, locking in an even worse outcome than if the position had been surrendered at the outset.[13] The crucial factor, then, will be which side is able to make the first

---

[11] Schelling, *Arms and Influence*, 43.

[12] Thomas C. Schelling, *The Strategy of Conflict* (Cambridge, MA: Harvard University Press, 1960), 22.

[13] Stephen Maxwell, *Rationality in Deterrence*, Adelphi Paper No. 50 (London: International Institute for Strategic Studies, 1968), 4.

move, leaving the other with the only "last clear chance" to avoid calamity.[14]

Finally, beyond committing oneself to a particular course, there is the tactic of issuing a "threat that leaves something to chance," wherein the final decision of whether to act is not altogether under the threatener's control.[15] This is a gambling technique that plays on the factor of risk-acceptance, assuming that the opposing side will choose to give in first. The standard image is of one person rocking a boat in order to elicit concessions from the other frightened occupants. Schelling uses the term "brinksmanship" to describe this strategy – the choice of "deliberately letting the situation get somewhat out of hand, just because its being out of hand may be intolerable to the other party and force his accommodation."[16] In keeping with the "chicken" scenario, this would be akin to one driver publicly consuming a large amount of alcohol before stepping into the car, creating doubt in his opponent's mind that he would be able to avoid collision even if he ultimately desired to do so. In the literature on deterrence, this phenomenon is called the "rationality of irrationality," since one can draw coercive power from the prospect of being potentially undeterrable.[17] Once again, while this can be a particularly potent strategy, it courts disaster by embracing irrationality even though one's opponent may have done the same or is fully expecting rational behavior in the crisis. Overall, it is important to remember that deterrence is fundamentally a psychological concept with its roots in capability, credibility, and resolve.

DETERRENCE THEORY IN THE COLD WAR

Nuclear weapons were first used as an instrument of compellence to end World War II. The bomb dropped on Hiroshima on 6 August 1945

---

[14] Herman Kahn, *Thinking about the Unthinkable* (London: Weidenfeld and Nicolson, 1962), 46.

[15] Schelling, *The Strategy of Conflict*, 188.   [16] Ibid., 200.

[17] Edward Rhodes, *Power and MADness: The Logic of Nuclear Coercion* (New York: Columbia University Press, 1989), 16.

killed 66,000 people immediately and tens of thousands more after-ward, ultimately resulting in Japan's surrender to the Allies.[18] As the Cold War began and the Soviet Union joined the nuclear club in 1949, the United States faced a threat to its homeland it had never experienced before. In response, America began to focus more on deterrence, beginning with President Eisenhower and John Foster Dulles' doctrine of massive retaliation, enunciated in 1954. Based on the premise that local defense was impossible against the overwhelming communist advantage in land power, Dulles argued that the United States should rely on strategic retaliation at places of its own choosing.[19] The difficulty with this position was that the Soviet Union was not dependent solely on its ground forces but was developing a formidable nuclear arsenal as well, resulting in a relationship that Donald Brennan coined as "mutual assured destruction," or MAD.[20] Many academics and policymakers questioned the credibility of American reliance on a nuclear response to a conventional attack, especially when the Soviets could retaliate in kind.[21] Richard Betts humorously remarked, "In a competition in risk taking, why should Americans do better at Russian roulette than the Russians?"[22] Eventually, Dulles phased out massive retaliation in 1957, though the dilemma of providing for the security of Europe remained.[23]

Put simply, the worry was that the superpowers' strategic arsenals could cancel each other out, enabling the Soviet Union to

---

[18] Lawrence Freedman, *The Evolution of Nuclear Strategy*, 2nd edition (London: Macmillan, in association with the International Institute of Strategic Studies, 1989), xv.

[19] John Foster Dulles, "Massive Retaliation," in *The Use of Force*, edited by Art and Waltz, 371.

[20] Wolfgang K.H. Panofsky, "The Mutual-Hostage Relationship between America and Russia," *Foreign Affairs* vol. 52, no. 1 (October 1973): 109.

[21] Robert Osgood, *Limited War: The Challenge to American Security* (Chicago: University of Chicago Press, 1957); Morton Halperin, *Limited War in the Nuclear Age* (Westport, CT: Greenwood Press, 1963); Robert Powell, *Nuclear Deterrence Theory* (Cambridge: Cambridge University Press, 1990), 13.

[22] Richard Betts, *Nuclear Blackmail and Nuclear Balance* (Washington DC: Brookings Institution Press, 1987), 13.

[23] Bernard Brodie, *Strategy in the Missile Age* (Princeton, NJ: Princeton University Press, 1959), 262.

take advantage of its conventional superiority, most likely through limited advances – called "salami tactics" – that would aggregate into significant gains.[24] Dubbed the "stability–instability" paradox, American strategic doctrine attempted to square this strategic circle by oscillating between a reliance on MAD and the development of war-fighting capabilities that would make even conventional aggression a dangerous prospect for the Soviets.[25] Not to be outdone in the battle of the acronyms, critics of strategies that relied on options such as tactical nuclear weapons to fight a "credible" war against the Soviets labeled this idea "nuclear utilization theory," or NUTs.[26]

US strategic thinkers were never quite able to achieve consensus on how to resolve this dilemma, simultaneously worrying that too much reliance on MAD would lack credibility, whereas too much confidence in fighting a "limited" conflict against the Soviets might actually increase the chance of war by making it easier to contemplate and plan for.[27] Over the decades, successive administrations reformulated old concepts, from Dulles' New Look and McNamara's Flexible Response, to the Schlesinger Doctrine and Brown's Countervailing Strategy. From time to time, some policymakers even brought up missile defense as a potential solution to the uneasy state of MAD. Ultimately, the United States adopted a hybrid approach incorporating elements of each strand of thought, maintaining the "tripwire"

[24] Henry Kissinger, *Nuclear Weapons and Foreign Policy* (New York: Harper and Brothers, 1957), 134; James J. Wirtz, "Counterproliferation, Conventional Counterforce and Nuclear War," *Journal of Strategic Studies* vol. 23, no. 1 (March 2000): 14.

[25] Robert Jervis, *The Illogic of American Nuclear Strategy* (Ithaca, NY: Cornell University Press, 1984), 29–34.

[26] Spurgeon M. Keeny Jr. and Wolfgang K.H. Panofsky, "MAD Versus NUTS: Can Doctrine or Weaponry Remedy the Mutual Hostage Relationship of the Superpowers?" *Foreign Affairs* vol. 60, no. 2 (winter 1981–82): 289; Eric Mlyn, "US Nuclear Policy and the End of the Cold War," in *The Absolute Weapon Revisited: Nuclear Arms and the Emerging International Order*, edited by T.V. Paul, Richard J. Harknett, and James J. Wirtz (Ann Arbor, MI: Michigan University Press, 1998), 192.

[27] G.W. Rathjens, "Flexible Response Options," *Orbis* vol. 18, no. 3 (fall 1974): 680; Lynne Etheridge Davis, "Limited Nuclear Options: Deterrence and New American Doctrine," in *Strategic Deterrence in a Changing Environment*, edited by Christoph Bertram (London: International Institute for Strategic Studies, 1981), 52.

force in Europe that would fight conventionally, triggering a broader strategic response if defeated.[28] While not resolving the underlying dilemma – since this tripwire force could not succeed in large-scale battle and the resulting nuclear attack would still devastate Europe – this strategy nevertheless contained enough of an irreversible commitment to fight to create a significant likelihood in the minds of the Soviets that a nuclear counterattack would occur despite its consequences and apparent "irrationality."[29]

Fortunately, the superpowers never had to play out this "doomsday" scenario, and today it is inconceivable that the former Soviet Union would carry out a conventional attack on Europe. Some in US policy circles claim that since "deterrence has been proven to work" during the Cold War, concern over rogue states acquiring WMD is misplaced.[30] In the words of former US Congresswoman Cynthia McKinney, "Clearly if our nuclear arsenal and conventional military superiority deterred the Soviet Empire, it can do the same to Korea or Iraq."[31] However, given the experiences of Hungary, Czechoslovakia, and Afghanistan, not to mention the scare during the Cuban Missile Crisis, it is difficult to argue that such recent history has raised deterrence to an "iron law." The fundamental dilemmas posed by the stability–instability paradox remain, and the answers are no more certain than before. The following section will address the factors that raise doubt about the continued applicability of "Cold War deterrence."

CHALLENGES TO DETERRENCE

On the face of it, nuclear deterrence has a simplicity that is quite compelling: the United States can promise certain and devastating

---

[28] Michael Quinlan, *Thinking about Nuclear Weapons* (London: Royal United Services Institute for Defence Studies, 1997), 21.

[29] Robert Jervis, "Why Nuclear Superiority Doesn't Matter," *Political Science Quarterly* vol. 94, no. 4 (winter 1979–80): 624.

[30] Kathleen C. Bailey, *Doomsday Weapons in the Hands of Many: The Arms Control Challenge of the 90s* (Chicago: University of Illinois Press, 1991), 80.

[31] Cynthia McKinney, "Should the US Have a Missile Defense System?" *American Legion Magazine* vol. 148, no. 1 (January 2000): 42.

retaliation in response to a WMD attack, and since no one in their right mind could tolerate such an outcome, the reliability of deterrence should hardly be at risk. This is the basic logic that Kenneth Waltz invokes when he offers the assurance that "not much is required to deter."[32] In fact, many scholars are so confident in the power of deterrence that they speak of it "with the reverence of a physical principle,"[33] a universal and timeless formulation that applies in any and all places.[34] Indeed, deterrence theory at times treats the concepts of capability and credibility like variables in a math equation that can be adjusted to somehow guarantee deterrence. Where credibility is lacking, increasing the level of force that can be brought to bear will compensate. Conversely, if the amount of military power available is unconvincing, commitment techniques can help to eliminate doubt over one's willingness to act. To these theorists, all that is needed is sensible leadership to strike this balance and the compelling logic of deterrence will do the rest.

What is more, some scholars often apply this confidence in deterrence across the spectrum of conflicts against any adversary the United States may encounter. Kenneth Waltz asserts that "Even the most troublesome and cruel leaders have shown themselves susceptible to deterrence."[35] The desire to simplify deterrence theory is understandable; grouping adversaries and relying upon certain assumptions has enormous predictive and prescriptive power.[36] Doing so enables policymakers to downplay the more complicated task of investigating who is being deterred and instead merely ensure

---

[32] Kenneth N. Waltz, "More May Be Better," in Scott D. Sagan and Kenneth N. Waltz, *The Spread of Nuclear Weapons: A Debate* (New York: W.W. Norton, 1995), 22.

[33] William C. Martel, "Deterrence and Alternative Images of Nuclear Possession," in *The Absolute Weapon Revisited*, edited by Paul et al., 215.

[34] See Ken Booth, *Strategy and Ethnocentrism* (London: Croom Helm, 1979), 41; Richard Rosencrance, "Strategic Deterrence Reconsidered," in *Strategic Deterrence in a Changing Environment*, edited by Bertram, 7.

[35] Kenneth N. Waltz, "A Reply," *Security Studies* vol. 4, no. 4 (summer 1995): 804.

[36] Keith B. Payne and Lawrence R. Fink, "Deterrence without Defense: Gambling on Perfection," *Strategic Review* vol. 17, no. 1 (winter 1989): 27–28; Rhodes, *Power and MADness*, 14.

that the American arsenal is terrifyingly decisive. At the same time, one must also consider that these WMD capabilities must have some substantial value to rogue states or they would not go through the risk and expense of their development. Many states likely see WMD as the only way to win a regional conflict with the United States, either by threatening their use to avoid battle altogether or by using them to prevail in an asymmetric fashion.[37] The remainder of this chapter will investigate the theoretical and historical reasons to maintain a healthy skepticism toward deterrence, exploring asymmetries of interest and risk-taking, commitment tactics, psychological effects and the rationality of the irrational, last resort attacks, and millenarian regimes.

Asymmetries of interest and running risks

One flaw of deterrence theory is that it posits a rational actor and then makes the assumption that a "rational" actor will act reasonably by not risking and perhaps provoking its own destruction. The historical record, however, shows that, from time to time, states are willing to accept enormous gambles, even ones that endanger national survival, for important causes. Thucydides described the famous dialogue in 416 BC between the Athenian spokesmen and the besieged Melians, the latter choosing to risk (and eventually suffering) annihilation and colonization by refusing to end their neutrality in the Second Peloponnesian war.[38] Likewise, Keith Payne recounts several instances of states suffering total societal destruction in the wake of war, ranging from the sacking of Carthage at the conclusion of the Third Punic War to the devastation of Kiev by Mongol warriors in 1240. According to Payne, "leaders in the past have known or believed that their decisions would affect the probability of utter

[37] Robert G. Joseph, "The Role of Nuclear Weapons in US Deterrence Strategy," in *Deterrence in the 21st Century*, edited by Max G. Manwaring (London: Frank Cass, 2001), 54.

[38] Thucydides, *The Peloponnesian War*, translated by Rex Warner (London: Cassell, 1954), 358–66; Donald Kagan, *On the Origins of War and the Preservation of Peace* (New York: Doubleday, 1995), 7–8.

societal destruction, at least for them and their society, but that prospect did not render threats thereof reliable instruments for deterrence or coercion."[39]

There are also numerous examples of weak states actually attacking the strong, believing that there were no other options open to them or that the resolve of their opponent was quite frail. One commentator, T.V. Paul, studied six asymmetric conflicts of the twentieth century from the Russo-Japanese War to the Falklands Crisis, observing: "The stronger powers in all the cases anticipated that their own overall superiority in power capability would act as a general deterrent preventing their weaker opponents from engaging in war."[40] Instead, factors beyond mere capability were at play, often with the weaker side hoping for a political victory or judging that the asymmetries of interest were sufficiently in their favor to make military success possible.[41] The Yom Kippur War of 1973 between Israel and Egypt, for example, was one instance of a stronger state simply not being able to understand that poor military prospects do not always outweigh other factors such as honor, prestige, or even a political gambit for sympathy, in the decision for war.[42] History is replete with accounts of states fighting against insurmountable odds in the name of intangible values such as

---

[39] Keith B. Payne, *Deterrence in the Second Nuclear Age* (Lexington, KY: The University Press of Kentucky, 1996), 97.

[40] T.V. Paul, *Asymmetric Conflicts: War Initiation by Weaker Powers* (Cambridge: Cambridge University Press, 1994), 62–164, 170.

[41] Andrew Mack, "Why Big Nations Lose Small Wars: The Politics of Asymmetric Conflict," *World Politics* vol. 27, no. 2 (January 1975): 175–200; Barry Wolf, *When the Weak Attack the Strong: Failures of Deterrence*, RAND Note (Santa Monica, CA: RAND, 1991), 9–11; Brad Roberts, "From Nonproliferation to Antiproliferation," *International Security* vol. 18, no. 1 (summer 1993): 161.

[42] Martin van Creveld, *Nuclear Proliferation and the Future of Conflict* (New York: The Free Press, 1993), 101; Paul, *Asymmetric Conflicts*, 9. Operation Desert Storm provides another example; some analysts believe that Saddam Hussein held firm in the face of coalition air strikes because at times in Middle Eastern political cultures it is better to be defeated (though not destroyed) than dishonored. See Adam Garfinkle, "An Observation on Arab Culture and Deterrence: Metaphors and Misgivings," in *Regional Security Regimes*, edited by Efraim Inbar (Albany, NY: State University of New York Press, 1995), 205.

dignity and freedom, including the American Confederacy, the Irish Easter Rising, and the Finns in 1940.[43]

Further, when a WMD threat is first being made, the opponent may sincerely believe that the United States will be deterred and it will never have to make good on its threat. After all, there is an important difference between running the risk of attack and actually suffering one; such a bet may not necessarily be irrational.[44] In most regional conflicts, it is likely that local opponents will show considerable resolve given that any war would probably involve their core interests whereas the stakes for the United States might be more peripheral in nature.[45] The best illustration of this confidence is once again a variation on the game of "chicken," with one driver as a convict on death row and the other a man with a family.[46] In such a match of wills, there will be an inherent advantage in brinksmanship to the side that feels it has "nothing left to lose." Of course, to take the analogy one step further and incorporate capabilities, it is probably appropriate to depict the American "family man" as driving a large truck relative to the regional adversary. In the words of Colin Gray, however, "The huge disparity in physical strength between the United States and Iraq, Iran, or North Korea is all but beside the point when there is perceived to be no less huge disparity (to the disfavor of the United States) in intensity of national interest at stake."[47] This is especially true when WMD are involved, which can act as a strategic equalizer, a sort of "bomb on the bumper" that would damage even the American truck in the event of a collision.

[43] Richard Ned Lebow and Janice Gross Stein, "Beyond Deterrence," *Journal of Social Issues* vol. 43, no. 4 (1987): 10.

[44] Wilkening and Watman, *Nuclear Deterrence in a Regional Conflict*, 3; Paul, *Asymmetric Conflicts*, 174; Charles L. Glaser and Steve Fetter, "National Missile Defense and the Future of US Nuclear Weapons Policy," *International Security* vol. 26, no. 1 (summer 2001): 67; Victor A. Utgoff, "Proliferation, Missile Defence and American Ambitions," *Survival* vol. 44, no. 2 (summer 2002): 91.

[45] Thomas G. Mahnken, "America's Next War," *The Washington Quarterly* vol. 16, no. 3 (summer 1993): 175; Wilkening and Watman, *Nuclear Deterrence in a Regional Context*, ix.

[46] Wilkening and Watman, *Nuclear Deterrence in a Regional Context*, 12, footnote 14.

[47] Colin S. Gray, *The Second Nuclear Age* (London: Lynne Rienner, 1999), 125–26.

It is certainly plausible to think of states that would care enough about a certain vital interest even to the point of risking national catastrophe. The oft-quoted Chinese general who told an American envoy, "In the end, you care more about Los Angeles than you do about Taipei," was demonstrating how asymmetries of interest strengthen their deterrent threat over a potential Taiwanese conflict.[48] The Chinese leadership clearly places extremely high priority on restoring its lost province, and hardly anyone would doubt that it is at least possible that China would risk a nuclear exchange to prevent Taiwan's independence. John Arquilla surmises, "This asymmetry of relative motivation could prove the most serious external constraint on regional deterrence, for if an opponent is relatively impervious to threats that raise the specter of higher costs and risks for aggression, then the fundamental calculus of deterrence is overturned."[49] In situations like these, it may be quite a gamble to assume that dominance in capabilities will compensate for an imbalance in interests and resolve.

The prospect of unpredictable leaders with unknown levels of risk-acceptance poses substantial problems for deterrence theory. Especially if states choose to hide their aggression until the last moment through a surprise attack, as Egypt did in the Yom Kippur War, there may not even be time for the defending state to issue an explicit deterrent threat.[50] To be sure, there is little question that the risks involved in attacking the United States with WMD would be extraordinary, but such a decision cannot be ruled out, especially when there is an imbalance in interests and resolve.[51] States in the past have accepted such supreme dangers, even on the level of putting

---

[48] Quoted in Patrick E. Tyler, "As China Threatens Taiwan, It Makes Sure US Listens," *New York Times*, 24 January 1996. See also James M. Lindsay and Michael E. O'Hanlon, *Defending America: The Case for Limited National Missile Defense* (Washington DC: Brookings Institution Press, 2001), 125.

[49] John Arquilla, "Bound to Fail: Regional Deterrence after the Cold War," *Comparative Strategy* vol. 14, no. 2 (April–June 1995): 127.

[50] Morgan, *Deterrence: A Conceptual Analysis*, 40.

[51] Lewis A. Dunn, *Controlling the Bomb: Nuclear Proliferation in the 1980s* (New Haven, CT: Yale University Press, 1982), 83.

their entire societies in mortal danger, and it would be remiss to assume that they never will do so again.

COMMITMENT TACTICS

While imposing audience costs in a brinksmanship contest can bolster resolve, as mentioned earlier in this chapter, if a leader's reputation becomes too invested in a particular stand, a "commitment trap" can develop that creates an obligation to follow through with a threat even into an undesired conflict.[52] Expectations and vulnerabilities can develop through imprudent posturing, making the fear of a domestic uprising owing to a retreat the greater danger than forging ahead with a risky war. For example, in the build-up to the Sino-Indian war of 1962, Nehru is quoted as having told a colleague, "If I give them [a negotiated settlement], I shall no longer be Prime Minister of India."[53] Beyond external constraints, internal psychological momentum can also bind decisionmakers to a commitment once it is made.[54] Feelings of pride and defiance can coalesce into a rigid determination to stay the course regardless of cost. In the Ussuri River border conflict between the Soviet Union and China in 1969, for example, both sides were determined not to be intimidated by nuclear blackmail and the subsequent military clashes were disturbingly close to escalating into full-scale war.[55]

Another commitment technique is to tie one's hands, not through audience costs, but by the actual pre-delegation of command authority, known in the deterrence literature as setting up a "doomsday machine" or issuing a "threat that leaves something to chance."[56]

---

[52] Sagan, "The Commitment Trap," 86.

[53] Quoted in Watman and Wilkening, *US Regional Deterrence Strategies*, 44–45.

[54] Irving L. Janis and Leon Mann, *Decision Making: A Psychological Analysis of Conflict* (New York: The Free Press, 1977), 287.

[55] Alfred D. Law, *The Sino-Soviet Dispute* (London: Associated University Presses, 1976), 277; Richard Wich, *Sino-Soviet Crisis Politics: A Study of Political Change and Communication* (Cambridge, MA: Harvard University Press, 1980), 166; Harry Gelman, *The Soviet Far East Buildup and Soviet Risk-Taking against China* (Santa Monica, CA: RAND, 1982), 41; Lyle J. Goldstein, "Do Nascent WMD Arsenals Deter? The Sino-Soviet Crisis of 1969," *Political Science Quarterly* vol. 118, no. 1 (spring 2003): 53–79. [56] Rhodes, *Power and MADness*, 155.

Essentially, the authority to carry out a deterrent threat is placed down the chain of command, usually out of a fear of the destruction of command/control links and the desire to shore up credibility by increasing the likelihood that there will be retaliation even should such an attack be successful. Shockingly, unknown to most observers, this strategy nearly led to the outbreak of war during the Cuban Missile Crisis. Recently released documents reveal that a Soviet submarine commander was on the verge of launching a nuclear-tipped torpedo in response to the American depth charges that were seeking to force him to the surface. Unaware of what was occurring on land, he is quoted as saying, "Maybe the war has already started up there, while we are doing somersaults here . . . We're going to blast them now! We will die, but we will sink them all. We will not disgrace our navy!"[57] Fortunately the commander relented after conferring with his other officers, though the incident should serve as a sobering reminder of the limited control over wartime situations and the dangers of pre-delegation. Employing commitment tactics can be very savvy, but can also be incredibly dangerous if one's opponent does the same or refuses to give in.

Psychological effects and the rationality of the irrational

Recognizing that cool, calculated decisionmaking will tend to strengthen deterrence, states may deliberately or implicitly cultivate a reputation for "irrational" behavior that paradoxically may be a very rational image to project.[58] Nikita Khrushchev is one famous example of a leader who sought to come across as slightly unstable in order to gain leverage in brinksmanship contests.[59] Beyond such partial deception, there are also many naturally occurring psychological biases and influences that could make a crisis – which by its

---

[57] Quoted in David Gonzalez, "At Cuba Conference, Old Foes Exchange Notes on 1962 Missile Crisis," *New York Times*, 14 October 2002.

[58] Patrick M. Morgan, "Saving Face for the Sake of Deterrence," in *Psychology and Deterrence*, edited by Robert Jervis, Richard Ned Lebow, and Janice Gross Stein (Baltimore, MD: The Johns Hopkins University Press, 1985), 128; Rhodes, *Power and MADness*, 45, 123.   [59] Schelling, *Arms and Influence*, 37.

very nature is inherently unstable – "get out of hand" in the heat of the moment.[60] The rationality of decisionmakers "may be degraded by factors of personal character or by such adverse circumstances as time pressure, fatigue, and anxiety."[61] Leaders can become desperate and panic, especially if extremist military cliques or domestic movements threaten their hold on power. Military factions might also push policy beyond the bounds the national leadership has set, as in the scenario of a "crazy colonel" independently lashing out with WMD to secure a sense of personal glory for landing a devastating blow against the West.[62] Scholars of the conflicts between the United States and North Korea in the late 1960s (assassination attempt on South Korean president Park Chung Hee in January 1968, seizure of the USS *Pueblo* in the same month, and the April 1969 downing of a US Navy EC-121) point out that Kim Il Sung was forced to purge his aggressive generals after their subversive policies brought the nation uncomfortably close to war with the United States.[63] During the Cuban Missile Crisis, another case study in the potential for disaster caused by organizational dysfunction, not only were the Soviet submariners on edge, but the US political leadership was under intense stress and constant pressure from some military hawks to pursue a more belligerent course.[64] More recently, the clashes between India

---

[60] Ibid., 97.

[61] Klaus Knorr, *The Power of Nations: The Political Economy of International Relations* (New York: Basic Books, 1975), 41.

[62] Stephen M. Meyer, "Small Nuclear Forces and US Military Operations in the Theater," in *Small Nuclear Forces and US Security Policy*, edited by Rodney M. Jones (Washington DC: Center for Strategic and International Studies, 1984), 164; George Quester, "The Future of Nuclear Deterrence," *Survival* vol. 34, no. 1 (spring 1992): 78.

[63] Dae-sook Suh, *Kim Il Sung* (New York: Columbia University Press, 1988), 239; Joseph S. Bermudez Jr., "The Democratic People's Republic of Korea and Unconventional Weapons," in *Planning the Unthinkable: How New Powers will Use Nuclear, Biological, and Chemical Weapons*, edited by Peter R. Lavoy, Scott D. Sagan, and James J. Wirtz (Ithaca, NY: Cornell University Press, 2000), 186–87.

[64] Sagan, "More Will Be Worse," in *The Spread of Nuclear Weapons*, 52; James G. Blight and David A. Welch, "Risking 'the Destruction of Nations': Lessons of the Cuban Missile Crisis for New and Aspiring States," *Security Studies* vol. 4, no. 4 (summer 1995): 824.

and Pakistan over Kashmir have led some analysts to fear that the tension and political stakes involved have made war possible despite the potential for nuclear escalation.[65] In sum, crises are often marked by surprises, mistakes, and catastrophic errors, all of which may work against the proper functioning of deterrence.

Even if leaders are functionally rational, there are numerous psychological biases and influences that can increase the likelihood of misperception and "sub-rational" behavior. It is important to recognize that deterrence is at root a psychological concept whose success requires a particular state of mind on the part of the opponent. In some cases, owing to psychological effects, the target of a deterrence policy may simply not understand, fully register, or believe a particular threat. They may be resorting to "wishful thinking," or only seeing what they expect or would like to see.[66] Closely related to this is the concept of "denial" or "defensive avoidance," which involves refusing to consider fully evidence that contradicts a decision that has already been made.[67] This type of "mental blinder" is known as a "motivated bias" since it satisfies a psychological need for peace of mind. In essence, when confronted with too many conflicting stimuli, a state of "cognitive dissonance" can develop, resulting in the distortion of information toward what one wants to believe in order to simplify an imminent decision or to cope with difficult and dangerous choices.[68] Through defensive avoidance, evidence to the contrary is explained away, and "the decision maker achieves a state of 'pseudocalm' at the expense of effective search and appraisal."[69]

[65] Waheguru Pal Sing Sidhu, "India's Nuclear Use Doctrine," in *Planning the Unthinkable*, edited by Lavoy et al., 143; Rajiv Chandrasekaran, "For India, Deterrence May Not Prevent War," *Washington Post*, 17 January 2002. See also Devin T. Hagerty, "Nuclear Deterrence in South Asia: The 1990 Indo-Pakistani Crisis," *International Security* vol. 20, no. 3 (winter 1995–96): 95.

[66] Robert Jervis, *Perception and Misperception in International Politics* (Princeton, NJ: Princeton University Press, 1976), 361.

[67] Robert Jervis, "Deterrence and Perception," *International Security* vol. 7, no. 3 (winter 1982–83): 29.

[68] Jervis, *Perception and Misperception in International Politics*, 382.

[69] Janis and Mann, *Decision Making*, 124.

For example, in the lead-up to the bombing of Pearl Harbor, Admiral Kimmel screened out various warning signs that were mixed in with other intelligence by rationalizing that the Japanese would not dare make a surprise attack. The term "pseudocalm" is appropriate because the perception of calm may actually be quite false; the Argentinian junta, for instance, was quite off target in their wishful thinking that Britain would allow their *fait accompli* in the Falklands to stand unchallenged.[70]

Based on his analyses of past deterrence failures, Richard Lebow observed that, "When leaders felt themselves compelled to pursue brinksmanship challenges, they frequently rationalized the conditions for their success."[71] Lebow analyzed the information bias in the decisions that led to World War I, concluding that Germany's hope for British neutrality in the event of war was nearly delusional.[72] Especially when several individuals are brought together to make a decision, a phenomenon known as "groupthink" can arise, often resulting in a concurrence-seeking tendency and the development of an illusion of invulnerability. Janis and Mann examined several examples of this psychological bias, including Chamberlain's inner circle in 1937–38, Truman in the lead-up to war in Korea, and Kennedy in the Bay of Pigs fiasco.[73] Once a state is committed to a certain policy, cognitive closure can set in, along with the conclusion that there are no other options available and that the risks involved with the chosen course are minimal.[74] Thus, it is always possible that even if a deterrent threat is credible and carefully communicated, the other side may simply not be listening or could misconstrue it as a bluff.

---

[70] Janice Gross Stein, "Calculation, Miscalculation, and Conventional Deterrence I: The View from Cairo," in *Psychology and Deterrence*, edited by Jervis et al., 108.

[71] Richard Ned Lebow, *Between Peace and War: The Nature of International Crisis* (Baltimore, MD: The Johns Hopkins University Press, 1981), 335.

[72] Ibid., 129–43.

[73] Janis and Mann, *Decision Making*, 129; Booth, *Strategy and Ethnocentrism*, 107.

[74] Robert Jervis, "Perceiving and Coping with Threat," in *Psychology and Deterrence*, edited by Jervis et al., 32; Frank C. Zagare and D. Marc Kilgour, *Perfect Deterrence* (Cambridge: Cambridge University Press, 2000), 44.

Finally, it may be that a state's leadership actually *is* mentally unbalanced, incapacitated, or following a nonrational method of decisionmaking. The infirmities of old age have affected numerous major political figures; US presidents Woodrow Wilson and Ronald Reagan are among those who required some assistance toward the end of their terms.[75] Several leaders in the past have abused drugs, including Hitler's prescription cocaine treatments, Mao's barbiturate addiction, and South Korean president Park Chung Hee's alcoholism. Recently declassified US State Department documents reveal that senior US officials considered Park dangerously unstable and prone to issuing "all sorts of orders when he begins drinking" that were fortunately ignored until he became sober.[76] There are further reports that Saddam Hussein relied on the advice of "soothsayers" to provide assistance in making his ill-fated military decisions during the 1990–91 Gulf War.[77] While instances of such erratic and unpredictable leaders may be rare, they are certainly dangerous if and when they do arise.[78] All in all, the potential for misperception and irrationality in crises, be it feigned, deliberate, or actual, poses a significant challenge to the proper functioning of deterrence.

Last resort attacks

Another weakness of traditional deterrence theory is that it has little to offer in situations where vital interests may actually be in conflict. Richard Betts explains, "The logic of deterrence is clearest when the issue is preventing unprovoked and unambiguous aggression . . . Deterrence is less reliable when both sides in a conflict see each other as the aggressor . . . Such situations are ripe for miscalculation."[79]

---

[75] Jerome D. Frank, *Sanity and Survival: Psychological Aspects of War and Peace* (London: The Cresset Press, 1967), 60.

[76] Keith B. Payne, *The Fallacies of Cold War Deterrence and a New Direction* (Lexington, KY: The University Press of Kentucky, 2001), 58–59.   [77] Ibid., 44.

[78] Yehezkel Dror, *Crazy States: A Counterconventional Strategic Problem* (Lexington, MA: Heath Lexington Books, 1971), xiii.

[79] Richard K. Betts, "The New Threat of Mass Destruction," *Foreign Affairs* vol. 77, no. 1 (January/February 1998): 33.

As the United States seems to be moving toward a strategic outlook wherein rogue state WMD possession alone is an unacceptable security threat, mutual recriminations and competing claims of acting in self-defense are likely. This development could be very dangerous, since if the United States poses a severe challenge to an opposing regime or its perceived interests, the adversary's leadership may place certain values such as honor and dignity above life and even national survival. Some states may be led by an unwavering belief in a powerful ideology or religious commitment, and there could be a readiness to sacrifice a great deal in its name.[80] Moreover, faced with a potentially humiliating outcome to a war with the United States and its allies, revenge may even become a primary motivating factor. A government in its death throes might attack nihilistically or become obsessed with a martyr complex, feeling that it might as well implement a sort of "Samson" strategy and attempt to bring down its enemies along with itself.[81] In the words of Secretary of Defense Perry, such regimes "may not buy into our deterrence theory. Indeed, they may be madder than MAD."[82]

The concept of "undeterrable" states with leaders willing to sacrifice everything has some historical precedent. Hitler, for instance, called for a scorched earth form of national self-destruction in his infamous Nero orders in March 1945.[83] A few months later, even after the atomic bomb devastated Hiroshima, some military leaders in Japan were contemplating a suicidal last stand, with the

---

[80] Dror, *Crazy States*, 7.

[81] Seymour M. Hersh, *The Samson Option: Israel, America and the Bomb* (London: Faber, 1991); Lewis A. Dunn, *Containing Nuclear Proliferation*, Adelphi Paper No. 263 (London: International Institute for Strategic Studies, winter 1991), 24, 26; Barry R. Schneider, "Strategies for Coping with Enemy Weapons of Mass Destruction," *Airpower Journal* (Special Edition 1996): 42; Avigdor Haselkorn, *The Continuing Storm: Iraq, Poisonous Weapons, and Deterrence* (New Haven, CT: Yale University Press, 1999), 151; James M. Lindsay and Michael E. O'Hanlon, "Correspondence," *International Security* vol. 26, no. 4 (spring 2002): 192.

[82] Quoted in Stephen J. Cimbala, *The Past and Future of Nuclear Deterrence* (Westport, CT: Praeger, 1998), 107.

[83] Albert Speer, *Inside the Third Reich* (New York: Macmillan, 1970), 440; Joachim Fest, *Speer: The Final Verdict* (London: Phoenix Press, 1999), 250–51.

war minister musing, "Would it not be wondrous for this whole nation to be destroyed like a beautiful flower?"[84] Such examples cast doubt on arguments that deterrence will always be sufficient to hold nations back from carrying out their WMD threat owing to the ruinous repercussions.[85] It is entirely possible that some leaders will be willing to "go down with their state" rather than accept the loss of power or experience military defeat.[86] Even Winston Churchill, notwithstanding his considerable confidence in the nuclear "balance of terror," still allowed for the "formidable admission" that such a deterrent did not apply to "lunatics or dictators in the mood of Hitler when he found himself in his final dugout."[87] In these circumstances, a final revenge attack may actually be "rational" in the mind of a desperate leader despite its consequences.

Many analysts concur, arguing prior to Operation Iraqi Freedom that Saddam Hussein would sooner start World War III than give up office voluntarily and that North Korea would likely launch a WMD attack in the event that the United States tried to eliminate its nuclear facilities.[88] Indeed, given the number of suicide bombers that are willing to sacrifice their lives in the Arab-Israeli conflict, is it really that hard to imagine that a given leader would not at some point volunteer his state to serve that role? Radovan Karadzic, former leader of the Bosnian Serbs, implied as much, threatening, "We are not prepared to give up our own self-defense. It is no problem to buy nuclear weapons on the world market. We will really carry it through. *We have nothing to lose.*"[89]

[84] Quoted in David McCullough, *Truman* (New York: Simon & Schuster, 1992), 459.

[85] Thomas L. Friedman, "Who's Crazy Here?" *New York Times*, 15 May 2001.

[86] Dunn, *Containing Nuclear Proliferation*, 24.

[87] Quoted in Fred Charles Iklé, "Can Nuclear Deterrence Last Out the Century?" *Foreign Affairs* vol. 51, no. 2 (January 1973): 269.

[88] Bermudez, "The DPRK and Unconventional Weapons," 197; James Dao, "Pentagon's Worry: Iraqi Chemical Arms," *New York Times*, 19 May 2002; Bradley Graham, " 'Scorched Earth' Plans in Iraq Cited," *Washington Post*, 19 December 2002; Michael R. Gordon, "Iraq Said to Plan Strategy of Delay and Urban Battle," *New York Times*, 16 February 2003; Rowan Scarborough, "Saddam Ready to Kill Iraqis, Blame US," *Washington Times*, 12 March 2003.

[89] Quoted in Philip L. Ritcheson, "Proliferation and the Challenge to Deterrence," *Strategic Review* vol. 23, no. 2 (spring 1995): 42 (italics in the original).

During the Cuban Missile Crisis, Che Guevara and Castro reportedly urged a preemptive strike on the United States, preferring to sacrifice Cuba and "die beautifully" in the fight against American imperialism.[90] As with the submarine commander, fortunately cooler heads prevailed and the Soviet vice-premier Anastas Mikoyan was able to overrule them, taking a much more conservative view of the situation.[91] As Keith Payne notes, however, "In future crises, leaders ready to 'die beautifully' may be in control of missiles, and their cost–benefit calculus will not permit the predictable functioning of deterrence."[92] Overall, while it may be true that rogue leaders will rarely risk massive retaliation since they "want to have a country that they can continue to rule," this simple logic becomes upended if regime change or unconditional surrender is the objective, which in many rogue states may end up resulting in the leader's death.[93]

Millenarian regimes

More troubling still is the potential that certain regimes will want to carry out WMD attacks regardless of whether their vital interests are threatened. Brad Roberts opines, "Proliferation may put strategic weapons in the hands of messianic leaders seeking to wage wars of ethnic or religious righteousness against what they perceive to be a corrupt, secular world . . ."[94] Millenarian states and religious fanatics might seek destruction for its own sake, lashing out against America and its allies in retribution or to serve some higher end. Ramzi Yousef, the mastermind behind the 1993 World Trade Center bombing, claimed that he was retaliating for US aid to Israel and hoped to kill 250,000 Americans.[95] Such states and groups may even welcome the

---

[90] Quoted in Blight and Welch, "Risking 'the Destruction of Nations,'" 842. See also Payne, *The Fallacies of Cold War Deterrence*, 50.

[91] Robert T. Kadish, Speech at the Military Appreciation Banquet, Fairbanks, Alaska, 2 March 2001.   [92] Payne, *The Fallacies of Cold War Deterrence*, 52.

[93] Waltz, "More May Be Better," 13; Wilkening and Watman, *Nuclear Deterrence in a Regional Context*, 36.

[94] Roberts, "From Nonproliferation to Antiproliferation," 161.

[95] Jessica Stern, "Terrorist Motivations and Unconventional Weapons," in *Planning the Unthinkable*, edited by Lavoy et al., 215–16.

consequences of devastating American reprisals, justifying them as an act of martyrdom in service of a deity or ideology.[96] A strong belief in an afterlife could create an extreme determination and willingness to sacrifice, brought about by the promise of great rewards after death.[97]

As with incapacitated leaders, while individuals, groups, or states with such a frame of mind are probably rather rare, even a low level of incidence is a major cause for concern given the potential effects of WMD. After all, it took just over a dozen hijackers to bring down the Twin Towers in New York, and there are similar networks of terror across the world. It is difficult to see how such covert organizations can be reliably deterred. In the words of former US Undersecretary of State John Bolton, the type of individuals who would crash airplanes into buildings are "not going to be deterred by anything."[98] Such a realization has profound implications for the durability of deterrence in regional conflicts.

These aspects of deterrence are particularly relevant to US strategy in the post-Cold War era. Adopting a preventive war doctrine and threatening regime change takes on a whole new meaning in light of the potential for last resort attacks. Missions to disarm an adversary are far more precarious if its leaders may have pre-delegated authority to use WMD under such circumstances. At the same time, the apparent growth in jihadist terrorist organizations, and the possibility of links between such groups and sympathetic state sponsors, raises the

[96] William E. Burrows and Robert Windrem, *Critical Mass: The Dangerous Race for Superweapons in a Fragmenting World* (London: Simon & Schuster, 1994), 19; Martel, "Deterrence and Alternative Images of Nuclear Possession," 221.

[97] Richard A. Falkenrath, Robert D. Newman, and Bradley A. Thayer, *America's Achilles' Heel: Nuclear, Biological, and Chemical Terrorism and Covert Attack* (Cambridge, MA: MIT Press, 1998); Hans M. Kristensen, *Nuclear Futures: Proliferation of Weapons of Mass Destruction and US Nuclear Strategy* (London: British American Security Information Council, March 1998), 19; Payne, *The Fallacies of Cold War Deterrence*, 49.

[98] William J. Broad, Stephen Engelberg, and James Glanz, "Assessing Risks, Chemical, Biological, Even Nuclear," *New York Times*, 1 November 2001.

specter of millenarian threats that are not easily deterred. The United States must strike a delicate balance between strengthening its own deterrent power and eliminating such threats without triggering a strategic reaction that could end up creating greater insecurity.

In the final analysis, there is no magic formula to ensure deterrence; in every instance the ultimate decision rests with the state being deterred. There are a variety of psychological, cultural, and political variables that can affect an adversary's reaction to a deterrent threat, and their response can never be guaranteed by any amount of military capability.[99] Keith Payne explains:

> The tremendous lethality of nuclear weapons may usefully focus leadership attention on occasion. Even very lethal threats, however, cannot bring to an end the enormous capacity of leaders to have poor judgment, impaired rationality, to pursue "unreasonable" goals and embrace unreasonable values, to be ignorant, passionate, foolish, arrogant, or selectively attentive to risks and costs, and to base their actions on severely distorted perceptions of reality.[100]

Any number of factors can create a deterrence deficiency: a state misperceiving the threat involved, purposefully manipulating the risk of war, or even actually desiring war. A regime may be "rational," yet act in ways that an opposing state finds quite unreasonable or even senseless.

In general, given the magnitude of US power, deterrence should work quite well, especially in cases of overt aggression against vital American interests, such as territorial defense of allies and the homeland. It is worth remembering, however, that deterrence has failed many times in the past, and even nuclear powers have come quite close to war despite the harrowing potential for escalation. In the case

[99] Gordon A. Craig and Alexander L. George, *Force and Statecraft: Diplomatic Problems of our Time*, 3rd edition (Oxford: Oxford University Press, 1995), 208; Garfinkle, "An Observation on Arab Culture and Deterrence," 205.

[100] Payne, *The Fallacies of Cold War Deterrence*, 75.

of actually resorting to WMD use, the exception would certainly prove the rule, upending any confidence in a stable order based on deterrence.[101] Overall, the burden of proof is clearly on the side that holds that such an attack could never occur. As A.J.P. Taylor notes, "A deterrent may work ninety-nine times out of a hundred. On the hundredth occasion it produces catastrophe."[102] Chapters 3 and 4 will investigate contemporary evidence of the likelihood of such a breakdown in deterrence.

[101] Richard K. Betts, "Universal Deterrence or Conceptual Collapse? Liberal Pessimism and Utopian Realism," in *The Coming Crisis: Nuclear Proliferation, US Interests, and World Order*, edited by Victor A. Utgoff (Cambridge, MA: MIT Press, 2000), 52.

[102] Quoted in Payne, *Deterrence in the Second Nuclear Age*, xi.

Part II   Crisis and conflict with Iraq and North Korea

We have seen that history is full of surprises; states attack unexpectedly, make rash decisions, and take astounding risks even in the face of military disaster. Such examples reveal the theoretical wrinkles in the assumption of rationality, and thereby raise considerable doubt over the reliability of deterrence itself. It remains to be seen, though, whether adding WMD to the equation will make deterrence a more reliable prospect. In the past, nearly without exception, states have only employed WMD when their opponents lacked a comparable capability, implying that restraint – or deterrence in some sense – would be likely if the potential to cause major destruction was mutual.[1] This has certainly been the case among the world's nuclear powers despite a few harrowing close calls.

How well, then, do deterrent threats hold up in asymmetric regional conflicts or crises when both sides possess WMD? While very few cases with such conditions exist, the next two chapters will investigate the United States and its interactions with Iraq and North Korea.[2] Both examples involve a wide range of implicit and explicit WMD threats, as well as efforts by participants to employ brinksmanship tactics in the hopes of gaining an advantage over their opponents. Fortunately WMD were never put to use, notwithstanding multiple failures of deterrence and compellence. I will examine the likely causes of such failures, as well as the equally relevant examples of apparent deterrence success.

---

[1] Kathleen Bailey, *Doomsday Weapons in the Hands of Many: The Arms Control Challenge of the 90s* (Chicago: University of Illinois Press, 1991), 63.

[2] Other crises with states such as Iran, Syria, and Libya all merit analysis, but lack the same level of explicit deterrent threats.

I conclude that both Iraq and North Korea sought to prevent US interference by posing the prospect of WMD retaliation, but important distinctions led to different results in each crisis. Iraq's chemical weapon (CW) arsenal was insufficient to deter the United States from attacking in the Gulf War of 1990–91, and likewise failed to prevent the US invasion in 2003. However, American counter-threats also went unheeded, and it appears likely that Iraq would have used WMD if US forces had moved on Baghdad in 1991, or if Iraqi forces had possessed them in 2003. Conversely, North Korea's opaque nuclear capability significantly constrained US freedom of action during the 1993–94 crisis, as did its ability to cause conventional devastation to an extent Iraq was never capable of. In the stand-off a decade later, North Korea's nuclear advances further augmented its deterrent power, an obvious and unfortunate object lesson for states such as Iran and Syria. Neither case provides a ringing endorsement of deterrence, demonstrating the significance of asymmetrical interests and the need for the United States to consider novel foreign policy strategies to counter the proliferation of WMD.

3 Iraq

This chapter explores the evolution of a bilateral relationship that started with a strategic partnership and descended into fifteen years of war and conflict, the repercussions of which continue to the present day. It first traces the bitter volley of threats and warnings that permeated the build-up and execution of Operation Desert Storm in 1990–91. Then, after a brief account of the tumultuous intervening years, it details the attempts at deterrence in Operation Iraqi Freedom, culminating in the overthrow of Saddam Hussein.

DESERT STORM (1990–91)

The strategic interaction between the United States and Iraq has always been complex. In the aftermath of World War II, monarchical Iraq for a time was a promising bulwark of stability in the Middle East, forming the core of the Baghdad Pact, a NATO-sponsored military alliance intended to quell communist and liberation movements in the region. The Iraqi revolution in 1958 came as quite a shock to the West, terminating Iraq's participation in the Baghdad Pact and ushering in years of turmoil. The subsequent violence was capped by a Ba'athist coup in 1968 that paved the way for Saddam Hussein's eventual accession to the presidency in 1979, the same year as the revolution in Iran. Given the West's extreme antipathy toward Ayatollah Khomeini, the United States was eager to assist Hussein in his quest for military power, particularly once war broke out between Iran and Iraq a year later.[1]

---

[1] For a full account of this support, see Kenneth R. Timmerman, *The Death Lobby: How the West Armed Iraq* (London: Fourth Estate, 1992); Leonard A. Cole, *The Eleventh Plague: The Politics of Biological and Chemical Warfare* (New York: W.H. Freeman, 1997), 81.

Despite the imperative to assist a de facto ally, the United States was never quite at ease with the rapid advancement of Iraq's WMD capabilities during this period, a tension that resulted in considerable controversy given the subsequent deterioration in relations.[2] Iraq's extensive use of CW during the war with Iran only exacerbated these misgivings, as it experimented with a whole range of toxins and nerve gases.[3] The conflict turned especially brutal toward the end, when Iraq fired more than 160 Scud missiles toward Tehran alone during the infamous "War of the Cities" in early 1988.[4] Hussein also stepped up the CW attacks, the most egregious of which occurred at Halabja in March of 1988, when a mixture of mustard gas and the nerve agents sarin, tabun, and VX killed over 5,000 Iraqi civilians, most of them Kurds.[5]

The Iraqi willingness to employ unconventional weapons became yet a greater worry once the remnants of the alliance with the United States fell apart and Iraq began to make preparations for the annexation of Kuwait. Hussein minced no words in attempting to capitalize on this fear, warning in May of 1990 that any military aggression against him would be met by a counterattack to "sweep away US influence in the region."[6] Around the same time he made a similar threat to Israel, alluding to his CW arsenal: "I swear to God that we shall burn half of Israel if it tries to wage anything against Iraq."[7] In a

[2] Barry Rubin, "The United States and Iraq: From Appeasement to War," in *Iraq's Road to War*, edited by Amatzia Baram and Barry Rubin (London: Macmillan, 1994), 257; Patrick E. Tyler, "Officers Say US Aided Iraq in War Despite Use of Gas," *New York Times*, 18 August 2002.

[3] David B. Ottaway, "In Mideast, Warfare with a New Nature," *Washington Post*, 5 April 1988; Dilip Hiro, *The Longest War: The Iran–Iraq Military Conflict* (New York: Routledge, 1991), 209.

[4] Thomas L. McNaugher, "Ballistic Missiles and Chemical Weapons: The Legacy of the Iran–Iraq War," *International Security* vol. 15, no. 2 (fall 1990): 5.

[5] Youssef M. Ibrahim, "Iran Reports New Iraqi Gas Raids, and Says Cities May be Hit Next," *New York Times*, 2 April 1988; Patrick E. Tyler, "Both Iraq and Iran Gassed Kurds in War, US Analysis Finds," *Washington Post*, 3 May 1990; Adel Darwish and Gregory Alexander, *Unholy Babylon: The Secret History of Saddam's War* (London: Victor Gollancz, 1991), 78; Christine Gosden, "Why I Went, What I Saw," *Washington Post*, 11 March 1998.

[6] Quoted in Amatzia Baram, "The Iraqi Invasion of Kuwait: Decision-Making in Baghdad," in *Iraq's Road to War*, edited by Baram and Rubin, 11.   [7] Ibid.

meeting with the American ambassador just prior to invading Kuwait, Hussein broadened his threat to include terrorist reprisals, stating, "We cannot come all the way to you in the United States, but individual Arabs may reach you."[8] Tariq Aziz, then Iraqi foreign minister, soon extended this admonition to all of America's allies, contending that Iraq would be "free of any moral constraint" if attacked.[9]

After occupying Kuwait, as tensions mounted toward war, Hussein also tried to raise the prospect of mass casualties, promising "whoever attacks Iraq will find in front of him columns of dead bodies which may have a beginning but may not have an end."[10] According to some reports, Iraq openly and ostentatiously loaded and then removed chemical weapons from aircraft in an attempt to deter US military action.[11] Once the coalition air strikes began, Hussein became even more explicit regarding the potential for WMD use, commenting in an interview with a CNN reporter, "I pray to God I will not be forced to use these [nonconventional] weapons, but I will not hesitate to do so should the need arise."[12] Al-Qadisiya, a prominent Iraqi newspaper, intoned a few days later, "We will use whatever power and weapons are at our disposal, starting from kitchen knives to weapons of mass destruction."[13] Even the Iraqi ambassador to the UN, Abd al-Amir al-Anbari, warned, "If the high-altitude bombings against Iraq are not stopped, we would have no choice but to resort to weapons of mass destruction."[14] Most dramatically of all, just before the coalition ground campaign, Hussein insinuated the possibility of imminent CW use by asking "the people of justice" to

---

[8] Quoted in Dilip Hiro, *Desert Shield to Desert Storm: The Second Gulf War* (New York: Routledge, 1992), 92.

[9] Quoted in Efraim Karsh and Inari Rautsi, *Saddam Hussein: A Political Biography* (London: Brassey's, 1991), 232.

[10] Quoted in Avigdor Haselkorn, *The Continuing Storm: Iraq, Poisonous Weapons, and Deterrence* (New Haven, CT: Yale University Press, 1999), 35.

[11] R. Jeffrey Smith, "US Warns of Retaliation if Iraq Uses Poison Gas," *Washington Post*, 9 August 1990; Karsh and Rautsi, *Saddam Hussein: A Political Biography*, 232.

[12] Quoted in Con Coughlin, *Saddam: The Secret Life* (London: Macmillan, 2002), 268.

[13] John Swain and James Adams, "Saddam Gives Local Commanders Go-Ahead for Chemical Attacks," *Sunday Times* (London), 3 February 1991.

[14] Quoted in Karsh and Rautsi, *Saddam Hussein: A Political Biography*, 260.

"forgive Iraq for any action they will initiate."[15] In essence, Hussein attempted initially to deter the United States and the coalition forces from intervening at all, and then from taking the war too far by threatening to launch CW attacks against allied troops, Israel, and Saudi Arabia.

The United States, for its part, was certainly not a silent recipient of such dire warnings. President George Bush wrote a letter to Saddam Hussein that was delivered to Tariq Aziz, stating that if chemical or biological weapons were used, "The American people would demand the strongest possible response. You and your country will pay a terrible price if you order such unconscionable action of this sort."[16] The envoy to that meeting, Secretary of State James Baker, made the most explicit counterthreat in person:

> If the conflict starts, God forbid, and chemical or biological
> weapons are used against our forces, the American people would
> demand revenge, and we have the means to implement this. This
> is not a threat, but a pledge that if there is any use of such
> weapons, our objective would not be only the liberation of
> Kuwait, but also the toppling of the present regime. Any person
> who is responsible for the use of these weapons would be held
> accountable in the future . . . we will not permit terrorism to be
> directed against Americans or against their partners in this
> coalition, and we will not allow any attempt to destroy Kuwaiti
> oilfields.[17]

After hostilities began in January, then Defense Secretary Richard Cheney reiterated the point, stressing that "were Saddam Hussein

---

[15] Quoted in Timothy V. McCarthy and Jonathan B. Tucker, "Saddam's Toxic Arsenal: Chemical and Biological Weapons in the Gulf Wars," in *Planning the Unthinkable: How New Powers Will Use Nuclear, Biological, and Chemical Weapons*, edited by Peter R. Lavoy, Scott D. Sagan, and James J. Wirtz (Ithaca, NY: Cornell University Press, 2000), 68.

[16] George Bush and Brent Scowcroft, *A World Transformed* (New York: Alfred A. Knopf, 1998), 442.

[17] Lawrence Freedman and Efraim Karsh, *The Gulf Conflict 1990–1991: Diplomacy and War in the New World Order* (London: Faber and Faber, 1993), 257.

foolish enough to use weapons of mass destruction, the US response would be absolutely overwhelming and devastating."[18]

Since there is no concrete evidence that Iraq resorted to WMD during the Gulf War, most analysts draw the conclusion that US threats to that effect were successful.[19] Indeed, if postwar accounts from the Iraqi leadership and military command are accurate, there is little doubt that they believed the coalition (as well as Israel) was prepared to use nuclear weapons or topple Hussein had Iraq attacked with CW.[20] This assessment, however, is usually unqualified, and presented without much direct evidence to substantiate such a significant finding. Sometimes the "proof" is as spurious as claiming that, since copies of President Bush's letter were found in several locations in Iraq, the threats therein must have been effective.[21] Very few commentators ask the decisive question of whether deterrence would have continued to hold firm if coalition forces had begun directly to threaten Hussein's grip on power with an attack on Baghdad itself.

Counterfactuals like this, of course, have no easy answers. One critical indicator of Hussein's intentions is the nature of his WMD

---

[18] Quoted in Robert Toth, "American Support Grows for Use of Nuclear Arms," *Los Angeles Times*, 3 February 1991.

[19] See, e.g., Kenneth N. Waltz, "More May Be Better," in Scott D. Sagan and Kenneth N. Waltz, *The Spread of Nuclear Weapons: A Debate* (New York: W.W. Norton, 1995), 13; Robin Ranger and David Wiencek, *The Devil's Brews II: Weapons of Mass Destruction and International Security*, Bailrigg Memorandum 17 (Lancaster: Centre for Defence and International Security Studies, 1997), 21; Daniel Byman, Kenneth Pollack, and Matthew Waxman, "Coercing Saddam Hussein: Lessons from the Past," *Survival* vol. 40, no. 3 (autumn 1998): 132; Robert G. Joseph and John F. Reichart, *Deterrence and Defense in a Nuclear, Biological, and Chemical Environment* (Washington DC: National Defense University Press, 1999), 19; Robert S. Litwak, *Rogue States and US Foreign Policy: Containment after the Cold War* (Baltimore, MD: The Johns Hopkins University Press, 2000), 41; Jan Lodal, *The Price of Dominance: The New Weapons of Mass Destruction and their Challenge to American Leadership* (New York: Council of Foreign Relations, 2001), 25.

[20] William M. Arkin, "Calculated Ambiguity: Nuclear Weapons and the Gulf War," *The Washington Quarterly* vol. 19, no. 4 (autumn 1996): 9; Robert W. Chandler with Robert J. Trees, *Tomorrow's War, Today's Decisions: Iraqi Weapons of Mass Destruction and the Implications of WMD-Armed Adversaries for Future US Military Strategy* (McLean, VA: AMCODA Press, 1996), 64; Cole, *The Eleventh Plague*, 128.

[21] Walter Pincus, "Military Study Mulled Deterrence of 'Fear,'" *Washington Post*, 5 July 2001.

capabilities and deployments at the time, for Iraq would hardly make such preparations without any intent for their use in combat or as a tool of deterrence. Much of our knowledge of these aspects comes from either UN weapons inspections or information from the defection in August 1995 of Hussein's son-in-law, Hussein Kamil Hassan al-Majid, who was in charge of Iraq's biological weapons (BW) program after its launch in 1985. We now know, for instance, that Iraq deployed 191 weapons (both aerial bombs and missiles) carrying BW to two sites before the Gulf War.[22] At least three separate BW agents were weaponized for use during war – developed to serve both tactical and strategic missions.[23] Moreover, as late as December 1990, Iraq was working on a spray tank to deliver anthrax by remotely piloted plane and had conducted field trials of munitions containing simulated anthrax and botulinum toxin.[24] According to Rolf Ekeus, then chief UN arms inspector, BW were "Baghdad's last trump card and could have been fired immediately – which is really unique. Bombs with biologically effective material were already stationed at military air bases and rocket launching sites. This is an absolute novelty – worldwide."[25]

As for CW preparation, there is evidence that Iraq had thirty CW Scud warheads ready for launch and even established chemical decontamination sites for protection.[26] UN inspections confirmed that Iraq deployed gas-filled 155mm artillery and 122mm multiple rocket rounds into the rear areas of the war theatre. Shockingly, Iraq's chemical weapons had no special visible markings, and were often stored in the same area as its conventional weapons.[27] Overall, given

[22] Raymond A. Zilinskas, "Iraq's Biological Warfare Program: The Past as Future?" in *Biological Weapons: Limiting the Threat*, edited by Joshua Lederberg (Cambridge, MA: The MIT Press, 1999), 141; Haselkorn, *The Continuing Storm*, 13; McCarthy and Tucker, "Saddam's Toxic Arsenal," 54.

[23] Anthony H. Cordesman, *Iran's Military Forces in Transition: Conventional Threats and Weapons of Mass Destruction* (Westport, CT: Praeger, 1999), 254.

[24] Chandler, *Tomorrow's War, Today's Decisions*, 78; McCarthy and Tucker, "Saddam's Toxic Arsenal," 53. However, the remotely piloted plane was probably not operational, and would have been quite vulnerable given US air superiority. See Zilinskas, "Iraq's Biological Warfare Program: The Past as Future?" 146.

[25] Quoted in Haselkorn, *The Continuing Storm*, 1–2.   [26] Ibid., 26, 37.

[27] Cordesman, *Iran's Military Forces in Transition*, 251.

the unlikely US initiation of WMD use, the extensive weaponization and deployment of Iraq's chemical-biological (CB) capability casts doubt on claims that such weapons were solely a deterrent against US nuclear strikes and would never be used first under any circumstances, as they were designed much more for war fighting than revenge attacks.

One crucial point of contention is whether or not Saddam Hussein actually pre-delegated control over any CB weapons to lower-level commanders, a "commitment tactic" normally used to enhance credibility. Some analysts argue that CB authority was quite circumscribed and probably released on a very strict basis, if at all.[28] However, the growing consensus on this issue is that Hussein did authorize local commanders to launch CW in the event of his death or the destruction of command-and-control links.[29] Recent scholarship reveals that Hussein probably hedged his bets against the dangers of unauthorized WMD use on the one hand, and the risk of a decapitation blow against him on the other, granting authority to a special unit commander to carry out a revenge attack in the event of a coalition nuclear strike.[30]

While uncertainty remains over whether Iraq would have actually escalated to WMD if Hussein's hold on power was jeopardized,

[28] Lawrence Freedman and Efraim Karsh, "How Kuwait was Won: Strategy in the Gulf War," *International Security* vol. 16, no. 2 (fall 1991): 34; Ranger and Wiencek, *The Devil's Brews II*, 43.

[29] Lewis A. Dunn, *Containing Nuclear Proliferation*, Adelphi Paper No. 263 (London: International Institute for Strategic Studies, winter 1991), 21; Elaine Sciolino, *The Outlaw State: Saddam Hussein's Quest for Power and the Gulf Crisis* (New York: John Wiley & Sons, 1991), 258; Hiro, *Desert Shield to Desert Storm*, 337; Chandler, *Tomorrow's War, Today's Decisions*, 90; Paul Bracken, *Fire in the East: The Rise of Asian Military Power and the Second Nuclear Age* (New York: Harper-Collins, 1999), 40; Haselkorn, *The Continuing Storm*, 49; Scott D. Sagan, "The Commitment Trap: Why the United States Should not Use Nuclear Threats to Deter Biological and Chemical Weapons Attacks," *International Security* vol. 24, no. 4 (spring 2000): 109; Joseph Cirincione, with John B. Wolfsthal and Miriam Rajkumar, *Deadly Arsenals: Tracking Weapons of Mass Destruction* (Washington DC: Carnegie Endowment for International Peace, June 2002), 279; Bob Drogin, " '91 Iraq Toxics Plan Reported," *Los Angeles Times*, 10 March 2003.

[30] McCarthy and Tucker, "Saddam's Toxic Arsenal," 76; Kenneth Pollack, "Why Iraq Can't Be Deterred," *New York Times*, 26 September 2002.

this reported contingency plan leads to the conclusion that it was certainly possible if not probable. This assessment is supported by British, US, and Israeli intelligence reports at the time that viewed CB attacks as likely in any event, and all but assured if Iraq was defeated and Hussein felt he was on the brink of being ousted.[31] Most telling, US Central Command's Situation Report on 24 February, the eve of the ground war, stated that it expected Iraq to initiate chemical operations within twenty-four hours.[32] Even the Soviet Union was fearful of a chemical response to the initiation of a ground war.[33] As Iraqi scholar Amatzia Baram put it, "The logic behind [Hussein's predelegation] is that he preferred Baghdad be annihilated rather than conquered by the allied forces."[34] Iraq clearly began "rocking the boat" with its missile attacks on Israel, and sent a particularly potent signal when it launched a missile[35] toward the Israeli nuclear facility

---

[31] Swain and Adams, "Saddam Gives Local Commanders Go-Ahead for Chemical Attacks"; Lisa Beyer, "Coping with Chemicals," *Time*, 25 February 1991; Tom Masland with Douglas Waller, "Are We Ready for Chemical War?" *Newsweek*, 4 March 1991; Michael R. Gordon and Bernard E. Trainor, *The General's War* (New York: Little, Brown and Company, 1995), 355; Haselkorn, *The Continuing Storm*, 59; Judith Miller, Stephen Engleberg, and William Broad, *Germs: The Ultimate Weapon* (London: Simon & Schuster, 2001), 113; Richard L. Russell, "CIA's Strategic Intelligence in Iraq," *Political Science Quarterly* vol. 117, no. 2 (summer 2002): 200.

[32] Arkin, "Calculated Ambiguity," 7.

[33] Hiro, *Desert Shield to Desert Storm*, 349. Primakov, the Soviet foreign minister, worried that Hussein suffered from a "Masada complex." See Rick Atkinson, *Crusade: The Untold Story of the Gulf War* (London: HarperCollins, 1994), 283.

[34] Amatzia Baram, "Saddam Husayn: Between his Power Base and the International Community," *Middle East Review of International Affairs* vol. 4, no. 4 (December 2000): 19.

[35] Notably, this missile – a Scud variant known as "al Hijarah" – was full of hardened concrete, an indication that it was capable of containing BW. See Ofra Bengio, *Saddam's World: Political Discourse in Iraq* (New York: Oxford University Press, 1998), 201; see also http://www.fas.org/nuke/guide/iraq/missile/al_hussein.htm. Avigdor Haselkorn concludes that this missile was not a mistake, but the indirect delivery of a last resort threat. According to Haselkorn, "Saddam was apparently hoping to convince his enemies that if they were thinking about toppling him, he was ready to bring Israel and perhaps the entire Middle East with him." See Haselkorn, *The Continuing Storm*, 72–75. Based on interviews with US government officials, if this was Hussein's intent, the message was not adequately communicated and the al Hijarah missile did not affect coalition war operations. Buster Glosson, phone interview with author, 26 August 2003; Brent Scowcroft, phone interview with author, 28 August 2003; James Baker, phone interview with author, 20 November 2003.

at Dimona. This was quite a dangerous decision, especially since Israel was barely restrained from striking back.[36] As Scott Sagan remarked, "How could Saddam Hussein have been *absolutely certain* that Israel would not retaliate with nuclear weapons? Governments take gambles, especially when they are in desperate straits."[37] In sum, it is not completely clear that Hussein was ever actually deterred; it is possible that "the fighting ended before the US (or, for that matter, Israeli) deterrence could be put to the test."[38]

When looked at in this way, the question is not simply whether Iraq was deterred from using WMD, but whether the United States itself was deterred (even partially) from achieving all of its objectives in Operation Desert Storm. While it is true that the United States never explicitly identified ousting Hussein as its war aim, there is ample evidence that this was highly desired; President Bush called upon the Iraqi people to "take matters into their own hands, to force Saddam Hussein, the dictator, to step aside," and even remarked that the American people did not want to "let Saddam get away."[39] With nearly all US analysts reassuring President Bush that Hussein would surely fall on his own, though, there was little reason to continue fighting even if much of the Iraqi army was in full retreat.[40] Moreover, there would have been other major obstacles in the way of taking the war to Baghdad. US policymakers noted (prophetically, it now appears) the risk of transforming Hussein into a nationalist hero, the costs of occupation when dealing with a hostile population, and the danger of opening the region up to Iranian influence through the "Lebanonization of

[36] Atkinson, *Crusade*, 84.

[37] Sagan, in *The Spread of Nuclear Weapons*, 129 (italics in the original).

[38] Haselkorn, *The Continuing Storm*, 85.

[39] Bush and Scowcroft, *A World Transformed*, 483; Atkinson, *Crusade*, 303. See also James A. Baker III, with Thomas M. DeFrank, *The Politics of Diplomacy* (New York: G.P. Putnam's Sons, 1995), 408 and Secretary of State Baker's comment that there is "unfinished business" in Gordon and Trainor, *The General's War*, 416.

[40] Michael Sterner, "Closing the Gate: The Persian Gulf War Revisited," *Current History* vol. 96, no. 606 (January 1997): 14; Andrew Cockburn and Patrick Cockburn, *Out of the Ashes: The Resurrection of Saddam Hussein* (London: Verso, 2000), 37.

Iraq."[41] At the same time, there were some military officers who did not want to call for a ceasefire, instead urging that a push toward Baghdad could be achieved with minimal casualties on both sides.[42] Even General Schwarzkopf commented in a postwar interview – later recanting after Colin Powell reminded him that he had an opportunity to air those views during the conflict – that his recommendation would have been to "continue the march" since the mission was not just to liberate Kuwait, but to destroy Iraq's offensive capabilities as well.[43]

President Bush, despite recognizing that there "hasn't been a clean end," felt that the original mission was accomplished and that pushing beyond it would be a political mistake, likely to result in the dissolution of the fighting coalition.[44] Granting that the dangers inherent in continuing war were quite legitimate, what is nevertheless amazing is that there is scarcely even a mention of the specter of WMD use that remained the Iraqi wildcard, nor of the intense danger that Israel would attempt unilaterally to destroy the Iraqi WMD capability if missile attacks continued. Indeed, there seems to be no public record whatsoever indicating that this unconventional last resort threat was even a partial reason for the cessation of hostilities.[45] This omission is

[41] Patrick E. Tyler, "Stirring the Iraqi Pot," *New York Times*, 21 March 1991; Yuen Foong Khong, "Vietnam, the Gulf, and US Choices: A Comparison," *Security Studies* vol. 2, no. 1 (autumn 1992): 89; Atkinson, *Crusade*, 300, 452; Baker, *The Politics of Diplomacy*, 435–37; Cockburn and Cockburn, *Out of the Ashes*, 24.

[42] Atkinson, *Crusade*, 475; Gordon and Trainor, *The General's War*, 423, 452, and 476. See also Kenneth M. Pollack, *The Threatening Storm* (New York: Random House, 2002), 46.

[43] R.W. Apple Jr., "Allies Destroy Iraqis' Main Force; Kuwait is Retaken after 7 Months," *New York Times*, 28 February 1991; Sterner, "Closing the Gate: The Persian Gulf War Revisited," 16. For Schwarzkopf's clarification, see H. Norman Schwarzkopf, with Peter Petre, *It Doesn't Take a Hero* (London: Bantam Press, 1992), 497; Colin L. Powell, with Joseph E. Persico, *A Soldier's Way* (London: Arrow Books, 1995), 524.

[44] Bush and Scowcroft, *A World Transformed*, 489; James Dao, "Senior Bush Defends '91 Decision on Iraq," *New York Times*, 1 March 2003.

[45] William L. Dowdy and Barry R. Schneider, "On to Baghdad? Or Stop at Kuwait? A Gulf War Question Revisited," *Defense Analysis* vol. 13, no. 3 (December 1997): 323; Samuel Berger, Caspar Weinberger, and Senator Joseph Biden, Hearing on Iraq before the Foreign Relations Committee, US Senate, Washington DC, 1 August 2002.

particularly surprising given how frank some of the same decision-makers were about expressing their concerns regarding Iraq's potential WMD threat in the lead-up to Operation Iraqi Freedom.[46] President Bush's closest advisors, though, insist that Iraq's suspected CB arsenal played no part in the Gulf War ceasefire decision.[47] Such disregard is unusual given the nearly universal alarm over Iraq's CB potential both before and during the war, but military strategists probably discounted the Iraqi threat because of the rudimentary design of its warheads and delivery methods.[48] Whether the ceasefire strategic assessment would have been the same had the US officials been aware of the true magnitude of the BW threat they faced is another matter.

As with any counterfactual analysis, while some conclusions are possible, one cannot make a definitive determination of who was successful in deterring whom. Identifying deterrence failures, fortunately, is a much easier task. On the Iraqi side, it certainly appears that Saddam Hussein misjudged the United States, especially in regard to his initial warning that a conflict against Iraq would turn into the "mother of all battles." His menacing threats to create "columns of dead bodies" did not stop coalition forces from following through with Desert Storm and ejecting the Iraqis from Kuwait, even with the knowledge (albeit underestimated) of Iraq's CB capability. Moreover, US forces were even confident enough to target Hussein himself with super-penetrator munitions, a remarkably foolhardy objective if they truly feared WMD retaliation in the wake of a decapitation strike.[49] On the American side, the United States was

---

[46] See Brent Scowcroft, "Don't Attack Saddam," *Wall Street Journal*, 15 August 2002; John Diamond, "Split over Iraq Grows More Public," *USA Today*, 19 August 2002. See also Avigdor Haselkorn, "Iraq's Bio-Warfare Option: Last Resort, Preemption, or a Blackmail Weapon?" *Biosecurity and Bioterrorism: Biodefense Strategy, Practice, and Science* vol. 1, no. 1 (2003): 19–26.

[47] Scowcroft, phone interview; Baker, phone interview.

[48] Gordon and Trainor, *The General's War*, 414; Russell, "CIA's Strategic Intelligence in Iraq," 200; Michael R. Gordon, "Iraq Said to Plan Tangling the US in Street Fighting," *New York Times*, 26 August 2002; Joby Warrick, "Uncertain Ability to Deliver a Blow," *Washington Post*, 5 September 2002.

[49] Byman, Pollack, and Waxman, "Coercing Saddam Hussein: Lessons from the Past," 141; Cockburn and Cockburn, *Out of the Ashes*, 34.

unable to deter Hussein from initially choosing to invade Kuwait, and then failed in attempting to compel him to withdraw; Hussein held his ground despite massive coalition forces aligned against him and American promises that his aggression would not stand. Significant controversy remains over how clear American threats were prior to the invasion of Kuwait, but regardless, it was an undeniably bold and aggressive move by Iraq against US interests.[50] Theoretically, it appears that Hussein believed that the asymmetries of interest involved were sufficient to enable a victory despite Iraq's inferior military capabilities. Saddam Hussein also took a major gamble in flouting Secretary of State Baker's threat to hold accountable those who commit terrorism against coalition partners or attempt to destroy Kuwaiti oilfields. Hussein did it all, apparently without fear of the consequences – raining missiles down on Israeli and Saudi cities, directing a (mostly failed) global terrorism effort, and setting oil wells ablaze in the last days of the war (causing one of the worst environmental disasters ever). Even if Iraq was aware of the Bush administration's private decision not to employ nuclear weapons in the event of an Iraqi CB attack, this is still the most unambiguous failure of a specific deterrent threat in the war.[51]

On the positive side of the ledger, it appears that US deterrent threats made Hussein think twice about using his WMD; after all, Iraqi restraint prevailed amidst a sweeping and humiliating defeat in the land war. While some analysts speculate that nonuse may have been a result of interrupted communications or a lack of atropine injectors to prevent self-contamination, this cannot fully explain the absence of CW in the long-range Scud launches or the scarcity of CW

[50] Thomas L. Friedman, "Envoy to Iraq, Faulted in Crisis, Says She Warned Hussein Sternly," *New York Times*, 21 March 1991; Darwish and Alexander, *Unholy Babylon*, 268, 270, 275; Janice Gross Stein, "Deterrence and Compellence in the Gulf, 1990–91: A Failed or Impossible Task?" *International Security* vol. 17, no. 2 (fall 1992): 152–56; Baram, "The Iraqi Invasion of Kuwait," 20; Cockburn and Cockburn, *Out of the Ashes*, 84; Said K. Aburish, *Saddam Hussein: The Politics of Revenge* (London: Bloomsbury, 2000), 282.

[51] Baker, *The Politics of Diplomacy*, 359; Bush and Scowcroft, *A World Transformed*, 463.

in the Kuwaiti front if mass devastation was Iraq's strategic intention.[52] It is much more likely that Hussein was concerned about an allied nuclear response, or the prospect of being forcibly ousted from power. At the same time, it also looks as if Hussein was able to force the United States to think twice about directly challenging his regime, even when pushing on to Baghdad would not have been a particularly taxing mission. There are many credible reasons for this restraint, and Iraq's CB may have been low on the list, but the fact that the coalition forces were equipped with gas masks and Israel inspected every missile attack for CW indicates an underlying fear that deterrence could fail. Even Colin Powell, then chairman of the Joint Chiefs of Staff, acknowledged that the possibility of a BW attack was his greatest nightmare during the war.[53] These fears would resurface over a decade later, when the United States did elect to march on Baghdad and force regime change, despite Iraq's renewed threat to use WMD.

IRAQI FREEDOM (2003)

As might be expected, relations between Iraq and the United States did not improve after the Desert Storm ceasefire agreement.[54] Arms inspections by the United Nations Special Commission (UNSCOM) were met with virtually immediate resistance and evasion by Iraqi officials. Iraqi forces brutally suppressed Kurdish uprisings in northern Iraq in 1991 and attacked Shi'a civilians in the south in 1992, prompting the United States to create safe havens and impose "no-fly zones" in both regions to restrict Iraq's military mobility. Iraq repeatedly bridled against these restraints, including initiating a build-up of troops on the Kuwaiti border in 1994 that required a US threat of large-scale strikes before Hussein agreed to withdraw. Two years

---

[52] Sciolino, *The Outlaw State*, 262; Stephen D. Bryen, "Ironic Chemistry: The UN Boosts Saddam's Threat," *Wall Street Journal*, 9 December 2002.

[53] Powell, *A Soldier's Way*, 503–04.

[54] For an excellent history of the litany of crises between the United States and Iraq in the decade following the 1990–91 Gulf War, see Daniel Byman and Matthew Waxman, *Confronting Iraq: US Policy and the Use of Force since the Gulf War* (Santa Monica, CA: RAND, 2000).

later, the United States actually launched a cruise missile strike to repel a second Iraqi incursion against Kurdish factions in the north. These incidents reveal an underlying Iraqi appreciation for deterrence, coupled with consistent attempts to probe its limits.

The biggest interwar conflict arose over the apparent failure of UNSCOM inspections. Frustrated with Iraq's repeated denials of access to suspected weapons facilities, President Clinton ordered Operation Desert Fox in December of 1998. According to Secretary of Defense William Cohen, the mission intended to diminish Iraq's capability to direct and protect its WMD programs, as well as delay its development of ballistic missiles capable of carrying CB weapons.[55] President Clinton justified the operation as necessary to bolster US credibility in the face of challenges by Saddam Hussein:

> If Saddam defies the world and we fail to respond, we will face a far greater threat in the future. Saddam will strike again at his neighbors; he will make war on his own people. And mark my words, he will develop weapons of mass destruction. He will deploy them, and he will use them. Because we are acting today, it is less likely that we will face these dangers in the future.[56]

Unfortunately, it is questionable whether Desert Fox was successful in achieving its goal of disarmament, and it hardly seemed to pose any threat whatsoever to Saddam Hussein's grip on power.[57]

After nearly three years of stalemate, the 11 September attacks dramatically increased US sensitivity to states developing WMD. President George W. Bush singled out Iraq as his prime concern, warning that if Saddam Hussein did not unambiguously disarm, "he'll

---

[55] William S. Cohen, Department of Defense News Briefing, 21 December 1998. Available at http://www.defenselink.mil/transcripts/1998/t12211998_t1221fox. html.

[56] William Clinton, Statement by the President, Office of the Press Secretary, 16 December 1998.

[57] See Fred Kaplan, "Strikes Didn't Finish Job US Set out to Do," *Boston Globe*, 21 December 1998; William M. Arkin, "Desert Fox Delivery; Precision Undermined its Purpose," *Washington Post*, 17 January 1999. See also Byman and Waxman, *Confronting Iraq*, 68.

find out" the consequences.[58] Bush was reportedly shocked by briefings in the wake of 11 September indicating that Al Qaeda was in the market for WMD and had reputed links to Iraqi agents.[59] At the time, defectors were the primary source of US intelligence regarding Iraqi WMD advances, revealing (perhaps with some self-interest) the supposed existence of secret underground BW labs and other hidden facilities.[60] The United States was aware of evidence to the contrary years before Iraqi Freedom,[61] but it was not until well after the war that US intelligence conceded the illusory nature of Iraq's WMD arsenal.[62]

[58] Quoted in Mike Allen, "Iraq's Weapons Could Make it a Target, Bush Says," *Washington Post*, 27 November 2001.

[59] Carla Anne Robbins and Jeanne Cummings, "How Bush Decided that Hussein Must Be Ousted from Atop Iraq," *Wall Street Journal*, 14 June 2002. It did not take long for these reputed links to fall into question and eventually become virtually discredited. See David Ignatius, "Dubious Iraqi Link," *Washington Post*, 15 March 2002; Walter Pincus, "No Link between Hijacker, Iraq Found, US Says," *Washington Post*, 1 May 2002; Dana Priest, "Al Qaeda–Iraq Link Recanted," *Washington Post*, 1 August 2004. Sadly, it appears that the build-up to Iraqi Freedom and the conflict itself has made these terrorist connections a reality. See William Safire, "Clear Ties of Terror," *New York Times*, 27 January 2003.

[60] See, e.g., Judith Miller, "An Iraqi Defector Tells of Work on at Least 20 Hidden Weapons Sites," *New York Times*, 20 December 2001; James Bone, "Iraq Sites for Bio-War Revealed by Defector," *The Times* (London), 12 July 2002; Michael Evans, "Secret Files on Baghdad's Weapons Plans," *The Times* (London), 29 August 2002; Johanna McGeary, "What Does Saddam Have?" *Time*, 16 September 2002.

[61] See, e.g., Karen DeYoung, "Baghdad Weapons Programs Dormant; Iraq's Inactivity Puzzles US Officials," *Washington Post*, 15 July 1999; Colum Lynch, "Iraqi Defector Claimed Arms were Destroyed by 1995," *Washington Post*, 1 March 2003; James Risen, "CIA Held Back Iraqi Arms Data, US Officials Say," *New York Times*, 6 July 2004. Douglas Jehl, "Report Warned Bush Team about Intelligence Doubts," *New York Times*, 6 November 2005.

[62] See Special Advisor to the Director of Central Intelligence, *Comprehensive Report on Iraq's Weapons of Mass Destruction* (30 September 2004). Available at http://www.cia.gov/cia/reports/iraq_wmd_2004/index.html. The possibility that Iraq diverted its WMD to Syria is an alternative theory, but one which has not yet been substantiated. See Bill Gertz, "Iraqi Weapons Pipeline Probed," *Washington Times*, 25 May 2004; Rowan Scarborough, "Saddam Agents on Syria Border Helped Move Banned Materials," *Washington Times*, 16 August 2004; Bill Gertz, "Photos Point to Removal of Weapons," *Washington Times*, 29 October 2004; Rowan Scarborough, "CIA Can't Rule out WMD Move to Syria," *Washington Times*, 27 April 2005. An addendum to the Comprehensive Report assessed that it was unlikely such a transfer took place. See Special Advisor to the Director of Central Intelligence, *Addendums to the Comprehensive Report* (March 2005), 1. Available at http://permanent.access.gpo.gov/DuelferRpt/Addendums.pdf.

In the spring of 2002, the United States began drawing up possible war plans for Iraq and President Bush made it clear that military force was under consideration, remarking "[Saddam Hussein] is a problem, and we're going to deal with him."[63] At a news conference, President Bush declared that he had made up his mind that "Hussein needs to go."[64] Meanwhile, Saddam Hussein was understandably trying to improve his standing in the Middle East, signing economic agreements with his neighbors and extending an olive branch to Kuwait.[65] For the United States, though, Hussein reprised his rhetoric from before the 1990–91 Gulf War, warning that any invading troops would be "buried in their own coffins."[66] At a war council meeting, Hussein allegedly disclosed to his officers that in the event of war he would respond with "everything," both on the battlefield and on "all other fronts."[67]

Listening to this rhetoric and observing the gradual US military build-up in the Gulf, the international community sought to slow down the push to war with calls for negotiation and a meeting at the UN Security Council. The US Congress also demanded hearings, arguing that President Bush could not conduct a military operation far beyond the scope of Operation Desert Fox without prior congressional authorization.[68] After considerable debate, the October 2002 US Joint Resolution authorizing force against Iraq was a huge victory for President Bush, cementing the credibility of his demand that Iraq disarm. The wording of the resolution indicated a loss of confidence in the ability of the United States to contain Iraq:

---

[63] Quoted in Dana Milbank and Mike Allen, "US Will Take Action against Iraq, Bush Says," *Washington Post*, 14 March 2002.

[64] Quoted in Bob Woodward, "President Bush Broadens Anti-Hussein Order," *Washington Post*, 16 June 2002.

[65] See Walter Pincus, "Hussein Tries to Mend Fences with Neighbors," *Washington Post*, 19 July 2002.

[66] Quoted in Howard Schneider, "Iraqi Leader Says Invaders will be 'Buried,'" *Washington Post*, 9 August 2002.

[67] Quoted in Arnaud de Borchgrave, "Commentary: Saddam Hussein's War Plan," *United Press International*, 10 July 2002.

[68] See James Dao, "Call in Congress for Full Airing of Iraq Policy," *New York Times*, 18 July 2002.

Whereas Iraq's demonstrated capability and willingness to use weapons of mass destruction, the risk that the current Iraqi regime will either employ those weapons to launch a surprise attack against the United States or its Armed Forces or provide them to international terrorists who would do so, and the extreme magnitude of harm that would result to the United States and its citizens from such an attack, combine to justify action by the United States to defend itself.[69]

Having previously promised never again to admit weapons inspectors, Saddam Hussein changed course in the face of a unanimous November 2002 Security Council resolution calling for their return.[70] President Bush described the resolution as a "final test" for Saddam Hussein, warning that disarmament must be "prompt and unconditional, or he will face the severest consequences."[71]

Despite high hopes riding on the shoulders of Hans Blix and Mohammed ElBaradei, the top UN inspection officials, Iraq could not break its habit of denying full and open access to inspectors. The United States quickly grew disillusioned with the process, publishing two reports (*Apparatus of Lies*[72] and *What Does Disarmament Look Like?*[73]) to highlight Iraq's deception and lack of cooperation. Then National Security Advisor Condoleezza Rice called the Iraqi weapons declaration a 12,200 page lie, describing the inspections regime as a giant shell game meant to fool the UN.[74] The pessimistic account of Hans Blix before the Security Council solidified these sentiments,

[69] US Government, *Joint Resolution to Authorize the Use of United States Armed Forces against Iraq*, Office of the Press Secretary, 2 October 2002.
[70] United Nations, Security Council Resolution 1441, UN Doc. S/RES/1441 (2002).
[71] Quoted in Julia Preston, "Security Council Votes, 15–0, for Tough Iraq Resolution," *New York Times*, 9 November 2002.
[72] US Government, *Apparatus of Lies* (Washington DC: 2003). Available at http://www.whitehouse.gov/ogc/apparatus/apparatus-of-lies.pdf.
[73] The White House, *What Does Disarmament Look Like?* (Washington DC: January 2003). Available at http://www.whitehouse.gov/infocus/iraq/disarmament/disarmament.pdf.
[74] Condoleezza Rice, "Why We Know Iraq is Lying," *New York Times*, 23 January 2003.

setting the stage for Secretary of State Colin Powell's pivotal presentation in early February 2003 laying out the US case for war.[75] Although Iraq eased its intransigence by permitting overflights, prompting Hans Blix to soften his assessment, the United States had settled on war, demanding not only disarmament but also that Hussein step down from power.

Unlike the prelude to Desert Storm, Iraq's threats prior to Iraqi Freedom were remarkably reserved and vague. For example, without any mention of CB weapons, an Iraqi aide promised suicide attacks in Iraq and beyond, turning the whole region into a "sea of resistance and danger for Americans."[76] Iraq's reticence was probably largely owing to the fact that anything more explicit would have been an acknowledgment of its WMD possession and thus would have invited calls for yet more invasive inspections. Once war began, however, reports began to circulate of a "red line" around Baghdad that would serve as a tripwire for CW use.[77] The United States military took these reports seriously and fully expected Iraq to turn to CB weapons as a form of last resort retaliation.[78]

---

[75] Colin Powell, Address to the UN Security Council, New York, 5 February 2003. Available at http://www.whitehouse.gov/news/releases/2003/02/20030205-1.html.

[76] Quoted in Ian Fischer, "Iraqi Aide Threatens Suicide Attacks," *New York Times*, 2 February 2003.

[77] See Bradley Graham, " 'Scorched Earth' Plans in Iraq Cited," *Washington Post*, 19 December 2002; Greg Jaffe, "Intelligence Suggests Hussein Allowed Chemical-Weapon Use," *Wall Street Journal*, 20 March 2003; David E. Sanger, "US Officials Fear Iraqis Plan to Use Gas on GIs," *New York Times*, 25 March 2003; Bernard Weinraub, "Army Reports Iraq is Moving Toxic Arms to its Troops," *New York Times*, 28 March 2003; Bill Gertz, "Coalition Still Wary of Chemical Weapons," *Washington Times*, 5 April 2003.

[78] See, e.g., Rowan Scarborough, "Saddam Would Hit Buildup of Troops," *Washington Times*, 17 June 2002; Mark Mazzetti and Kevin Whitelaw, "Six Deadly Fears," *US World and News Report*, 17 February 2003. In fact, there are reports that Hussein actually did attempt to order a CW attack, even though Iraq may have lacked the capability to carry it out. See Bryan Bender, "Regime Ordered Chemical Attack, Investigator Says," *Boston Globe*, 8 August 2003. Analysts believe either reports of Iraq's pre-delegation orders may have been a bluff to attempt to deter the United States or perhaps the Iraqi Special Republican Guard was providing faulty information to its commanders. See Walter Pincus and Dana Priest, "Hussein's Weapons May Have Been Bluff," *Washington Post*, 1 October 2003; Charles Krauthammer, "Calling Iraq's Bluff," *Washington Post*, 30 January 2004.

In response, the United States sought to defuse the CB threat through offensive attacks, defensive precautions, and deterrence. The most direct route was for US forces to strike first and destroy any WMD stockpiles before they could be used.[79] Alternatively, US troops were equipped with the specialized suits, vehicles, and treatments necessary to fight even in a contaminated battlefield environment.[80] Finally, beyond attempting to convince Iraqi officials that employing their CB capabilities would be futile, US officials also threatened general retaliation as well as personalized punishment for those responsible. Around the time of the US congressional debates, for instance, two senior US senators disclosed that US officials had warned Saddam Hussein that he and his country could face "annihilation" if Iraq employed WMD during the war.[81] The United States also initiated an intense campaign involving speeches, leaflets, and even e-mails that threatened war crimes trials for any Iraqi official carrying out an order to use WMD.[82] President Bush gave several speeches reinforcing this message, declaring in one: "An Iraqi regime faced with its own demise may attempt cruel and desperate measures. If Saddam Hussein orders such measures, his generals would be well advised to refuse those orders. If they do not refuse, they must understand that all war criminals will be pursued

---

[79] James Dao, "Pentagon's Worry: Iraqi Chemical Arms," *New York Times*, 19 May 2002.

[80] See John J. Lumpkin, "US Sees Limit to Iraqi Chemical Threat," *Philadelphia Inquirer*, 14 July 2002.

[81] Joyce Howard Price, "US Reprisal to be 'Annihilation,'" *Washington Times*, 9 September 2002. In reality, as in Desert Storm, the American options for retaliation would have been rather limited given the profound reluctance to resort to nuclear weapons and the already extensive conventional bombing plans. See Bradley Graham, "As US Girds for Worst in Iraq, Retaliation isn't Clear-Cut Issue," *Washington Post*, 29 January 2003.

[82] Vince Crawley, "US to Iraq: Using Weapons of Mass Destruction Would Be a Mistake," *ArmyTimes.com*, 13 August 2002; Thomas D. Grant, "For an Iraq Amnesty," *Washington Post*, 20 August 2002; Walter Pincus, "US Effort Aimed at Iraqi Officers," *Washington Post*, 30 September 2002; James Drummond and Edward Alden, "Rumsfeld Orders Extra Forces to Mideast," *Financial Times* (London), 13 January 2003; Thom Shanker and David Johnston, "US Lists Iraqis to Punish, or to Work with," *New York Times*, 26 February 2003.

and punished."[83] In essence, the United States carried out a multi-faceted strategy intended both to strip whatever Iraqi WMD did exist of their coercive power, and to persuade Iraqi officials not to execute orders to carry out WMD attacks. Using the terminology from chapter 2, this counterbalanced the commitment tactic of pre-delegation and provided some defensive protection in the event that deterrence failed through a last resort attack.

From a broader perspective, Iraqi Freedom pitted the US compellent threat that Iraq admit inspectors unconditionally and depose Saddam Hussein against the Iraqi deterrent threat to make it extremely costly for the United States to do so by force. Where Iraq miscalculated, it appears, is in thinking that its latent CB threat and the costs of occupation would deter the United States from invading Baghdad as it may have in 1991. Even though the US military was indeed fearful of the potential for casualties from CB weapons, the previously mentioned US precautions had diluted this threat to an acceptable level. If anything, the United States was more concerned about the conventional challenges of waging an urban war campaign against Iraqi guerilla fighters.[84] Given the desire of the Iraqi leadership not to be overthrown, the balance of interests probably favored Iraq, but President Bush and other US officials were deeply committed to their course and believed that the costs of occupation would be manageable.

The obvious lesson from Iraqi Freedom for other states singled out by the United States as national security threats was that conventional military strength coupled with limited WMD capabilities would not suffice to deter the US military. The other two members of the so-called "axis of evil" could hardly fail to note this disturbing result and adjust their deterrence strategies accordingly. The next chapter details how North Korea dealt with this problem, demonstrating the vastly increased leverage bestowed by nuclear weapon capabilities.

---

[83] George W. Bush, Remarks on Iraq, Cincinnati, Ohio, 7 October 2002; see also George W. Bush, "Taking Action to Strengthen Small Business," St. Louis, Missouri, 22 January 2003.

[84] See Robin Wright, "An Iraqi Campaign Faces Many Hurdles," *Los Angeles Times*, 10 March 2002; Mark Thompson, "Going Door to Door," *Time*, 16 September 2002.

4 North Korea

Thankfully free from outright war, the US relationship with North Korea over the past dozen years has nevertheless been just as strained and combative as that with Iraq. Edging uncomfortably close to war during the first plutonium reprocessing crisis in 1993–94, both sides reached an uneasy truce that fell apart dramatically a decade later. Deterrent and compellent threats underlay all of the negotiations, with nuclear overtones that were not present to the same extent in the Persian Gulf. This chapter analyzes both crises, drawing lessons as to how WMD affect real-world conflict situations.

THE FIRST CRISIS (1993–94)

Even though its nuclear research program dates back to the 1950s, by the mid-1980s North Korea's main communist benefactors – China and the Soviet Union – were providing less than certain defense support, leading the Democratic People's Republic of Korea (DPRK) to decide to develop a secret nuclear weapons capability as a deterrent against US military intervention.[1] During a covert refueling of the Yongbyon reactor in 1989, US intelligence agencies estimate that the

---

[1] Victor D. Cha, "The Second Nuclear Age: Proliferation Pessimism Versus Sober Optimism in South Asia and East Asia," *Journal of Strategic Studies* vol. 24, no. 4 (December 2001): 91. Of course, relations between the United States and North Korea were patchy throughout the Cold War. North Korea pursued a succession of dramatically erratic and brazen provocations, ranging from a commando raid on the South Korean Blue House (1968), the illegal seizure of an American electronic intelligence vessel named the USS *Pueblo* (1968), the downing of a navy EC-121 reconnaissance plane, killing thirty (1969), the brutal axe murder of two American officers over the pruning of a tree in the De-Militarized Zone (1976), and blowing up half of the South Korean cabinet with a bomb in Rangoon (1983), just to name a few. See Richard K. Betts, "What Will it Take to Deter the United States?" *Parameters* vol. 21, no. 4 (winter 1995–96): 79, footnote 4; Chuck Downs, *Over the Line: North Korea's Negotiating Strategy* (Washington DC: AEI Press, 1999), 119–62.

DPRK extracted and potentially reprocessed approximately ten to twelve kilograms of plutonium, sufficient fissile material for at least two nuclear devices, depending on the design.[2] US officials also suspect North Korea of having produced a wide range of CB weapons – an estimated stockpile of 2,500 to 5,000 tons – and ballistic missiles with nearly intercontinental range.[3] Overall, North Korea's WMD programs remain largely a mystery to the outside world, and are becoming even more so now that the DPRK has expelled all International Atomic Energy Agency (IAEA) inspectors from the country.

Diplomatically, ever since Reagan's "modest initiative" in 1988, the United States has sought to engage North Korea, all the while communicating a tough stance of firm resolve and deterrent power. Relations were improving dramatically in December of 1991, when North and South Korea concluded the Joint Declaration on the Denuclearization of the Korean Peninsula, providing for mutual inspections and renouncing both nuclear reprocessing and uranium enrichment.[4] Unfortunately, after a promising initial meeting in New York in January of 1992, IAEA inspections later that year at Yongbyon uncovered evidence that three plutonium separations may have taken place in 1989, prompting accusations of cheating and demands for evidence of the missing plutonium.[5] The United States presented satellite photos indicating further deception in February of 1993, enraging members of Congress and leading North Korea to announce its intention to withdraw from the Nonproliferation

---

[2] Joseph S. Bermudez Jr., "Exposing North Korea's Secret Nuclear Infrastructure – Part Two," *Jane's Intelligence Review* vol. 11, no. 8 (August 1999): 42; Joseph S. Bermudez Jr., *The Armed Forces of North Korea* (New York: I.B. Tauris, 2001), 8.

[3] Joseph S. Bermudez Jr., "The Rise and Rise of North Korea's ICBMs," *Jane's International Defense Review* vol. 32, no. 7 (1 July 1999); Joseph S. Bermudez Jr., "The Democratic People's Republic of Korea and Unconventional Weapons," in *Planning the Unthinkable*, edited by Peter R. Lavoy, Scott D. Sagan, and James J. Wirtz (Ithaca, NY: Cornell University Press, 2000), 191.

[4] Marcus Noland, *Avoiding the Apocalypse: The Future of the Two Koreas* (Washington DC: Institute for International Economics, 2000), 147.

[5] Don Oberdorfer, *The Two Koreas: A Contemporary History* (London: Warner Books, 1997), 270.

Treaty (NPT). As Korea expert Don Oberdorfer put it, "The announcement of the withdrawal was treated as an incomprehensible
act of defiance and an ominous sign that North Korea was hell-
bent on the production of nuclear weapons."[6] Some on Capitol Hill
and in the American media began pressing for tough counteraction,
including the consideration of military options.[7] Talks recommenced later that year, culminating in a joint statement that sus-
pended the North Korean withdrawal threat one day before it was to
take effect.

With this temporary reprieve in hand, the IAEA returned to its
demand for full inspections, even though North Korea was actively
seeking a middle ground that allowed a continuity of monitoring but
forbade investigation into its prior potential diversion of fissile material.[8] Some bargaining took place, as the United States raised the
option of providing a proliferation-resistant light water reactor and
discussed the possible tradeoff of inspections in return for a suspen-
sion of the US–South Korean military training known as Team Spirit
Exercises. Talks were never consistent, however, and soon broke
down amidst reports of a North Korean military build-up along the
De-Militarized Zone (DMZ) between the Koreas, triggering a reconsideration of sanctions by the United States. With inspections still on
hold, the IAEA announced that its monitoring equipment would soon
run out of film and batteries, placing at risk the ability to ensure that
North Korea would not remove more plutonium from its reactor.
About this time, in November of 1993, President Clinton claimed on
NBC's "Meet the Press" that "North Korea cannot be allowed to
develop a nuclear bomb."[9] South Korean president Kim Young Sam

---

[6] Ibid., 280.
[7] Robert S. Litwak, *Rogue States and US Foreign Policy: Containment after the Cold War* (Baltimore, MD: The Johns Hopkins University Press, 2000), 210.
[8] Michael J. Mazarr, *North Korea and the Bomb: A Case Study in Nonproliferation* (London: Macmillan, 1995), 128.
[9] Quoted in Bermudez, "The DPRK and Unconventional Weapons," 189. Later, after various US officials speculated that North Korea already had at least one bomb, the White House said that Clinton had misspoken. See Oberdorfer, *The Two Koreas*, 295.

backed this firm position, stating, "North Korea's nuclear development should be stopped by all means."[10]

Relations continued to plummet with the start of the new year, as the United States prepared to send reinforcements to the peninsula and began to plan for Team Spirit Exercises. A new visit by the IAEA in March of 1994 failed to guarantee that plutonium had not been reprocessed since its previous inspection, but fortunately seemed able to preserve the continuity of its monitoring capabilities.[11] Talks remained stymied, and became heated when a North Korean official broadcast declared that the new military steps by the United States and South Korea had "pushed the situation to a very dangerous brink of war."[12] The most dramatic remark, however, came from Park Yong Su, a North Korean official who made the now famous warning to his South Korean counterpart during negotiations at the DMZ "truce village" of Panmunjom: "Seoul is not far from here. If a war breaks out, it will be a sea of fire. Mr. Song, it will probably be difficult for you to survive."[13] As in the dialogue leading up to Desert Storm, the United States responded forcefully to this deterrent threat, with Secretary of Defense William Perry issuing a sharp warning that the United States intended to stop North Korea from developing a substantial arsenal of nuclear weapons even at the potential cost of another war on the Korean Peninsula.[14]

As if tensions were not high enough, crisis struck in April 1994 when Kim Il Sung announced that North Korea would shut down the major reactor at Yongbyon a second time so that spent fuel rods from its core could be removed, potentially permanently erasing evidence of its past defueling. Surprisingly, Kim coupled this revelation with

---

[10] Quoted in Andrew Mack, "A Nuclear North Korea," *World Policy Journal* vol. 11, no. 2 (summer 1994): 28.   [11] Mazarr, *North Korea and the Bomb*, 155.

[12] Quoted in T. R. Reid, "North Korea Warns of 'Brink of War,' " *Washington Post*, 23 March 1994.

[13] Quoted in J.F.O. McAllister, "Pyongyang's Dangerous Game," *Time*, 4 April 1994. See also Oberdorfer, *The Two Koreas*, 304.

[14] R. Jeffrey Smith, "Perry Sharply Warns North Korea," *Washington Post*, 31 March 1994.

two remarkably conciliatory interviews in which he disowned the "sea of fire" comment by calling it "a mistake," renounced any nuclear ambitions, and called for a recommencement of talks with the United States.[15] Focusing on North Korea's actions rather than its words, the United States proved that Perry's statement was far from empty rhetoric; along with harsh economic sanctions, subsequent accounts now reveal that the United States was also contemplating a preemptive attack – readying a war plan that called for the precision bombing of the Yongbyon facility, hoping to destroy it and entomb the plutonium without causing a meltdown.[16] As the United States considered its military options, the IAEA responded to North Korea by emphasizing that it would be imperative for its inspectors to have complete access during the defueling to ensure that no diversion of fuel rods took place. It also requested samples from the reactor's fuel rods to determine the amount of plutonium unloaded in the 1989 shutdown.[17] The DPRK agreed to allow inspectors to view the defueling, but refused the sampling request.

When unloading of the fuel rods began in mid-May, proceeding at a pace that made proper IAEA monitoring impossible, chief inspector Hans Blix declared that confidence over the control of reactor fuel had been irreversibly lost. With this news, the pressure rose further and the United States pushed its case for economic sanctions to the international community, stating that the DPRK had "crossed the point of no return."[18] North Korea promptly responded that it would "rather accept a war" than give up its defense secrets,

---

[15] Quoted in Leon V. Sigal, *Disarming Strangers: Nuclear Diplomacy with North Korea* (Princeton, NJ: Princeton University Press, 1998), 111.

[16] Ashton B. Carter and William J. Perry, *Preventive Defense: A New Security Strategy for America* (Washington DC: Brookings Institution Press, 1999), 128; Ashton B. Carter and William J. Perry, "Back to the Brink," *Washington Post*, 20 October 2002; Selig S. Harrison, *Korean Endgame: A Strategy for Reunification and US Disengagement* (Princeton, NJ: Princeton University Press, 2002), 122; William J. Perry and Ashton B. Carter, "The Crisis Last Time," *New York Times*, 19 January 2003.

[17] Paul Leventhal and Steven Dolley, "The North Korean Nuclear Crisis," Nuclear Control Institute, 16 June 1994. Available at http://www.nci.org/n/nkib2.htm.

[18] Quoted in Leventhal and Dolley, "The North Korean Nuclear Crisis."

and that "sanctions mean war, and there is no mercy in war."[19] Just two days later the US ambassador ordered his family out of Seoul and met with the commander of US forces in Korea to map out evacuation plans.[20] Relations were in a free-fall, as North Korea withdrew from the IAEA and again hinted at leaving the NPT.

Conservatives in the American press were outraged, and began another strong push for the consideration of military strikes.[21] The US military command was indeed weighing that very option in a major strategy session, and on 18 June President Clinton met with his national security advisors to finalize an "Action Plan" for a substantial expansion of American military forces in and near Korea.[22] Around this time former president Jimmy Carter was en route to Pyongyang on a mission to try and find a face-saving way for North Korea to avert the looming war, and upon meeting with Kim Il Sung the two worked out a plan to keep inspectors in place and start a new round of talks.[23] Perry testified to Congress that he was just in the process of presenting several alternative build-up plans to President Clinton for his final approval at the very hour they got word from Carter that the North Koreans were prepared to sit down and negotiate an agreement.[24] Though many in Washington were infuriated by Carter's intervention, his trip helped to break the diplomatic logjam and bring about a round of talks that eventually culminated in the Agreed Framework in October of 1994.

Most analysts and the direct participants agree that the danger of war during these two months was quite high. Robert Litwak opines, "Given the mutual mistrust and the absence of regular contact between North Korea and the United States, the May–June

[19] Quoted in Oberdorfer, *The Two Koreas*, 311.

[20] Harrison, *Korean Endgame*, 117.

[21] Charles Krauthammer, "Get Ready for War," *Washington Post*, 3 June 1994; Sigal, *Disarming Strangers*, 117.   [22] Harrison, *Korean Endgame*, 118.

[23] See Douglas Brinkley, *The Unfinished Presidency* (New York: Penguin Putnam, 1998), 400–10.

[24] William Perry, Hearing on Security Implications of the Nuclear Agreement with North Korea before the Senate Armed Services Committee, US Senate, Washington DC, 26 January 1995.

1994 crisis carried a significant risk of inadvertent military escalation through misperception and miscalculation."[25] Since the conflict was defused before it could get too far out of hand, it is difficult to judge how actively deterrence – and compellence – were at play. On the one hand, a DPRK preemptive attack seemed extremely unlikely, despite the comment of one North Korean colonel to a US officer that "We are not going to let you do a build-up."[26] On the other hand, the likelihood of an unprovoked US military attack appeared equally remote, especially given US casualty estimates of a prospective war. Perry noted that he and General Shalikashvili (chairman of the Joint Chiefs of Staff) had concluded that a preemptive attack "was very likely to incite the North Koreans to launch a military attack on South Korea," effectively removing the military option from further consideration.[27] There were certainly not many attractive options, and even the alternative of sanctions carried a very real threat of a devastating war. In a hearing before Congress, Perry testified that he took the DPRK "sea of flames" rhetoric seriously enough to lead him to recommend to the president that any imposition of sanctions on North Korea should be accompanied by an immediate augmentation of US military forces in the Republic of Korea.[28]

Essentially, using the theoretical framework from chapter 2, the DPRK successfully communicated the impression (feigned or actual) of irrationality, leading to the quite rational outcome of deterrence power against the United States. Though North Korea certainly was

[25] Litwak, *Rogue States and US Foreign Policy*, 216.

[26] Quoted in Oberdorfer, *The Two Koreas*, 326. There is some evidence that the North Korean military was moving to a war footing, conducting unusual training exercises in response to the US reinforcement measures. See Mitchell Reiss, *Bridled Ambition* (Washington DC: Woodrow Wilson Center Press, 1995), 271.

[27] Steven Greenhouse, "Perry Says US Considered Bombing North Korean Reactor," *The Houston Chronicle*, 25 January 1995; Carter and Perry, *Preventive Defense*, 128–29. Despite this conclusion, in November 2002 former president Bill Clinton reportedly told an audience at the University of California's Davis campus that, eight years before, "we literally threatened to attack and planned to attack North Korea if they didn't end their nuclear weapons program." See Carl Limbacher, "Clinton: I Threatened to Attack North Korea," *NewsMax.com*, 24 November 2002.

[28] Perry, Hearing on North Korea, 26 January 1995.

deficient in overall strategic capabilities and could not threaten the US homeland directly, its abundant artillery batteries located within striking distance of Seoul (and therefore US troops as well) were a potent weapon that was extremely worrisome for American warplanners. Moreover, the DPRK had a sufficient compelling interest in protecting its nascent nuclear program and avoiding sanctions that would further cripple its economy to make the threat of all-out war credible. In the final analysis, to the United States, the imperative to discover North Korea's potential to produce a handful of nuclear weapons was simply not worth the risk of a major conflict. US Ambassador Laney and General Luck both saw a diplomatic arrangement as the most prudent outcome, commenting, "Why are we going to risk killing a million people? A bomb or two can't even do that."[29] In fact, Perry implied a tacit consent to a limited DPRK arsenal, conceding in April of 1994, "Our policy right along has been oriented to try to keep North Korea from getting a significant nuclear-weapon capability." Regarding the one to two weapons the United States already suspected the DPRK of possessing, Perry said, "We don't know anything we can do about that. What we can do something about, though, is stopping them from building beyond that."[30]

At the same time, if we reverse perspective, it becomes apparent that the United States had a fair amount of deterrence leverage itself. Or, more accurately, the United States had a strong coercive stance that combined elements of compellence (the demand that North Korea freeze its nuclear program) and deterrence (a warning not to attack South Korean or US forces).[31] Of course, we will never know how events would have played out if North Korea had not sat down to talks, but Perry and his colleague Ashton Carter insist that they were prepared to risk war if the Agreed Framework had fallen

[29] Quoted in Sigal, *Disarming Strangers*, 122.

[30] Quoted in Mark Thompson, "Well, Maybe a Nuke or Two," *Time*, 11 April 1994.

[31] Yuen Foong Khong, "Strategic Coercion in East Asia: The Cases of Cambodia and North Korea," in *Strategic Coercion: Concepts and Cases*, edited by Lawrence Freedman (Oxford: Oxford University Press, 1998), 129.

through. Most US officials involved in the crisis likewise maintain that the North Korean threat of war did not deter them from pursuing their objective of restraining further DPRK nuclear development.[32] North Korea did ultimately have to offer concessions to reach a compromise, implying that there was some fear that continued "stonewalling" on their part could lead to a military strike on Yongbyon or international sanctions, despite the DPRK threat of war in response.

Especially given the almost total lack of knowledge of the DPRK leadership, it is quite hard to determine which side felt the greater deterrence pressure; for two states facing the imminent prospect of catastrophic war, both seemed willing to stand firm over certain baseline negotiating positions no matter what. Deterrence theory would generally predict a more cautious approach, though this was perhaps an instance of both sides employing commitment techniques and thereby locking themselves into positions from which it became increasingly difficult to make a graceful retreat. Theory aside, even if deterrence worked successfully in this case, the potential for war in the spring of 1994 was disturbingly high. Robert Gallucci, the chief negotiator of the Agreed Framework with North Korea, felt "[t]here was every indication at the time that President Clinton would have used force rather than allow the North Koreans to separate more plutonium to produce nuclear weapons."[33] Perry himself said in a 1999 news conference, "We were literally within a day of imposing severe sanctions on North Korea – sanctions that they said would be equivalent to an act of war. We were within a day

---

[32] Joel Wit, interview with author, 18 August 2003; William Perry, phone interview with author, 21 August 2003; Robert Gallucci, phone interview with author, 22 August 2003. For a more in-depth assessment, see William M. Drennan, "Nuclear Weapons and North Korea: Who's Coercing Whom?" in *The United States and Coercive Diplomacy*, edited by Robert J. Art and Patrick M. Cronin (Washington DC: United States Institute of Peace Press, 2003). See also Joel S. Wit, Daniel Poneman and Robert Gallucci, *Going Critical: The First North Korean Nuclear Crisis* (Washington DC: Brookings Institution Press, 2004).

[33] Quoted in David E. Sanger and James Dao, "North Korea Says it Regains Access to its Plutonium," *New York Times*, 23 December 2002.

of making major additions to our troop deployments in Korea, and we were about to undertake an evacuation of American civilians from Korea."[34] Lieutenant General Howard Estes, the senior US Air Force officer in Korea, admitted, "Inside we all thought we were going to war."[35]

Perhaps both the United States and North Korea were engaged in a high-stakes bluff and neither would have actually stayed the course into conflict. The costs of war for both sides would have been immense, resulting in the virtual annihilation of Seoul and the eventual demise of the DPRK regime, along with considerable military casualties. It is hard to escape the imagery of the game of "chicken" described in chapter 2, with each driver attempting to convince the other that they were too invested in the crisis to swerve. Over the following decade, the United States and North Korea would repeat this test of wills time and time again. As the bomb on North Korea's bumper became ever more real and menacing, the credibility of the United States to demand disarmament even at the risk of war diminished in kind. Although a final resolution to this drama may yet unfold, events a decade later made clear North Korea's increasing deterrence leverage.

THE SECOND CRISIS (2002–05)

The Agreed Framework quelled the reprocessing crisis of 1994 by freezing (at least on paper) the North Korean nuclear program, but it hardly brought an end to the persistent tension and heated exchanges on the Korean Peninsula. Border flare-ups actually appeared to increase following the agreement, with the downing of an American helicopter in December of 1994 and a major incident involving the infiltration of a DPRK spy submarine into South Korean waters less than two years later. DPRK missile development continued apace, and the United States was caught off-guard by the North Korean test

---

[34] Quoted in Kim Myong Chol, "Kim Jong Il's Military Strategy for Reunification," *Comparative Strategy* vol. 20 (2001): 404.
[35] Quoted in Oberdorfer, *The Two Koreas*, 306.

of a three-stage rocket launched over Japan in 1998, reputedly to send a satellite into space.[36] Suspicions also began to mount that North Korea was in the midst of a covert expansion of its nuclear program involving the construction of a uranium enrichment facility, thereby bypassing the plutonium-producing reactor at Yongbyon that was shut down by the Agreed Framework. American attention focused on a remote site named Kumchangri, and after protracted negotiations and payment of a hefty fee, US inspectors gained access to what turned out to be a largely abandoned site.[37] Though embarrassed, the United States was not convinced of North Korean compliance with the Agreed Framework, and as a result its terms went largely unfulfilled, with most phases far behind schedule.

The failed investigation at Kumchangri made the North Korean acknowledgment in October of 2002 that it had built a clandestine uranium enrichment facility in contravention of the Agreed Framework all the more dramatic. Presented with what observers have described as incontrovertible evidence from an American envoy, North Korea initially chose angrily to deny the allegation but apparently eventually decided (though it later returned to a position of denial) that acknowledging the program was inevitable and could perhaps force the United States into much sought-after bilateral negotiations. So began a high-stakes cycle of threats, demands, and freewheeling diplomacy that often seemed on the verge of spiraling out of control, highlighting the complex deterrence interactions between the two states.

[36] After its 1998 test, North Korea agreed to a moratorium on missile launches that lasted until February 2003, when it fired a rocket (believed to have possibly been a long-range cruise missile) into the sea to coincide with the inauguration of the new South Korean president. Besides its progress in intercontinental missiles, intelligence reports from the South Korean Defense Ministry declare that North Korea is producing and deploying new intermediate ballistic missiles with a range of 1,800 to 2,500 miles. See Anthony Faiola, "N. Korea Deploying New Missiles with Longer Range, South Says," *Washington Post*, 9 July 2004; Thom Shanker, "North Korean Missile Said to Advance; US is Unworried," *New York Times*, 5 August 2004.

[37] Noland, *Avoiding the Apocalypse*, 159; Chol, "Kim Jong Il's Military Strategy for Reunification," 357.

Discovery of the clandestine uranium enrichment facility confirmed US fears that North Korea had never given up its ambitions to become a nuclear power. As disconcerting as this revelation was, the more immediate danger remained the status of any plutonium that may have been diverted from the Yongbyon reactor, a supply frozen by the Agreed Framework which had the potential to provide the fuel for thirty or more nuclear weapons.[38] Recriminations and demands flared, with the United States calling for an immediate dismantling of North Korea's nuclear program and the DPRK insisting upon direct negotiations and a nonaggression pact from the United States. Both sides claimed a sense of betrayal, as the US evidence of deception was countered by North Korean charges that the United States was not upholding its side of the Agreed Framework and that Bush's "axis of evil" rhetoric was overtly threatening. Faced with a refusal to enter into bilateral talks, North Korea warned that it might recommence testing missiles and began making conflicting statements regarding its nuclear status, perhaps exercising a little deliberate ambiguity to raise the stakes.[39]

As in 1993–94, US–DPRK relations fell into a destructive pattern of brinksmanship that escalated the situation to dangerous levels. After the DPRK rejected a last appeal by the IAEA for inspections of the new plant, South Korea and the United States decided to cut off shipments of oil mandated by the Agreed Framework. Then, in December 2002, just as US and Spanish special operations forces were boarding a ship carrying North Korean missiles to Yemen, the DPRK announced that it was lifting the freeze on Yongbyon and two other reactors imposed by the 1994 agreement. This move was particularly alarming in Washington, because it meant that these plants could resume producing spent fuel rods that might then be

---

[38] Doug Struck, "Crisis Could Push N. Korea to Expel Nuclear Inspectors," *Washington Post*, 14 November 2002.

[39] See, e.g., Howard W. French, "North Korean Radio Asserts Country Has Nuclear Arms," *New York Times*, 18 November 2002; Howard W. French, "North Korea Clarifies Statement on A-Bomb," *New York Times*, 19 November 2002.

reprocessed into weapons-grade plutonium at a rate sufficient to make more than fifty nuclear bombs a year.[40] Initially, North Korea stopped short of kicking out the IAEA inspectors charged with ensuring that Yongbyon's existing spent fuel rods remained in place. However, two weeks later it chose to remove all of the surveillance cameras and seals from the cooling pond where the fuel rods were stored, stripping them of their monitoring capabilities.[41]

Having effectively returned to the crisis situation of 1994, both sides began to ratchet up their rhetoric. Building off of President Bush's statement that North Korea's decision to reactivate an idle reactor was "unacceptable," Secretary of Defense Donald Rumsfeld intimated that the United States was still capable of winning two major regional conflicts simultaneously, a fairly direct hint to North Korea given the war planning taking place over Iraq.[42] The DPRK responded in kind, warning of "uncontrollable catastrophe" and "merciless punishment" if negotiations did not occur.[43] The North Korean defense minister, Kim Il Chol, asserted that the United States was pushing the crisis to the "brink of a nuclear war" and that there would be a "fight to the end" if the United States provoked a conflict.[44]

North Korea wasted no time in creating some provocations of its own. In the last week of December 2002, it officially expelled the IAEA inspectors and moved about a thousand fresh fuel rods into Yongbyon, an unmistakable signal of willingness to recommence production of

---

[40] Bill Gertz, "North Korea Can Build Nukes Right Now," *Washington Times*, 22 November 2002.

[41] Sanger and Dao, "North Korea Says it Regains Access to its Plutonium."

[42] Quoted in David Stout, "Bush and Seoul Call North Korea Nuclear Plan 'Unacceptable,'" *New York Times*, 13 December 2002; David Stout, "Rumsfeld Says, if Necessary, US Can Fight 2 Wars at Once," *New York Times*, 23 December 2002.

[43] Quoted in Howard W. French, "North Korea Warns the US to Negotiate or Risk 'Catastrophe,'" *New York Times*, 24 December 2002; Howard W. French, "US Gets Warning from North Korea," *New York Times*, 25 December 2002.

[44] Quoted in Christopher Torchia, "N. Korea Warns US Risking Nuclear War," *Washington Post*, 24 December 2002; Peter S. Goodman, "N. Korean Official Threatens 'Fight to the End' with US," *Washington Post*, 25 December 2002.

plutonium.[45] Shortly thereafter, the DPRK confirmed its intention to withdraw from the Nonproliferation Treaty, perhaps a redundant move that nevertheless carried significant symbolic weight. When US satellites began detecting trucks that appeared to be moving the previously quarantined stockpile of 8,000 nuclear fuel rods out of storage at Yongbyon, observers questioned whether North Korea had tossed aside all restraints as they would now be capable of producing weapons-grade plutonium by the end of March 2003.[46] Alongside the announcement that it would resume "normal operations" at Yongbyon, the DPRK attempted to reassure the world that such work would "at the present stage" only be used for electricity generation.[47]

The United States found little solace in such claims, and the commander of American forces in the Pacific sent a request to Washington for additional air and naval forces to serve as a deterrent against North Korea.[48] Pentagon officials were careful to mention that such preparations did not signal imminent military action, though the redeployment of twenty-four B-52 bombers to the Pacific island of Guam likely added to North Korea's insecurity. This was the first military response in the escalating crisis, and the diplomatic tension increased in kind. President Bush told reporters that while he believed it was possible to achieve a peaceful resolution to the crisis, "all options are on the table" if diplomacy failed to prevent North Korea from resuming its efforts to build nuclear weapons.[49] The DPRK renounced the build-up of American "aggression troops" and warned that such moves could lead to a nuclear war that would

---

[45] Peter S. Goodman, "N. Korea Moves to Activate Complex," *Washington Post*, 27 December 2002; James Brooke, "North Korea Says it Plans to Expel Nuclear Monitors," *New York Times*, 28 December 2002.

[46] David E. Sanger and Eric Schmitt, "Satellites Said to See Activity at North Korean Nuclear Site," *New York Times*, 31 January 2003.

[47] Howard W. French, "North Korea Restarts Reactor with Ability to Fuel Arms," *New York Times*, 6 February 2003.

[48] Eric Schmitt and David E. Sanger, "Admiral Seeks Deterrent Force in Korea Crisis," *New York Times*, 1 February 2003.

[49] Quoted in James Dao, "Bush Urges Chinese President to Push North Korea on Arms," *New York Times*, 9 February 2003.

reduce both Koreas "to ashes."[50] The danger of an accidental or quickly escalating conflict grew even more real as a North Korean MiG fighter jet intruded into South Korean airspace for the first time in twenty years. Only a few weeks later, in March 2003, four North Korean fighter jets intercepted an unarmed American spy plane on a surveillance mission, leading the United States to consider ordering the addition of armed fighter escorts to dissuade future interference.

By the spring of 2003, American intelligence resources were focused intently on trying to uncover any evidence of whether North Korea was reprocessing its spent plutonium. Since reprocessing was the supposed "red line" in the 1993–94 crisis, analysts were disturbed to pick up signs of increasing activity around Yongbyon's reprocessing plant, indicating that there might not be the same degree of North Korean restraint as occurred the decade before.[51] The level of American resolve in holding back the DPRK nuclear program was also uncertain, with some administration officials hinting that the United States might be tacitly accepting a nuclear North Korea, and would instead focus its resources on preventing any sale of missile technology or fissile material.[52] Complicating efforts to craft an informed US strategy were the vague and often contradictory reports concerning North Korean progress in reprocessing. For instance, efforts to discover evidence of krypton gas (a tell-tale byproduct of plutonium reprocessing that is emitted into the atmosphere) were generally inconclusive or conflicted with reports that the DPRK was having difficulty even starting up its reprocessing facility.[53]

[50] Ibid.
[51] David E. Sanger, "US Sees Quick Start of North Korean Nuclear Site," New York Times, 1 March 2003.
[52] Doug Struck and Glenn Kessler, "Foes Giving in to N. Korea's Nuclear Aims," Washington Post, 5 March 2003; Sonni Efron, "US Said to be Resigned to a Nuclear Korea," Los Angeles Times, 5 March 2003; David E. Sanger, "Bush Shifts Focus to Nuclear Sales by North Korea," New York Times, 5 May 2003.
[53] Glenn Kessler and Walter Pincus, "N. Korea Stymied on Plutonium Work," Washington Post, 20 March 2003; Bill Gertz, "2nd N. Korean Nuclear Site Not Likely," Washington Times, 22 July 2003; Douglas Frantz, "N. Korea's Nuclear Success is Doubted," Los Angeles Times, 9 December 2003.

High hopes for scheduled talks between the United States, North Korea, and China in April 2003 were dashed when the negotiations ended a day early amidst some of the most provocative comments to date. According to reports of the exchange, the North Korean negotiator told an American envoy outside of the official session that the DPRK already possessed nuclear weapons, had begun making bomb-grade plutonium, and that the decision over whether it would market its nuclear materials or conduct an atomic test would depend on American actions.[54] Once the dust settled from this unexpected confrontation, discussion began to focus on a possible package of US security guarantees and economic assistance in return for DPRK nuclear disarmament. The difficulty, though, just as in 1994, was that neither side seemed willing to take the first steps down this road. New evidence of North Korean reprocessing, coupled with the perception of an increasingly hard-line approach to negotiation, led many Bush administration advisors to consider giving up on a diplomatic solution and instead move to impose sanctions and a tight economic blockade to force compliance.

Over the summer of 2003, progress toward a round of much-anticipated six-nation multilateral talks, eventually scheduled for late August, gave the prospects for a diplomatic resolution new life. Bringing the other regional actors to the negotiating table was a primary objective of the United States, which believed that only a united front opposing North Korean nuclear advances would persuade it to change its path. Toward that end, the United States worked hard to rally its allies to take an active role in breaking the deadlock with North Korea. In a joint statement with South Korea's new president Roh Moo Hyun, Bush declared that the two countries "will not tolerate nuclear weapons in North Korea" and threatened the use of "further steps" in response.[55] Soon after, Bush met with

---

[54] David E. Sanger, "North Korea Says it Now Possesses Nuclear Arsenal," *New York Times*, 25 April 2003.

[55] Quoted in Joseph Curl, "North Korea Gets Stern Warning," *Washington Times*, 15 May 2003.

Japanese prime minister Junichiro Koizumi and issued a similar warning against the DPRK building additional weapons.

While such summits gave the appearance of a united front, the threats were left deliberately vague largely because both Japan and South Korea remained nervous about the consequences that could follow from taking too coercive a stance against the DPRK. Instead, the Pacific allies put into motion a gradual program of economic restrictions, initiated partly by Japan cracking down on companies that had long been suspected of providing North Korea with equipment used in the development of WMD.[56] Building off this, the United States devoted a great deal of diplomatic effort to recruiting a broad range of participants for its Proliferation Security Initiative, an international partnership created to intercept WMD shipments from suspect states like North Korea.[57] The same group also sought to implement a parallel program called the DPRK Illicit Activities Initiative, meant to crack down on North Korea's narcotics trade, counterfeiting, money laundering, and other illegal financial activities.[58] For the United States, getting other important players like China and Russia on board has been a daunting task, mostly because of their proximity and relatively close relationship with the DPRK. For those two regional actors, fear of a massive refugee crisis in the wake of a collapse of the North Korean government is tempered only by the equal concern of a nuclear "domino" effect resulting in the decision of South Korea and Japan to pursue their own nuclear weapons programs.

As a more direct security measure, the United States announced that it was initiating a major realignment of American troop deployments on the Korean Peninsula, moving many of its soldiers further away from the DMZ. Such a shift, Pentagon officials argued, would save lives from the anticipated artillery barrage along

---

[56] Sachiko Sakamaki and Doug Struck, "Japan Cracks down on Firms Tied to N. Korea," *Washington Post*, 22 May 2003.   [57] See chapter 7.

[58] Steven R. Weisman, "US to Send Signal to North Koreans in Naval Exercise," *New York Times*, 18 August 2003.

the DMZ in the event of war and preserve a fighting force capable of a decisive counterattack.[59] However, as the Cold War amply demonstrated, even reputedly defensive measures can be threatening because of the cover they might provide for offensive plans. In response, North Korea announced for the first time that it was seeking a "nuclear deterrent" to ease the burden of its million-man army, and disclosed that it was making significant progress toward producing enough plutonium for several nuclear bombs.[60]

This backdrop was far from ideal for the multilateral talks, and they broke down in similar fashion to the round a few months earlier. The addition of new participants did little to transform the fundamental dilemma which was that North Korea was unwilling to bargain away its nuclear program without security guarantees, and the United States would not offer such immunity until it was sure the DPRK was disarmed and unable to transfer WMD abroad. The DPRK rejected a joint accord offered by South Korea, Japan, and the United States laying out a "coordinated" set of steps toward disarmament, preferring instead "simultaneous" moves that did not leave it open to attack.[61] A North Korean counterproposal raising the prospect of a nuclear freeze in return for energy aid was likewise turned down by President Bush as inadequate.[62] A visit by an unofficial US delegation in January 2004 resolved little, and even resulted in North Korea denying the existence of the uranium enrichment facility that had sparked the entire controversy a year and a half earlier.[63] Consequentially, plans for a follow-up round of multilateral

---

[59] Howard W. French, "Official Says US Will Reposition its Troops in South Korea," *New York Times*, 3 June 2003.

[60] David E. Sanger, "North Korea Says it Has Made Fuel for Atom Bombs," *New York Times*, 15 July 2003.

[61] Glenn Kessler, "US Agrees to Statement on North Korea Talks," *Washington Post*, 8 December 2003; Sang-hun Choe, "North Korea Rejects US Nuclear Proposal," *Philadelphia Inquirer*, 15 December 2003.

[62] Soo-Jeong Lee, "Bush Rejects N. Korea's Offer of Nuclear Programs Freeze for Energy," *Washington Post*, 10 December 2003.

[63] Barbara Demick, "N. Korea Denies it Has a Warhead," *Los Angeles Times*, 13 January 2004; Philip P. Pan, "Nuclear Talks Clouded by N. Korea's Denial of Enrichment Effort," *Washington Post*, 25 February 2004.

talks nearly fell through, and these talks were largely ineffectual when they did finally occur in late February 2004.[64]

Nevertheless, multilateral talks continued in June 2004, and the US position appeared to soften somewhat. American negotiators put forward a conditional set of incentives modeled after the Libyan agreement, promising aid immediately after a commitment by Kim Jong Il to dismantle the DPRK plutonium and uranium weapons programs.[65] After the North Korean acceptance, China, Russia, Japan, and South Korea would send tens of thousands of tons of heavy fuel oil to North Korea, and the United States would offer a "provisional" guarantee not to invade the country or seek to topple the DPRK.[66] Rather than being set on an open-ended time-frame like the Agreed Framework, this "preparatory period of disarmament" would last only for a three-month grace period, which would terminate if international inspectors were not granted access to suspected nuclear sites. The North Korean reaction to this proposal was mixed; according to some observers, the DPRK took a hard-line stance, threatening nuclear tests and once again denying the existence of the covert uranium enrichment facility.[67] Others, however, perceived a much more accommodating posture, citing a DPRK statement that it would "show flexibility" if the United States agreed to participate in providing energy assistance.[68] Ultimately, this new initiative ground to a halt, with North Korea labeling it as a "sham offer" that expected the DPRK to disarm and submit to inspections before it received significant economic benefits from the concessions offered by the other regional powers.[69]

[64] Joseph Kahn, "North Korea Says it is against More Talks," New York Times, 30 August 2003; Barbara Demick, "N. Korea Says it Will Be a No-Show at Six-Party Talks," Los Angeles Times, 10 December 2003; Joseph Kahn, "Diplomats See Modest Progress in North Korea Nuclear Talks," New York Times, 28 February 2004.

[65] David E. Sanger, "US to Offer North Korea Incentives in Nuclear Talks," New York Times, 23 June 2004.   [66] Ibid.

[67] Bill Gertz and Nicholas Kralev, "Pyongyang Takes a Hard-Line at Six-Way Talks," Washington Times, 26 June 2004.

[68] Philip P. Pan, "N. Korea Says it Can 'Show Flexibility,' " Washington Post, 26 June 2004.

[69] David E. Sanger, "North Korea Seems to Reject Butter-for-Guns Proposal from US," New York Times, 25 July 2004.

After multilateral talks in the summer of 2004, both the United States and North Korea hardened their positions. In late August 2004, North Korea called President Bush a "fascist tyrant" and "human trash."[70] Two months later, Colin Powell rejected the North Korean suggestion that the United States provide "up front" benefits as an inducement for a return to talks.[71] Then, in February 2005, responding to a statement by Condoleezza Rice describing North Korea as an "outpost of tyranny," the DPRK announced unambiguously that it possessed nuclear weapons as a deterrent against an alleged hostile American strategy, rejecting the prospect of further multilateral talks.[72] Despite this shocking declaration, the United States held firm to its position rejecting bilateral talks and continued to insist on complete disarmament as a precondition for any deal.

Far from such an outcome, North Korea further augmented its nuclear forces, claiming to have extracted yet more fissile material from a shutdown of the Yongbyon reactor in April 2005.[73] In response, the United States alluded to seeking political support for the imposition of sanctions against North Korea if talks remained deadlocked.[74] After a series of conciliatory measures on both sides, talks did eventually recommence in July 2005, culminating two months later in a ground-breaking joint statement in which North Korea agreed to abandon its nuclear weapons programs in return for economic bene-

---

[70] Quoted in Glenn Kessler, "N. Korea Continues Criticism of Bush," *New York Times*, 25 August 2004.

[71] Glenn Kessler, "US Rejects North Korean Conditions for Dismantling Nuclear Programs," *New York Times*, 23 October 2004.

[72] See DPRK Ministry of Foreign Affairs Statement, 10 February 2005. Available at http://news.bbc.co.uk/2/hi/asia-pacific/4252515.stm. See also James Brooke, "North Korea Says it Has Nuclear Weapons and Rejects Talks," *New York Times*, 10 February 2005.

[73] David E. Sanger, "Steps at Reactor in North Korea Worry the US," *New York Times*, 18 April 2005; James Brooke, "North Koreans Claim to Extract Fuel for Nuclear Weapons," *New York Times*, 12 May 2005.

[74] See Mark Magnier, "Rice Puts Pressure on N. Korea," *Los Angeles Times*, 21 March 2005; David E. Sanger, "White House May Go to UN over North Korean Shipments," *New York Times*, 25 April 2005.

fits and a security guarantee.[75] Widely hailed as a promising sign of diplomatic progress, the agreement lacked a timeline for disarmament and side-stepped the issue of when North Korea would receive a light-water nuclear reactor, the base bargain from the original Agreed Framework. Sure enough, just as a decade previously, the devil is in the details of implementation, and the inconclusive follow-up negotiations in November 2005 led many to question whether the September agreement was merely a tactic for the DPRK to buy time in solidifying its nuclear arsenal or striking a better deal.

When comparing the two crises with North Korea, what is most illuminating is how the DPRK in the second crisis crossed virtually every "red line" established as grounds for war by the United States in the first. North Korea expelled IAEA inspectors, restarted the Yongbyon reactor, proceeded with reprocessing, and announced its nuclear capability, all with hardly any reaction (beyond ineffectual protests) from the United States and its allies. This change is likely attributable to a gradual shift in North Korean interests and capabilities, enhancing its credibility in the contest of deterrence.

First, North Korea has successfully capitalized on the ambiguity surrounding its development of nuclear weapons. Victor Cha provides a very useful illustration of this underlying uncertainty, depicting the North Korean WMD program in metaphorical terms as potentially a shield meant to provide protection from attack, a sword intended for aggressive or revisionist purposes, or a badge to serve as a symbol of prestige as well as confer leverage in talks.[76] Without knowing the true intentions behind North Korea's nuclear program, the United States is loath to risk a catastrophic war over what could merely be a defensive precaution. North Korea's unwillingness to bargain may not necessarily imply bad faith; after all, it has very legitimate security concerns and may not find the US security

---

[75] People's Republic of China, Ministry of Foreign Affairs, Joint Statement of the Fourth Round of the Six-Party Talks, 19 September 2005.

[76] Victor D. Cha, "North Korea's Weapons of Mass Destruction: Badges, Shields, or Swords?" *Political Science Quarterly* vol. 117, no. 2 (summer 2002): 211.

guarantees believable. As Barry Schneider humorously remarked, "as the saying goes, just because you are paranoid, does not mean someone is not out to get you. North Korean fears of preemption are not entirely misplaced . . ."[77] North Korea sees the US *National Security Strategy*, the "axis of evil" appellation, and President Bush's admission that he "loathes Kim Jong Il" collectively as a virtual declaration of war that threatens the very existence of its country.[78] With such pressure from the world's sole superpower bearing down on a reclusive state with few allies, its interests in maintaining a nuclear deterrent are very credible and consequently hold great deterrent power.

Second, North Korea's military capability to devastate Seoul and other regional US allies remains as robust as ever. Even though the DPRK would likely ultimately lose any conflict with the United States, it could exact a heavy price in the fighting. The commander of US forces in Korea, General Leon LaPorte, estimated that the DPRK possesses more than 800 missiles capable of striking the Korean Peninsula and surrounding countries.[79] Add to this an estimated 10,000 artillery pieces, and it becomes clear that North Korea can wreak devastation in the region regardless of whether it has nuclear weapons. General LaPorte emphasized the asymmetric nature of North Korea's threat, which the United States estimates is based on a 120,000-strong special operations force and a doctrine of using CW as munitions.[80] Though the United States and South Korea

---

[77] Barry R. Schneider, *Radical Responses to Radical Regimes: Evaluating Preemptive Counter-proliferation*, McNair Paper No. 41 (Washington DC: National Defense University Press, May 1995), 32.

[78] Doug Struck, "For North Korea, US is Violator of Accords," *Washington Post*, 21 October 2002; Julia Preston, "North Korea Demands US Agree to Nonaggression Pact," *New York Times*, 25 October 2002; Bob Woodward, "A Course of 'Confident Action,'" *Washington Post*, 19 November 2002; James T. Laney and Jason T. Shaplen, "How to Deal with North Korea," *Foreign Affairs* vol. 82, no. 2 (March/April 2003): 20.

[79] Leon LaPorte, *This Week with George Stephanopoulos*, ABC News Transcripts, 27 July 2003.

[80] Bill Gertz, "US Commander Fears N. Korea Would Sell Nukes," *Washington Times*, 18 November 2003.

have far superior air forces and well-trained armies, the sheer numbers the DPRK can bring to bear in terms of both manpower and artillery mean that any war would be incredibly costly.

Just as important, North Korea's nuclear assets remain effectively immune from American air attack. The very dearth of intelligence that exacerbates the crisis with North Korea also frustrates the ability to resolve it by force. With ambiguous data surrounding North Korea's emission of krypton, US analysts appear unsure as to whether Yongbyon is the primary reprocessing facility or whether an alternate hidden plant exists.[81] Moreover, there seems to be even less certainty over the location of the uranium enrichment plant that sparked the current controversy in October 2002.[82] North Korea is masterful in its concealment and deception, moving sensitive materials beneath the Earth's surface where spy satellites cannot easily detect them. This burrowing strategy is extensive; South Korea estimates that the North has more than 8,000 underground installations, including 500 kilometers of tunnels.[83] Assuming for the moment that American and South Korean intelligence agencies have secret knowledge of the location of North Korean nuclear sites, it is highly doubtful that these areas will be vulnerable to conventional air strikes. Not only are underground facilities shielded from prying electronic eyes, but states can construct them to be virtually impervious to aerial bombardment. The US campaign in Afghanistan demonstrated that even multiple attacks with large fuel-air explosive bombs often leave hardened enclaves protected by natural rock formations unscathed. Worse still, even if the United States could locate and destroy such sites it will be next to

---

[81] David E. Sanger and Howard W. French, "North Korea Prompts US to Investigate Nuclear Boast," *New York Times*, 1 May 2003; David E. Sanger and Thom Shanker, "North Korea Hides New Nuclear Site, Evidence Suggests," *New York Times*, 20 July 2003.

[82] John Diamond, "N. Korea Keeps US Intelligence Guessing," *USA Today*, 10 March 2003.

[83] Kongdan Oh and Ralph C. Hassig, *North Korea: Through the Looking Glass* (Washington DC: Brookings Institution Press, 2000), 108.

impossible for it to track down the reprocessed plutonium North Korea has removed from the Yongbyon reactor, which could be dispersed and hidden virtually anywhere in the country. Thus, while the United States could undoubtedly cause substantial damage to North Korea's nuclear facilities, air strikes alone would be unlikely to destroy the plutonium that the DPRK could use either for sale abroad or for future manufacture into nuclear weapons.

On the opposing side, the United States also has significant interests at stake in the confrontation. Of primary concern is the disturbing possibility that North Korea may see nuclear weapons as a commodity for sale to shore up its failing economy. The United States cannot lightly brush aside such an option, raised by the North Korean negotiator at the April 2003 talks with the United States, given the extensive history of DPRK proliferation activities, most notably the reports of its sale of uranium to Libya in early 2001.[84] Over the past decade North Korea has cooperated with Pakistan by exchanging missile parts in return for gas centrifuges and machinery to assist in enriching uranium.[85] Furthermore, once such technology or material is out of the country, there is little control over its final destination, as proved by recent revelations of deals for missile and nuclear technology among Pakistan, Iran, and Saudi Arabia.[86] North Korea's arms contacts extend far and wide, from Yemen to Germany and China, and there is little doubt that there would be many interested buyers for weapons-grade plutonium or a completed nuclear device.[87]

---

[84] David E. Sanger and William J. Broad, "Evidence is Cited Linking Koreans to Libya Uranium," *New York Times*, 23 May 2004. But see Dafna Linzer, "US Misled Allies about Nuclear Export," *Washington Post*, 20 March 2005.

[85] David E. Sanger, "In North Korea and Pakistan, Deep Roots of Nuclear Barter," *New York Times*, 24 November 2002.

[86] Douglas Frantz, "Iran Closes in on Ability to Build a Nuclear Bomb," *Los Angeles Times*, 4 August 2003; Joby Warrick, "Iran Admits Foreign Help on Nuclear Facility," *Washington Post*, 27 August 2003; David R. Sands, "Israeli General Says Saudis Seek to Buy Pakistan Nukes," *Washington Times*, 23 October 2003; David E. Sanger and William J. Broad, "From Rogue Nuclear Programs, Web of Trails Leads to Pakistan," *New York Times*, 3 January 2004.

[87] Bill Gertz, "China Ships North Korea Ingredient for Nuclear Arms," *Washington Times*, 17 December 2002; Bill Gertz, "N. Korea Ship Gets Arms in and out,"

At the same time, despite being designated as a prime proliferation threat, there is scant evidence that North Korea has sought to export any of its WMD capabilities. Even the alleged 2001 Libyan sale consisted of uranium which could not have been used for nuclear fuel unless it was enriched in centrifuges. Moreover, as Victor Cha and David Kang have noted, the link between North Korea and the rest of the "axis of evil" has primarily been financial – related to missile sales.[88] North Korean ties to terrorist entities have also largely dissipated, with the main grounds for keeping the DPRK on the US list of state sponsors of terrorism being its lack of support for international efforts to combat terror. The US State Department's *Country Reports on Terrorism* acknowledges that North Korea has not sponsored any terrorist acts since the bombing of the Korean Airlines flight in 1987.[89] North Korea's relative restraint in selling WMD certainly should not inspire confidence that such a policy will continue, especially in light of direct threats to the contrary and evidence of limited sales, but it at least tempers allegations that North Korea is primarily interested in nuclear technology for financial gain. As with its nuclear intentions more generally, the ambiguity surrounding North Korea's intentions to proliferate weighs strongly against the United States being willing to initiate an attack to prevent uncertain contingencies.

The United States also fears the potential chaos that would likely follow from the fall of Kim Jong Il's regime. As an instructive analogy, immediately preceding the invasion of Iraq, satellite imagery showed a heavy flow of traffic into Syria that some officials believe may have consisted of material from Hussein's weapons program.[90]

Washington Times, 18 February 2003; Nicholas Kralev, "North Korea Offers Nigeria Missile Deal," *Washington Times*, 29 January 2004.

[88] Victor D. Cha and David C. Kang, "The Korea Crisis," *Foreign Policy* no. 136 (May/June 2003): 20, 22. This may be because transferring any nuclear know-how would be an enormously risky proposition given the extent of US concern.

[89] US Department of State, *Country Reports on Terrorism, 2004* (Washington DC: April 2005), 90. See also James Miles, "Waiting out North Korea," *Survival* vol. 44, no. 2 (summer 2002): 42.

[90] Douglas Jehl, "Iraq Removed Arms Material, Aide Says," *New York Times*, 29 October 2003. But see Special Advisor to the Director of Central Intelligence, *Addendums to the Comprehensive Report* (March 2005), 1. Available at http://permanent.access.gpo.gov/DuelferRpt/Addendums.pdf.

Similarly, if North Korea produces and disperses nuclear devices in remote locations to avoid detection and possible destruction, it will be extremely difficult to keep track of weapons stolen by factions looking to turn a quick profit on the black market in the midst of a civil war or coup. As with direct exports, this form of indirect proliferation would also pose a severe threat to the United States if a terrorist group ever tried to make an American city a nuclear target.

These significant concerns notwithstanding, the threat to US vital interests are only potential and probabilistic. Without some outward display of aggression, as Iraq amply provided in Kuwait, it will be extremely problematic for the United States to initiate hostilities, even if North Korea makes significant strides in its WMD arsenal. For instance, were the DPRK to conduct a nuclear test, or otherwise demonstrate its nuclear weaponization, the muted international reaction to the shutdown of Yongbyon in April 2005 – netting perhaps yet more fissile material – indicates that a renewed push for economic sanctions would likely be the only reaction. In the language of deterrence theory, the United States has the "last clear chance" to avoid disaster.

Thus far, the DPRK has not flexed its nuclear muscle to provide cover for military action, though the Korean People's Army has never been particularly risk-averse in asserting sea boundaries, challenging US reconnaissance missions, and destabilizing the tense stand-off at the DMZ through infiltrations and efforts at intimidation. Even if the United States would consider an attack on DPRK nuclear facilities, the potential for reprisals against Seoul makes the choice virtually unthinkable. Given sufficient provocation, however, such as the DPRK choosing to sell WMD or initiate its own attacks, the United States might be forced to wage war nonetheless. Overall then, as traditional deterrence theory would predict, it appears that both North Korea and the United States possess powerful defensive deterrent forces but lack the ability to use them offensively. The United States has been unable to compel the DPRK to disarm, or even freeze its nuclear development; North Korea has been unwilling to attack

South Korea or seek to compel unification. The danger arises on the margins, surrounding the potential for WMD proliferation or transfer to terrorists. Part III of this book will address the strategic options for responding to these very real threats.

Part III **Responding to the threat**

The preceding chapters suggest that although deterrence is still a powerful force in international affairs, it may be operating in ways deleterious to US security. Specifically, the proliferation of WMD is expanding the number of states capable of making substantial deterrent threats. Thankfully WMD have not been used on the battlefield against the United States, but in the tense conflicts with Iraq and North Korea, they are certainly being used at the negotiating table. In fact, virtually every military engagement involving the United States over the past decade or so – ranging from the Bosnian war to Operation Desert Fox – has involved open references to unconventional warfare.[1]

Of course, as the wars in Iraq demonstrated, the United States is not easily deterred, especially when an adversary undertakes open aggression or has limited WMD capabilities. Generally speaking, the immense military advantages the United States enjoys will be more than sufficient to persuade any adversary that the costs of aggressive action would far outweigh any benefits.[2] However, the crises with

---

[1] See Philip L. Ritcheson, "Proliferation and the Challenge to Deterrence," *Strategic Review* vol. 23, no. 2 (spring 1995): 42; Henning Riecke, "NATO's Non Proliferation and Deterrence Policies: Mixed Signals and the Norm of WMD Non-Use," *Journal of Strategic Studies* vol. 23, no. 1 (March 2000): 46; Robert D. Critchlow, "Whom the Gods Would Destroy: An Information Warfare Alternative for Deterrence and Compellence," *Naval War College Review* vol. 53, no. 3 (summer 2000): 27.

[2] For advocates of this view, see Stephen M. Walt, "Containing Rogues and Renegades: Coalition Strategies and Counterproliferation," in *The Coming Crisis: Nuclear Proliferation, US Interests, and World Order*, edited by Victor A. Utgoff (Cambridge, MA: MIT Press, 2000), 211; Jan Lodal, *The Price of Dominance: The New Weapons of Mass Destruction and their Challenge to American Leadership* (New York: Council of Foreign Relations, 2001), 100; James H. Lebovic, "The Law of Small Numbers: Deterrence and National Missile Defense," *The Journal of Conflict Resolution* vol. 46, no. 4 (August 2002): 465; John J. Mearsheimer and Stephen M. Walt, "An Unnecessary War," *Foreign Policy* no. 134 (January/February 2003): 50–59.

North Korea reveal the limits of this perspective. The United States can hardly make its conventional forces more fearsome, and there are substantial moral restraints against using its nuclear arsenal in all but the most extreme situations. As a result, the excessive power of American nuclear weapons may paradoxically make an adversary's threat to use WMD more credible. Expecting that any US counterattack would remain conventional, a regional power may be more likely to resort to nonconventional weapons.[3] Recognition of this potential "failure" of deterrence is the very foundation of North Korea's deterrence success against the United States. Unable to match the overwhelming conventional superiority of the United States, other states are clearly taking note of this attempt to balance the calculus of deterrence. Iran, for instance, has embarked on an ambitious effort to offset American military advantages, working on producing anti-ship technology, long-range missiles, and possibly even nuclear weapons.[4]

Perhaps, as some suggest, the United States should embrace the universalization of deterrence, adopting a defensive mindset and avoiding situations that could result in a rogue state feeling driven to

---

[3] Lewis A. Dunn, "Rethinking the Nuclear Equation: The United States and the New Nuclear Powers," *The Washington Quarterly* vol. 17, no. 1 (winter 1994): 10. This was in fact the strategy of several "red teams" that participated in a US war gaming exercise; see Frank Tiboni, "War Game Stuns US Strategists," *Defense News*, 12 May 2003.

[4] Iran's nuclear program has received intense scrutiny recently. For further details on its WMD and missile build-up, see International Atomic Energy Agency, *Implementation of the NPT Safeguards Agreement in the Islamic Republic of Iran*, IAEA Doc. GOV/2004/83 (November 2004). Available at http://www.iaea.org/ Publications/Documents/Board/2004/gov2004-83_derestrict.pdf; Shahram Chubin, "Does Iran Want Nuclear Weapons?" *Survival* vol. 37, no. 1 (spring 1995): 97; Anthony H. Cordesman, *Iran's Military Forces in Transition: Conventional Threats and Weapons of Mass Destruction* (Westport, CT: Praeger, 1999), 4; Michael Dobbs, "A Story of Iran's Quest for Power," *Washington Post*, 13 January 2002; Scott Peterson, "Iran's Nuclear Challenge: Deter, not Antagonize," *Christian Science Monitor*, 21 February 2002; Joby Warrick and Glenn Kessler, "Iran's Nuclear Program Speeds Ahead," *Washington Post*, 10 March 2003; Massimo Calabresi, "Iran's Nuclear Threat," *Time*, 17 March 2003; Scott Peterson, "Behind Diplomacy, Iran Sees a Fight Coming," *Christian Science Monitor*, 31 March 2005; Dafna Linzer, "Iran is Judged 10 Years from Nuclear Bomb," *Washington Post*, 2 August 2005; Bill Gertz, "US says Tehran is Pursuing Nuke Arms," *Washington Times*, 25 November 2005.

make use of WMD.[5] The United States could then declare explicit red lines such as crossborder aggression or WMD transfer to terrorists, theoretically keeping dangerous states in their "box." As discussed in chapter 1, however, deterrence can enable various forms of undesirable behavior, such as a rogue state pursuing limited coercive military operations against a neighboring country that might not clearly qualify as aggression. States with deficient military capabilities are often adept at "designing around" deterrent strategies, making only gradual advances so that no single step on its own would merit retaliation.[6] In effect, universalizing WMD deterrence would open a Pandora's box of uncertainty over what would or would not be defended, with each side hoping – or gambling – that the other had enough restraint to keep the fighting on a conventional level.

Moreover, granting a rogue state a form of sanctuary could allow its government or terrorist networks within it to bide their time in preparing a surprise attack that would have as little warning as potential for being deterred. During the war in Afghanistan, for instance, there were numerous accounts of Al Qaeda trying desperately to develop WMD. Subsequently, raids on various labs and hideouts revealed bioterror manuals, videos of experiments with chemical agents, a diagram for a "dirty" radiological bomb, and even low-grade uranium-238.[7] Even though Osama bin Laden claims to desire

[5] Robert S. Litwak, *Rogue States and US Foreign Policy: Containment after the Cold War* (Baltimore, MD: The Johns Hopkins University Press, 2000), 152; William Raspberry, "Our Insane Focus on Iraq," *Washington Post*, 9 September 2002; *New York Times*, "In Defense of Deterrence," 10 September 2002. See also Morton A. Kaplan, *System and Process in International Politics* (New York: John Wiley & Sons, 1957), 50; Pierre Gallois, *The Balance of Terror: Strategy for the Nuclear Age* (Boston, MA: Houghton Mifflin, 1961), 8–9.

[6] Alexander L. George and Richard Smoke, *Deterrence in American Foreign Policy: Theory and Practice* (New York: Columbia University Press, 1974). See also Elli Lieberman, *Deterrence Theory: Success or Failure in Arab-Israeli Wars?* McNair Paper No. 45 (Washington DC: Institute for National Strategic Studies, National Defense University, October 1995), 35, 58.

[7] Colum Lynch, "Bin Laden Sought Uranium, Jury Told," *Washington Post*, 8 February 2001; Mike Boettcher, "Evidence Suggests Al Qaeda Pursuit of Biological, Chemical Weapons," *CNN*, 14 November 2001; Bob Woodward, Robert G. Kaiser, and David B. Ottaway, "US Fears Bin Laden Made Nuclear Strides," *Washington Post*, 4

chemical and nuclear weapons only to deter American use of the same, Al Qaeda's development of such weapons would be of grave concern.[8]

In sum, in an era of mass globalization, enabling a few individuals to kill thousands and potentially millions, perhaps through covert means, the containment "box" is becoming more porous than ever – hardly a sturdy barrier against creeping regional threats and terrorism. Unfortunately, security interests no longer end at one's border, for the dangers can come from all directions at any time, and the harm caused can be virtually irreparable. The United States cannot necessarily afford the luxury of relying on the threat of punishment to deter the use of WMD; chemical, biological, and nuclear weapons have taken the rungs out of the escalation ladder, creating a world in which the first break in the WMD taboo is likely to be catastrophic. The next several chapters shift away from theory and history toward an analysis of the foreign policy options available to the United States in combating these new threats. After laying out the broad strategies to choose from, I will focus on the legal and practical aspects of the most important and controversial options: preventive war and interdiction.

Footnote 7 (cont.)

    December 2001; Judith Miller, "Qaeda Videos Seem to Show Chemical Tests," *New York Times*, 19 August 2002; Neil Doyle, "Al Qaeda Nukes are Reality, Intelligence Says," *Washington Times*, 28 October 2002; Associated Press, "Bin Laden Said to Have Sought Nuclear Arms," *Baltimore Sun*, 30 December 2002; Josh Meyer, "Al Qaeda Feared to Have 'Dirty Bombs,'" *Los Angeles Times*, 8 February 2003.

[8] David Willman and Alan C. Miller, "Nuclear Threat is Real, Experts Warn," *Los Angeles Times*, 11 November 2001; Bill Gertz, "CIA Says Al Qaeda Ready to Use Nukes," *Washington Times*, 3 June 2003. Similar concerns surround the WMD ambitions of Iraqi insurgents in the wake of Iraqi Freedom. See Bob Drogin, "The Other Weapons Threat in Iraq," *Los Angeles Times*, 10 October 2004.

5 Counterproliferation strategies

The proliferation of WMD is a multilayered phenomenon, fueled by indigenous research and development, global trade, arms sales, and covert transfers to nonstate actors. Defending against such a complex threat, in turn, involves a wide array of legal, institutional, and strategic mechanisms. Besides relying on deterrence, states can adopt export controls to reduce proliferation generally, build missile defenses and other passive defenses to minimize the damage from a WMD attack, take military action to disarm a potential adversary, or police the channels proliferators use to exchange weapons. Collectively, these are known as "counterproliferation" strategies, aimed at preparing the United States and its allies to operate effectively against WMD-armed adversaries.[1] While such measures will never eliminate the potential for a WMD attack, they are ways to manage risk and enable the United States to continue to support international stability in a confident manner. This chapter will briefly examine the range of counterproliferation strategies under review and development.

EXPORT CONTROLS

The use of export controls to prevent potential adversaries from acquiring advanced weaponry has always been the most sensible first line of defense in US counterproliferation efforts. During the

---

[1] See US Government, *The National Security Strategy of the United States of America* (Washington DC: September 2002), 14. See also US Department of Defense, *Proliferation: Threat and Response* (Washington DC: January 2001), 69; National Defense University, *The Counterproliferation Imperative: Meeting Tomorrow's Challenges* (Washington DC: November 2001), 2; William J. Perry, "Preparing for the Next Attack," *Foreign Affairs* vol. 80, no. 6 (November/December 2001): 33. Export controls are generally not included under the counterproliferation heading, but I do so for the sake of organization.

Cold War, the United States created the Coordinating Committee for Multilateral Export Controls to deny sophisticated technology to the Soviet Union, and a veritable alphabet soup of arms control agencies and treaties are in place today to limit the spread of WMD, including the Missile Technology Control Regime (MTCR), the Nuclear Suppliers Group (NSG), and the Enhanced Proliferation Control Initiative (EPCI).[2] While effective to an extent, the trouble is that increasingly proliferation is fueled by "dual-use" items, goods with civilian purposes that also have military applications.[3] Blocking equipment such as centrifuges or x-ray machines can be extraordinarily politically sensitive given the humanitarian benefits of their legitimate medical use. Also, companies and governments, often more attuned to the immediate prospect of financial gain than the long-term security risks of questionable sales, do not always ensure that buyers are using exported products for their intended

---

[2] See US Department of Defense, *Threat and Response*, 70–77. To secure and regulate foreign sources of fuel and technological expertise, the United States primarily relies on the Cooperative Threat Reduction Program. By finding new employment for former nuclear scientists and dismantling ageing nuclear forces, this initiative aims to stem the flow of hardware and scientific expertise from the former Soviet Union to prospective WMD clients. See Michael Krepon, "Moving away from MAD," *Survival* vol. 43, no. 2 (summer 2001): 87. The Department of Energy has also initiated a $450 million campaign to retrieve nuclear materials that the United States and the Soviet Union sent around the world for use in research reactors; see Matthew L. Wald and Judith Miller, "Energy Department Plans a Push to Retrieve Nuclear Materials," *New York Times*, 26 May 2004. Parallel to this effort, the United States in June 2002 made a major financial and political commitment to the G8 Partnership against the Spread of Weapons of Mass Destruction, whose mission is to raise over $20 billion by 2012 to help maintain control over this dismantlement process. By August 2004, the Partnership had raised about $18.5 billion. See US Department of State, Bureau of Nonproliferation, "Fact Sheet: The G8 Global Partnership against the Spread of Weapons and Materials of Mass Destruction" (24 August 2004). Available at http://www.state.gov/t/np/rls/fs/34967.htm. See also Sam Nunn and Michele Flournoy, "A Test of Leadership on Sea Island," *Washington Post*, 8 June 2004.

[3] David Albright, "A Proliferation Primer," *The Bulletin of Atomic Scientists* vol. 49, no. 5 (June 1993): 14. For instance, in 2000 Japan imposed export controls on its PlayStation2 video game system because it could process high-quality images quickly, a feature much in demand for advanced missile guidance systems. See Patrick M. Morgan, *Deterrence Now* (Cambridge: Cambridge University Press, 2003), 234.

purpose.[4] Iraq in particular shocked the world with the degree to which it was able quietly to procure the precursors to its arsenal of WMD prior to the 1990–91 Gulf War, often directly from suppliers in the West.[5] Similarly, the Nonproliferation Treaty (NPT) enables states to acquire sophisticated nuclear reactors and technology that are ostensibly for civilian power production, but which a state can ultimately divert to weapons development either in secret or if it chooses to terminate NPT safeguards. This potential loophole has led to proposals to place the supply of fissile material under international control, rather than continue to promote complete indigenous development.[6]

Even if it were possible to reach international agreement over how to restrict dual-use items and regulate fissile material, the reality is that we live in a post-proliferation world, and so in a sense the horse is out of the barn. North Korea is effectively a nuclear state, likely to be in possession of sufficient reprocessed plutonium to create nearly a dozen bombs and possibly hard at work developing enriched uranium as well.[7] Most analysts also suspect Iran, notwithstanding repeated agreements with the European Union to suspend its nuclear

---

[4] US General Accounting Office, *Post-Shipment Verification Provides Limited Assurance that Dual-Use Items are Being Properly Used*, GAO-04-357 (Washington DC: January 2004).

[5] Kenneth R. Timmerman, *The Death Lobby: How the West Armed Iraq* (London: Fourth Estate, 1992); David Kay, "Denial and Deception Practices of WMD Proliferators: Iraq and Beyond," *The Washington Quarterly* vol. 18, no. 1 (winter 1995): 85–105; Robert W. Chandler with Robert J. Trees, *Tomorrow's War, Today's Decisions: Iraqi Weapons of Mass Destruction and the Implications of WMD-Armed Adversaries for Future US Military Strategy* (McLean, VA: AMCODA Press, 1996), 129, 154.

[6] See, e.g., United Nations, *A More Secure World: Our Shared Responsibility*, Report of the Secretary-General's High-level Panel on Threats, Challenges and Change (2004), 44; George Bush, Remarks on Weapons of Mass Destruction Proliferation, Fort Lesley J. McNair, National Defense University, Washington DC: 11 February 2004. Available at http://www.whitehouse.gov/news/releases/2004/02/20040211-4.html.

[7] See Glenn Kessler, "More N. Korean Bombs Likely, US Official Says," *Washington Post*, 16 July 2004; David E. Sanger and William J. Broad, "North Korea Said to Expand Arms Program," *New York Times*, 6 December 2004; Robert S. Norris and Hans M. Kristensen, "North Korea's Nuclear Program, 2005," *Bulletin of the Atomic Scientists* vol. 61, no. 3 (May/June 2005): 64–67.

development,[8] of being well on its way toward mastering the uranium enrichment process and hence on the verge of becoming a shadow, if not actual, nuclear power.[9] The international arms bazaar of Pakistani nuclear mastermind Dr. A.Q. Khan may be no more, but it certainly appears to have had brisk sales while it was open for business.[10] This does not mean that export controls are futile; the success of Dr. Khan demonstrates how crucial it is to prevent a future repetition of such proliferation. However, barring a disarmament agreement along the lines of that reached with Libya,[11] in which Iran and North Korea agree to give up their weapons programs in return for aid and improved relations with the West (which appears fairly unlikely, despite the September 2005 agreement with North Korea), export controls will not turn back the clock on these nascent nuclear states.

MISSILE DEFENSES

Given the enormous challenges inherent in export controls, US government officials are giving much more attention and funding to national missile defense (NMD) programs.[12] Often maligned as a pipe

---

[8] See Karl Vick, "Iran's Leader Backs Deal on Inspections," *Washington Post*, 4 November 2003; Peter Ford, "Europe Persuades Iran to Cool Nuclear Program – For Now," *Christian Science Monitor*, 16 November 2004; Elaine Sciolino, "Europe Gets Iran to Extend Freeze in Nuclear Work," *New York Times*, 26 May 2005.

[9] See International Atomic Energy Agency, *Implementation of the NPT Safeguards Agreement in the Islamic Republic of Iran*, IAEA Doc. GOV/2004/83 (November 2004). See also Barbara Slavin, "Iran's Nuke Plans May Be Unstoppable," *USA Today*, 30 August 2004; Douglas Frantz, "Iran Moving Methodically toward Nuclear Capability," *Los Angeles Times*, 21 October 2004.

[10] See Central Intelligence Agency, *Unclassified Report to Congress on the Acquisition of Technology Relating to Weapons of Mass Destruction and Advanced Conventional Munitions*, 1 July–31 December 2003 (2004). Available at http://www.cia.gov/cia/reports/721_reports/pdfs/721report_july_dec2003.pdf. See also David E. Sanger and William J. Broad, "From Rogue Nuclear Programs, Web of Trails Leads to Pakistan," *New York Times*, 3 January 2004; William J. Broad and David E. Sanger, "Pakistani's Black Market May Sell Nuclear Secrets," *New York Times*, 21 March 2005.

[11] See James G. Lakely, "Libya Will Dismantle its Weapons," *Washington Times*, 20 December 2003.

[12] James Dao, "Pentagon Optimistic about Missile Shield," *New York Times*, 15 April 2002; Greg Miller, "US Claims 90% Hit Rate in Missile Plan," *Los Angeles Times*, 19 March 2003; Bradley Graham, "General Says Missile Defense Could Be Ready Soon," *Washington Post*, 28 April 2004; Helen Dewar, " 'Realistic' Missile Tests Ordered," *Washington Post*, 18 June 2004.

dream that seeks to "hit a bullet with a bullet," skeptics claim that the low reliability of such a system[13] combined with its susceptibility to countermeasures[14] means that it is unlikely to provide many strategic benefits.[15] One group of analysts asserts, "Confidence in the effectiveness of the planned NMD system would not be high enough to increase US freedom of action beyond the level already achieved through deterrence."[16] Other skeptics of NMD, including nuclear deterrence theorist Robert Powell, believe that a moderately effective NMD will decrease American security by making the United States bolder in its interactions with rogue states, thereby increasing the risk of a nuclear attack in response.[17] Still other critics point out that if American NMD ambitions are too extensive or seen as too effective, Russia and China may compensate by building up their missile arsenal, possibly producing an overall net loss in security.[18]

On the opposing side of this debate are those who feel that any uncertainty over accuracy will affect the enemy as well, and it is worth "raising the admission price" of potential WMD attacks as high as possible.[19] According to this position, US missile defenses could act as a "psychological deterrent," providing important insurance

[13] Thus far, test results of the fledgling missile defense system in Alaska have not been promising. See David Stout and John H. Cushman, "Defense Missile for US System Fails to Launch," *New York Times*, 16 December 2004.

[14] See, e.g., William J. Broad, "Achilles' Heel in Missile Plan: Crude Weapons," *New York Times*, 27 August 2001.

[15] William J. Broad, "The Nuclear Shield: Repelling an Attack," *New York Times*, 30 June 2000; Richard L. Garwin, "A Defense that Will Not Defend," *The Washington Quarterly* vol. 23, no. 3 (summer 2000): 110; Gordon R. Mitchell, *Strategic Deception: Rhetoric, Science, and Politics in Missile Defense Advocacy* (East Lansing, MI: Michigan State University Press, 2000); Bradley Graham, "Scientists Raise Doubts about Missile Defense," *Washington Post*, 16 July 2003; Paul Richter, "Missile Defense System Doubts," *Los Angeles Times*, 22 January 2004.

[16] George Lewis, Lisbeth Gronlund, and David Wright, "National Missile Defense: An Indefensible System," *Foreign Policy* no. 117 (winter 1999–2000): 128.

[17] Robert Powell, "Nuclear Deterrence Theory, Nuclear Proliferation, and National Missile Defense," *International Security* vol. 27, no. 4 (spring 2003): 88.

[18] Dean Wilkening, *Ballistic-Missile Defence and Strategic Stability*, Adelphi Paper 334 (Oxford: Oxford University Press, International Institute for Strategic Studies, 2000), 8.

[19] Henry Kissinger, *Does America Need a Foreign Policy?* (New York: Simon & Schuster, 2001), 69; US Department of Defense, *Nuclear Posture Review* (Washington DC: 31 December 2001).

against attack by raising the prospect in an adversary's mind that using its WMD-missile force could bring about all of the costs inherent in US retaliation without any of the "benefit" of causing damage to American interests.[20] As James Lindsay and Michael O'Hanlon put it, "even a porous missile defense could enhance deterrence by forcing an attacker with limited capability to contemplate the possibility that any attack would be futile and fatal."[21] With such a system in place, rogue states would be less inclined to engage in blackmail or extreme coercive measures under the cover of deterrence, realizing that the United States might feel secure enough to respond with military force regardless of whether the threat was a bluff or not. This viewpoint meshes with Robert Powell's central premise – that robust defensive capabilities would make the US willingness to use force offensively more credible – but reaches the opposite conclusion that greater freedom of action is advantageous to American foreign policy. The prospect of such an outcome has resulted in much of the international opposition to NMD by those interested in keeping American military might as constrained as possible.

Both sides of the argument have merit, and ultimately the decision will come down to technical feasibility, and what level of insurance against missile attack is worth the expense involved. In brinksmanship situations, if an adversary is hoping to deter the United States, will it likely rely heavily on a long-range missile threat? Given the wide range of alternative means for harming the United States, as demonstrated by the 11 September attacks, there is an understandable concern that missile defenses might embody a "Maginot Line" mentality that aggressive states could easily bypass

---

[20] Jerome H. Kahan, "Deterrence and Warfighting in an NBC Environment," in *The Niche Threat: Deterring the Use of Chemical and Biological Weapons*, edited by Stuart E. Johnson (Washington DC: National Defense University Press, 1997), 54; Stephen J. Hadley, "A Call to Deploy," *The Washington Quarterly* vol. 23, no. 3 (summer 2000): 100; Philip Gordon, "Bush, Missile Defence and the Atlantic Alliance," *Survival* vol. 43, no. 1 (spring 2001): 18.

[21] James M. Lindsay and Michael E. O'Hanlon, *Defending America: The Case for Limited National Missile Defense* (Washington DC: Brookings Institution Press, 2001), 20.

altogether. Moreover, as an alternative to long-range missiles, rogue states may also develop cruise missiles that are far more difficult to defend against and perfectly suited for carrying biological weapons.[22] Nevertheless, the unique coercive power of missiles justifies further testing of new defensive technologies, especially with the greater success of boost-phase missile defense systems.[23] Stripping rogue states of a secure belief in their ability to deliver WMD by missile will undoubtedly reduce the force of their deterrent threats. The crucial issue will be how NMD technologies develop and whether they are cost-effective compared with countering the other threats faced by the United States.

PASSIVE DEFENSES

Considering the fallibility of export controls and missile defenses, should a WMD attack ever occur it is imperative to try and limit its destructiveness through the use of passive defenses. On the battlefield, the ability of US military forces to survive a WMD attack and continue with their mission (which would likely then include regime change) will make rogue state leaders more reluctant to put deterrence to the test. Military gaming exercises show that chemical and biological weapon (CB) detection and defense capabilities can significantly boost US resolve, giving soldiers confidence that they can fight and win in a contaminated environment.[24] Reversing perspective, war games in which teams were assigned to play the role of a regional adversary revealed that the US ability to operate in a WMD environment had a

---

[22] Kathleen C. Bailey, *Doomsday Weapons in the Hands of Many: The Arms Control Challenge of the 90s* (Chicago: University of Illinois Press, 1991), 103; Chandler, *Tomorrow's War, Today's Decision*, 178; Barry R. Schneider, *Future War and Counterproliferation: US Military Responses to NBC Proliferation Threats* (Westport, CT: Praeger, 1999), 126; Rex R. Kiziah, *Assessment of the Emerging Biocruise Threat*, Future Warfare Series No. 6 (Maxwell Air Force Base, AL: Air War College, August 2000).

[23] See, e.g., Frank J. Gaffney Jr., "Go Navy Missile Defense," *Washington Times*, 1 March 2005.

[24] Robert G. Joseph, "The Role of Nuclear Weapons in US Deterrence Strategy," in *Deterrence in the 21st Century*, edited by Max G. Manwaring (London: Frank Cass, 2001), 58.

major impact on the adversary's decision over whether to resort to unconventional weapons.[25] Similar to the psychological deterrent power of missile defenses, effective passive defense measures are likely to create uncertainty in the mind of an adversary that their WMD use would succeed, causing them to fear inviting repercussions without any military gain. To reinforce this perception, the US Department of Defense is developing and fielding a range of sensors, masks, decontamination systems, and medical kits for soldiers in combat.[26] New protective suits and masks are standard issue for American infantry, and many soldiers also receive vaccinations against smallpox.[27] The US military is also gradually expanding its training for operations involving WMD, including the use of simulations, the construction of Humvees that protect against and detect CB, the creation of special response teams and medical units, and the exploration of new operational tactics to limit vulnerability.[28] While there are surely shortcomings in certain areas and significant room for improvement, assessments that coalition soldiers in Operation Iraqi Freedom were

[25] Robert G. Joseph and John F. Reichart, "NBC Military Planning: Lessons Learned from Analysis and Wargaming," in *Countering the Proliferation and Use of Weapons of Mass Destruction*, edited by Vincent J. Jodoin and Alan R. Van Tassel (New York: McGraw-Hill, 1998), 185.

[26] Edward M. Spiers, *Weapons of Mass Destruction: Prospects for Proliferation* (London: Macmillan, 2000), 134; US Department of Defense, *Threat and Response*, 85–90; John Hendren, "Pentagon Battles Unknown Preparing for a Toxic War," *Los Angeles Times*, 29 September 2002; Teresa Riordan, "Plastic Pods for Biological Attacks," *New York Times*, 30 September 2002. See generally *Chem-Bio Defense Quarterly Magazine* for information on the latest advances in CB defense.

[27] Vicki Kemper, "Vaccine Program Going Well, Military Reports," *Los Angeles Times*, 14 February 2003; Matthew Cox and William Matthews, "The Best Protective Gear in the World?" *Air Force Times*, 24 February 2003.

[28] US Department of Defense, Chemical and Biological Defense Program, *Annual Report to Congress and Performance Plan* (Washington DC: April 2003); Ann Scott Tyson, "For Army, a New Primer in Chemical War," *Christian Science Monitor*, 21 October 2002; John Diedrich, "SpaceCom Improves Ability to Dodge Scuds," *Colorado Springs Gazette*, 31 January 2003; George Coryell, "New Humvee Protects against All Chemical, Biological Warfare," *Tampa Tribune*, 11 March 2003. One particularly interesting project involved a competition sponsored by the Defense Advanced Research Projects Agency that set a $1 million reward for a team that could construct an unmanned land vehicle capable of navigating across 200 miles of open desert without any human assistance. See Rene Sanchez, "Robot Race is Giant Step for Unmanned Kind," *Washington Post*, 10 March 2004.

reasonably well prepared to withstand a chemical weapons attack reflected well on America's progress in CB defense capabilities.[29]

At home, the United States is a soft target with many points of vulnerability. Bioterrorism against agriculture, chemical attacks on public transportation systems or at public events, and even suitcase nuclear weapons all remain major fears. Particularly after the anthrax attacks in the autumn of 2001 and subsequent reports of a plot to detonate a "dirty bomb" in a US city, the threat of WMD has without question become a US domestic concern. In response, training, investment, and innovation directed toward the US military should be mirrored in homeland security efforts to improve the skills and equipment of first-responders and Civil Support Teams in major cities.[30] When compared with the billions of dollars spent on NMD, these efforts can justifiably be described as offering "more 'anti-bang' for the buck."[31] Unfortunately, despite significant progress in some areas, many experts believe that the United States has a long way to go in providing an adequate homeland security framework.[32]

This is not to say that the United States has failed to take steps to protect itself; at least on the surface the Bush administration

[29] Matt Kelley, "Iraq Can Make Chemical Weapons that Penetrate US Protective Gear," *Associated Press*, 17 November 2002; Peter Baker, "But What if the Iraqis Strike First?" *Washington Post*, 23 January 2003; Romesh Ratnesar, "Can They Strike Back?" *Time*, 3 February 2003; Tony Capaccio, "Iraq Probably Can't Mount Major Chemical Attack, General Says," *Bloomberg.com*, 4 March 2003.

[30] See Richard A. Falkenrath, Robert D. Newman, and Bradley A. Thayer, *America's Achilles' Heel: Nuclear, Biological, and Chemical Terrorism and Covert Attack* (Cambridge, MA: MIT Press, 1998); Bill Miller, "Denver Stages Mock Terror Attack," *Washington Post*, 23 February 2002.

[31] Richard Betts, "Universal Deterrence or Conceptual Collapse? Liberal Pessimism and Utopian Realism," in *The Coming Crisis: Nuclear Proliferation, US Interests, and World Order*, edited by Victor A. Utgoff (Cambridge, MA: MIT Press, 2000), 79.

[32] See, e.g., Jim A. Davis and Barry R. Schneider, eds., *The Gathering Biological Warfare Storm* (Maxwell Air Force Base, AL: USAF Counterproliferation Center, April 2002); Council on Foreign Relations, *America Still Unprepared – America Still in Danger*, 17 October 2002; Stephen Smith, "US Farms Called Vulnerable to Terrorism," *Boston Globe*, 22 November 2002; Brad Knickerbocker, "Risk of Terrorism to Nation's Food Supply," *Christian Science Monitor*, 24 December 2002; Ceci Connolly, "Readiness for Chemical Attack Criticized," *Washington Post*, 4 June 2003; Spencer S. Hsu, "Anthrax Alarm Uncovers Response Flaws," *Washington Post*, 17 March 2005.

appears to understand the need for developing such technologies, having requested billions of dollars to protect the nation against bioterrorism. Project Bioshield is meant to encourage private firms to conduct research into new vaccines against threats such as anthrax, and to experiment with novel techniques like artificial antibodies potentially to treat smallpox after infection.[33] Likewise, the Department of Homeland Security has implemented many important reforms, particularly in the area of border control.[34] Through the Container Security Initiative, the United States has recently reformed its customs rules to require every shipping company importing cargo to provide US officials with advance information on each container on its ships, along with other security measures.[35] On the positive side, border control is being substantially aided by the development of portable pager-sized nuclear detection devices that can sense minute amounts of radioactive material.[36] Unfortunately, producing comparable biological weapon detectors is proving much more of a challenge, prompting research into advanced technologies such as tissue-based biosensors as well as specialized environmental and public health monitoring systems to improve detection speed and sensitivity.[37] As with missile defense, homeland security measures

[33] Vicki Kemper, "Senate Approves $5.6 Billion for 10-Year 'Bioshield' Project," *Los Angeles Times*, 20 May 2004. See also Dee Ann Divis, "BioWar: Biowatch Expansion Developing," *Washington Times*, 24 February 2005.

[34] See US Department of Homeland Security, *Securing our Homeland* (Washington DC: 2004); US Department of Homeland Security, *National Response Plan* (Washington DC: December 2004). Available at http://www.dhs.gov/interweb/assetlibrary/NRP_FullText.pdf.

[35] Mark Hosenball and Evan Thomas, "High-Seas Hunting," *Newsweek*, 23 December 2003.

[36] Barton Gellman, "Fears Prompt US to Beef up Nuclear Terror Detection," *Washington Post*, 3 March 2002; Steven Johnson, "Stopping Loose Nukes," *Wired* vol. 10, no. 11 (November 2002). Available online at http://www.wired.com/wired/archive/10.11/nukes.html; Anthony L. Kimery, "Searching for 'Dirty Bombs,'" *Insight Magazine*, 21 January 2003; Joby Warrick, "Bush to Seek Funds for Fighting 'Dirty Bombs,'" *Washington Post*, 30 January 2003; Philip Shenon, "Border Inspectors to Look for Radioactive Material," *New York Times*, 1 March 2003.

[37] US Department of Defense, *Threat and Response*, 119; Judith Miller, "US is Deploying a Monitor System for Germ Attacks," *New York Times*, 22 January 2003; Spencer S. Hsu, "Sensors May Track Terror's Fallout," *Washington Post*, 2 June 2003.

are prudent not only to save American lives if the unthinkable does occur, but also to reduce the force of WMD threats generally.

COUNTERFORCE

Fearing that none of these largely defensive measures will be adequate, some commentators maintain that the risk of certain states using WMD or supplying them to terrorists may be substantial enough to justify disarmament by air strikes or outright invasion.[38] Generally speaking, this option is not new to US military planners, who seriously contemplated contingency plans to destroy the nuclear facilities of the Soviet Union at the start of the Cold War[39] and China in the early 1960s.[40] After a period of limited interest over the subsequent few decades, the build-up to Iraqi Freedom brought renewed attention to the strategic and legal aspects of forcible disarmament. Secretary of Defense Donald Rumsfeld articulated a modern version of the classic counterforce doctrine, claiming "[i]t is not possible to defend against every threat, in every place, at every conceivable time. Defending against terrorism and other emerging threats requires that we take the war to the enemy."[41]

The challenge will be how to make this offensive outlook militarily successful and politically viable, given that "we can expect future WMD target sets to be large, extremely difficult to find, hardened, well-protected, and located next to things or people we do not

[38] See, e.g., Michael J. Glennon, "Preempting Terrorism: The Case for Anticipatory Self-Defense," *The Weekly Standard* vol. 7, no. 19 (28 January 2002); William C. Bradford, " 'The Duty to Defend Them': A Natural Law Justification for the Bush Doctrine of Preventive War," *Notre Dame Law Review* vol. 79 (2004): 1470; John C. Yoo, "Using Force," *University of Chicago Law Review* vol. 71, no. 3 (summer 2004): 794.

[39] See Russell D. Buhite and William Christopher Hamel, "War for Peace: The Question of an American Preventive War against the Soviet Union, 1945–1955," *Diplomatic History* vol. 14, no. 3 (summer 1990): 367–84.

[40] See William Burr and Jeffrey T. Richelson, "Whether to 'Strangle the Baby in the Cradle': The United States and the Chinese Nuclear Program, 1960–64," *International Security* vol. 25, no. 3 (winter 2000–01): 54–55, 68.

[41] Donald H. Rumsfeld, "Transforming the Military," *Foreign Affairs* vol. 81, no. 3 (May/June 2002): 20–32.

want to damage or injure."[42] Iran's suspected enrichment facilities, for instance, are effectively immune from air strikes, hidden in large government complexes and other secret locations.[43] Novel tunneling techniques have given rogue states the ability to bury bunkers and compartments, reinforced to withstand intensive bombing, far beneath the Earth's surface; indeed, there are now more than 1,100 such facilities known to be in existence.[44] To be fair, advances have taken place on the detection side as well – including sophisticated techniques such as hyperspectral imaging, seismic sensing, and gravimetry – that may help uncover even well-hidden underground construction efforts.

Confronted with the prospect of deeply buried targets, the US Department of Defense is reconsidering the employment of tactical nuclear weapons, leading to fierce debate in Congress over whether to fund further research, development, and possible testing of such an option.[45] Some analysts argue that only nuclear weapons are powerful enough to penetrate shielded and hardened facilities, and could

---

[42] Chandler, *Tomorrow's War, Today's Decisions*, 156. See also Marc Dean Millot, "Facing the Emerging Reality of Regional Nuclear Adversaries," *The Washington Quarterly* vol. 17, no. 3 (summer 1994): 48.

[43] See Sharon Squassoni, "Iran's Nuclear Program: Recent Developments," Congressional Research Service, March 2004. Available at http://www.ceip.org/files/projects/npp/pdf/Iran/crsirannuclear3-04_04.pdf. See also David E. Sanger, "US vs. a Nuclear Iran," *New York Times*, 12 December 2004.

[44] Eric M. Sepp, *Deeply Buried Facilities: Implications for Military Operations*, Occasional Paper No. 14 (Maxwell Air Force Base, AL: Air War College, May 2000), 5; US Department of Defense, *Nuclear Posture Review*; Michael A. Levi, *Fire in the Hole: Nuclear and Non-Nuclear Options for Counterproliferation*, Working Paper No. 31 (Washington DC: Carnegie Endowment for International Peace, November 2002), 8; David A. Fulghum, "Iraq's Hidden Weapons 'Are Likely Underground,'" *Aviation Week & Space Technology*, 16 December 2002.

[45] Paul Richter, "US Works up Plan for Using Nuclear Arms," *Los Angeles Times*, 9 March 2002; Walter Pincus, "US Nuclear Arms Stance Modified by Policy Study," *Washington Post*, 23 March 2002; Walter Pincus, "US Explores Developing Low-Yield Nuclear Weapons," *Washington Post*, 20 February 2003; Dan Stober, "Nuclear 'Bunker Busters' Sought," *San Jose Mercury News*, 23 April 2003; Carl Hulse, "Senate Votes to Lift Ban on Producing Nuclear Arms," *New York Times*, 21 May 2003; William J. Broad, "Facing a Second Nuclear Age," *New York Times*, 3 August 2003; Julian Coman, "Pentagon Wants 'Mini-Nukes' to Fight Terrorists," *Sunday Telegraph* (London), 26 October 2003; John Diamond and Tom Squitieri, "House Panel Says No to Nuke Funding," *USA Today*, 10 June 2004; Helen Dewar, "Senate Passes $447 Billion Defense Bill," *Washington Post*, 24 June 2004;

have the added advantage of creating temperatures likely to inciner-
ate any CB materials that are contained therein.[46] Furthermore, advocates of tactical nuclear weapons believe that by being "usable" and
thereby more credibly threatened, they will contribute to deterrence
more than thermonuclear devices that would create unacceptable
levels of damage.[47] However, there is a growing consensus that such
a strategy will fall prey to the same flaws that have foiled plans for
tactical nuclear weapons before, from nuclear artillery to neutron
bombs: no matter how tiny, they simply cannot be used without
causing intolerable radioactive fallout.[48] As an alternative, military
research labs are developing new conventional options such as pene-
trating "thermobaric" bombs (called BLU-118Bs), advanced munitions that can repeatedly strike the same precise location to reach far
beneath the surface, and bombs that employ a "hard target smart
fuze" to delay detonation until deep underground.[49]

Associated Press, "Senate Approves Money for New Nuclear Weapon," *Los Angeles Times*, 2 July 2005. James Sterngold, "US Alters Nuclear Weapons Policy," *San Francisco Chronicle*, 28 November 2005.

[46] Thomas M. Dowler and Joseph S. Howard II, "Stability in a Proliferated World," *Strategic Review* vol. 23, no. 2 (spring 1995): 28; Walter Pincus, "Nuclear Strike on Bunkers Assessed," *Washington Post*, 20 December 2001; Levi, *Fire in the Hole*, 22. Conventional weapons, by contrast, may simply only succeed in dispersing the CB materials, causing widespread collateral damage.

[47] David G. Savage, "Nuclear Plan Meant to Deter," *Los Angeles Times*, 11 March 2002; Amy Scott Tyson, "Nuclear Plan Changes Calculus of Deterrence," *Christian Science Monitor*, 14 March 2002; Richard T. Cooper, "Making Nuclear Bombs 'Usable,'" *Los Angeles Times*, 3 February 2003.

[48] Robert W. Nelson, "Low-Yield Earth-Penetrating Nuclear Weapons," *Journal of the Federation of American Scientists* vol. 54, no. 1 (January/February 2001): 1–5; William J. Broad, "Call for New Breed of Nuclear Arms Faces Hurdles," *New York Times*, 11 March 2002; Rose Gottemoeller, "On Nukes, We Need to Talk," *Washington Post*, 2 April 2002; Michael M. May and Zachary Haldeman, *Effectiveness of Nuclear Weapons against Buried Biological Agents* (Stanford, CA: Center for International Security and Cooperation, June 2003).

[49] Andrew Koch, "Dual Delivery is Key to Buried Targets," *Jane's Defence Weekly* vol. 33, no. 10 (8 March 2000); US Department of Defense, *Threat and Response*, 90; National Defense University, *The Counterproliferation Imperative*, 30; Andre C. Revkin, "Advanced Armaments," *New York Times*, 3 December 2001; John F. Burns, with Eric Schmitt, "US Forces Join Big Assault on Afghan Stronghold," *New York Times*, 3 March 2002; Levi, *Fire in the Hole*, 17–20; Walter Pincus, "Future of US Nuclear Arsenal Debated," *Washington Post*, 4 May 2003.

Even if the United States could contain the fallout from a nuclear strike, there is still the serious danger of releasing WMD from the attack and causing collateral damage. During Operation Desert Fox in 1998, then Secretary of Defense William Cohen left many Iraqi CB facilities off the target list, remarking, "We're not going to take a chance and try to target any facility that would release any kind of horrific damage to innocent people."[50] This is a significant lesson for any rogue state hoping to secure sanctuary for its WMD. As a result, extensive research is underway on technologies like high-power microwave weapons (that would disable the electricity and communications of a facility), high-temperature incendiaries (that would seek to burn up any released material), and special foam (that would seal off a site and render it unusable without releasing its contents) to disable a target without emitting WMD.[51] Given that even the most protected underground sites require contact with the surface, the prospects for "functional defeat," or isolating a facility by destroying its electronics or support systems, are rather promising.[52]

In the end, if there are too many targets to be able to place confidence in even the most thorough of air campaigns to destroy them all, then a preemptive attack runs the risk of provoking the very attack it intended to foreclose. The reliability of target identification ought to be tempered by the experience of the 1990–91 Gulf War, after which target planners were shocked at how badly they underestimated the

---

[50] Quoted in Steven Lee Myers, "The Targets: Jets Said to Avoid Poison Gas Sites," *New York Times*, 18 December 1998.

[51] Bryan Bender, "USA Planning Warhead to Hit CB Weapons," *Jane's Defence Weekly* vol. 31, no. 12 (24 March 1999); John Hendren, "US Studies Foam Bombs among Options to Isolate Chemicals," *Los Angeles Times*, 18 July 2002; David A. Fulghum, "Microwave Weapons May Be Ready for Iraq," *Aviation Week & Space Technology*, 5 August 2002; Michael Smith, "Saddam to be Target of Britain's 'E-Bomb,'" *Daily Telegraph* (London), 26 August 2002. For an overview of the advances in counterforce technologies, see Barry R. Schneider, *Counterforce Targeting Capabilities and Challenges*, Counterproliferation Paper No. 22 (Maxwell Air Force Base, AL: Air War College, August 2004).

[52] Sepp, *Deeply Buried Facilities*, 10, 23–28; Levi, *Fire in the Hole*, 21.

number of Iraqi WMD facilities.[53] Conversely, the apparent overestimation of Iraqi WMD stockpiles during Iraqi Freedom also does little to instill faith in the ability of the intelligence community to develop an accurate target set.[54]

Granted an outright invasion would probably bypass the uncertainties of intelligence and collateral damage problems, uprooting a state's WMD development in its entirety, but it would also likely increase the risk of devastating reprisals and last resort attacks. As strong as US military forces are, all wars are incredibly costly in both financial and human terms, and would likely be even more so if WMD were involved. The heavy burdens of occupation, as demonstrated by the aftermath of Iraqi Freedom, would also serve as a severe limiting factor on carrying out missions of regime change and disarmament. The crucial question is whether it is worth risking or waging a war to eliminate a potential threat before it becomes truly imminent. Chapter 6 will explore these strategic difficulties, as well as the legal aspects of counterforce.

INTERDICTION

Given these grim conclusions – the failure of export controls, the uncertainty of defenses, and the impracticality of counterforce – it is crucial that the United States has robust interdiction capabilities to prevent the transfer of WMD. Recognizing this need, President Bush announced on 31 May 2003 in Krakow, Poland the Proliferation Security Initiative (PSI), a multinational effort to equip states to

---

[53] Chandler, *Tomorrow's War, Today's Decisions*, 154; Schneider, *Future War and Counterproliferation*, 155; Andrew Cockburn and Patrick Cockburn, *Out of the Ashes: The Resurrection of Saddam Hussein* (London: Verso, 2000), 96; Buster Glosson, *War with Iraq: Critical Lessons* (Charlotte, NC: Glosson Family Foundation, 2003), 287.

[54] Walter Pincus, "US Has Still Not Found Iraqi Arms," *Washington Post*, 26 April 2003; Barton Gellman, "Frustrated, US Arms Team to Leave Iraq," *Washington Post*, 11 May 2003; Greg Miller, "Analysis of Iraqi Weapons 'Wrong,'" *Los Angeles Times*, 31 May 2003; Michael Duffy, "Weapons of Mass Disappearance," *Time*, 9 June 2003; Barton Gellman, "Iraq's Arsenal Was Only on Paper," *Washington Post*, 7 January 2004.

prevent WMD proliferation.[55] The founding participants of the PSI issued a "Statement of Interdiction Principles," identifying specific areas of cooperation, particularly in sharing intelligence information and providing mutual consent in interdiction missions.[56] Already the PSI has had some notable successes, including the September 2003 interception of a freighter bound for Libya with a shipment of parts for centrifuges used in uranium enrichment, which some observers believe was responsible for Libyan leader Muammar Gaddafi's decision to accept inspections and disarm.[57]

The PSI is meant to "be consistent with existing national legal authorities and international law and frameworks."[58] Generally, while a state has complete jurisdiction over its airspace, territory, and internal waters, its authority diminishes in relation to the distance from its coastline.[59] Under the principle of exclusive flag state jurisdiction, vessels on the high seas[60] or aircraft beyond a state's territorial seas "are subject to no authority except that of the State whose flag they fly."[61]

[55] See US Department of State, Bureau of Nonproliferation, Press Release, "The Proliferation Security Initiative" (May 2005). Available at http://www.state.gov/t/np/rls/other/46858.htm.

[56] See The White House, Office of the Press Secretary, "Fact Sheet: Proliferation Security Initiative: Statement of Interdiction Principles" (4 September 2003). Available at http://www.state.gov/t/np/rls/fs/23764.htm.

[57] See Robin Wright, "Ship Incident May Have Swayed Libya," Washington Post, 1 January 2004. There are other more long-term explanations for Gaddafi's change of heart as well. See David Gargill, "The Libya Fallacy: The Iraq War is Not What Disarmed Qaddafi," Harper's Magazine, November 2004. Available at http://www.findarticles.com/p/articles/mi_m1111/is_1854_309/ai_n8573894.

[58] US Department of State, Bureau of Nonproliferation, "Fact Sheet: Proliferation Security Initiative Frequently Asked Questions (FAQ)," (24 May 2004). Available at http://www.state.gov/t/np/rls/fs/32725.htm

[59] See Daniel H. Joyner, "The Proliferation Security Initiative: Nonproliferation, Counterproliferation and International Law," Yale Journal of International Law vol. 30, no. 2 (summer 2005): 525–26.

[60] According to the UN Law of the Sea Convention, the high seas are beyond a state's "exclusive economic zone," which is a maximum of 200 nautical miles from its twelve-mile territorial sea. See United Nations Convention on the Law of the Sea, art. 3, 57, 86, UN Doc. A/CONF. 62/122, opened for signature 10 December 1982, 1833 UNTS 397 (1994) (hereinafter UNCLOS).

[61] S.S. Lotus Case (Fr. v. Turk.), PCIJ (ser. A) No. 9 (7 September 1927), 25. This principle was codified in UNCLOS, art. 92(1). See also Michael Byers, "Policing the High Seas: The Proliferation Security Initiative," American Journal of International Law vol. 98, no. 3 (July 2004): 527, footnotes 9, 13.

For maritime interdiction, the primary exceptions to this rule are listed in Article 110 of the UN Convention on the Law of the Sea (UNCLOS), granting warships the right to board and search a vessel when there is reasonable ground for suspecting that it is engaging in piracy, slave trading, unauthorized broadcasting, lacks a flag, or is flying a false flag.[62] Thus, unless one is willing to expand the definition of piracy to include WMD proliferation, which is probably quite a stretch,[63] this means that UNCLOS bars any state from interdicting suspected WMD traffickers on the high seas without the consent of the ship's flag state.

The potential consequences of this restriction were brought into sharp relief in December 2002, when US intelligence identified an unflagged North Korean freighter (the *So San*) crossing the Arabian Sea and contacted the Spanish government to request that its navy stop the vessel and inspect it for illicit cargo.[64] Spanish special forces boarded the ship, uncovering a cache of Scud missiles hidden beneath sacks of cement. Shortly thereafter, Yemeni government officials came forward and claimed ownership, declaring that they had purchased the missiles from North Korea for defensive purposes. Since international law does not bar such a sale, the United States and Spain allowed the *So San* to proceed, accepting an agreement from the Yemeni president not to make further purchases. This incident was disturbing not for its specific facts – the boarding itself was legal because the ship was flagless – but rather because it highlighted the limited legal authority that would exist for similar operations in the future. If the *So San* had been flying a North Korean flag, and refused to consent to boarding, UNCLOS would prohibit interdiction, even if there was a strong certainty that it carried WMD.

Making the best of its limited legal authority, the PSI is focusing on streamlining the process for acquiring the consent of flag states to

[62] UNCLOS, art. 110(1).   [63] Joyner, "The Proliferation Security Initiative," 35.

[64] See Jofi Joseph, "The Proliferation Security Initiative: Can Interdiction Stop Proliferation?" *Arms Control Today* vol. 34, no. 5 (June 2004): 7; Thom Shanker, "Threats and Responses: Arms Smuggling; Scud Missiles Found on Ship of North Korea," *New York Times*, 11 December 2002.

board their vessels, thereby bypassing UNCLOS altogether. Besides the provisions addressing mutual consent in the PSI's "Statement of Interdiction Principles,"[65] the United States has signed six ship-boarding agreements including some of the world's major shipping registry states, establishing bilateral procedures for boarding vessels suspected of carrying WMD or related materials.[66] Modeled after counternarcotics arrangements, these agreements have the effect of limiting the number of flag states a proliferating state can rely upon in transporting illicit materials under the protection of UNCLOS. Indeed, by August 2005 the PSI had ship-boarding agreements with states representing more than 60 percent of the global commercial shipping fleet.[67] Despite this initial progress, securing the assent of the remaining key shipping registry states could be difficult given that many states that offer "flags of convenience" (allowing registration with little regulation or oversight) are highly dependent on the earnings from such transactions and may be reluctant to grant consent.[68] Unless the United States can reach ship-boarding agreements with virtually all flag states, traffickers will retain options for shipping WMD effectively immune from interdiction authority.[69] Moreover, even if universal participation were possible, the most likely proliferators, such as Pakistan, Iran, and North

[65] The White House, "Fact Sheet: Proliferation Security Initiative: Statement of Interdiction Principles."

[66] The United States has signed agreements with Liberia (11 February 2004), Panama (12 May 2004), the Marshall Islands (13 August 2004), Croatia (1 June 2005), Cyprus (25 July 2005), and Belize (4 August 2005). Each of these agreements enables a party to request that the other confirm the nationality of the ship in question and, if needed, authorize interdiction. For the text of the agreements, see the US Department of State Ship Boarding Agreements website. Available at http://www.state.gov/t/np/c12386.htm.

[67] See US Department of State, Office of the Spokesman, Media Note, "The United States and Belize Proliferation Security Initiative Ship Boarding Agreement" (4 August 2005). Available at http://www.state.gov/r/pa/prs/ps/2005/50787.htm.

[68] See Andreas Persbo and Ian Davis, *Sailing into Uncharted Waters? The Proliferation Security Initiative and the Law of the Sea* (London: British American Security Information Council Research Report, June 2004), 8–9. Available at http://www.basicint.org/pubs/Research/04PSI.htm.

[69] See Joel A. Doolin, "Operational Art for the Proliferation Security Initiative," unpublished final paper at the Naval War College (2004), 5. Available at http://www.fas.org/man/eprint/doolin.pdf.

Korea, could always elect to transport WMD shipments under their own flag, thereby guaranteeing that consent would not be forthcoming.

Realistically, if the United States were to receive intelligence reports indicating that a North Korean ship was transporting a completed nuclear device on the high seas, lack of consent would surely not be a barrier to its decision to interdict. This poses a gap between the stated objectives of the PSI and its legal authority to achieve them. The threat posed by WMD is simply too great to allow a pocket of immunity under UNCLOS to prevent all interdiction efforts without consent, regardless of the magnitude of the threat. The notion that some states should profit from lending the use of their flag as a shield against inspection is likewise untenable in an age of WMD. Instead, as I argue in chapter 7, there should be a global norm against WMD proliferation that is all-inclusive, holding any state that transports WMD responsible, regardless of nationality.

This is not meant to imply that interdiction will suffice as an exclusive or even primary strategy to combat WMD. Interdiction missions require extraordinary intelligence, timing, and coordination to be successful. Detecting plutonium is incredibly difficult given its faint radiation emission,[70] and monitoring biological and chemical weapons is even more challenging since their precursor elements are often dual-use in nature, posing the same dilemmas that plague export control decisions.[71] Far preferable are negotiated disarmament agreements and confidence-building measures that could eliminate the desire of states to acquire WMD in the first place. However, given the limitations of counterproliferation strategies illustrated in this chapter, if states do choose to develop and sell WMD, interdiction may be the last viable line of defense against their use. The alternative of active disarmament operations is far more dangerous, invasive, legally questionable, and likely to spur yet further proliferation to deter such action.

---

[70] See Nuclear Threat Initiative, "Interdicting Nuclear Smuggling," available at http://www.nti.org/e_research/cnwm/interdicting/index.asp; Michael Levi, "Uncontainable: North Korea's Loose Nukes," *New Republic*, 26 May 2003.

[71] Ashley Roach, interview with author, 25 October 2004.

6   Preemptive and preventive war

If the United States believes that WMD are too dangerous to rely on deterrence alone as protection, then one potential solution is to deny rogue states WMD altogether. With states already in possession of WMD, the only way to achieve this objective may be disarmament by negotiation or force. Given the obvious incentives for designated "rogue" states to retain WMD for their deterrent power, a solution by the former route will be rare. Unfortunately, as this chapter demonstrates, the practical and legal difficulties with the latter option are equally daunting.

The US *National Security Strategy* (NSS) states that America must identify and destroy threats before they reach its borders, reserving a right of military preemption even in the absence of an imminent attack. According to the NSS, while the decision to preempt may be necessitated by modern technology and new adversaries, its justification is not novel:

> The United States has long maintained the option of preemptive actions to counter a sufficient threat to our national security. The greater the threat, the greater is the risk of inaction – and the more compelling the case for taking anticipatory action to defend ourselves . . . To forestall or prevent such hostile acts by our adversaries, the United States will, if necessary, act preemptively.[1]

Former National Security Advisor Condoleezza Rice affirmed this viewpoint in an October 2002 speech, claiming "There has never been

---

[1] US Government, *The National Security Strategy of the United States of America* (Washington DC: September 2002), 15.

a moral or legal requirement that a country wait to be attacked before it can address existential threats."[2] This may be the case in principle, but American historical practice suggests that there is little to no precedent for the United States attacking preemptively, with the exception of the Spanish-American War and more recent military operations like Iraqi Freedom.[3] Instead, the United States has traditionally only reacted to acts of aggression, restricting its offensive action to limited covert operations.

To be precise, the concept articulated by the NSS – also known as the Bush Doctrine – is more appropriately termed preventive war. A preemptive action, by contrast, is based on incontrovertible evidence that an enemy attack is imminent, leading the targeted state to strike first in order to attain an advantage. As common sense would suggest, there can be little expectation for a state to wait and absorb the first blow when war is at hand. The inherent danger with such a strategy, though, is that it is based on the supposition of intended harm, and thus could bring about a war that perhaps might have been averted through eleventh-hour diplomacy or a last-minute change of heart by the suspected aggressor state. There may be standards of imminence that truly do equate to actual attack, such as missiles en route, but generally preemption seeks to precede the initiation of conflict sufficiently to gain a decisive edge. As such, if two states share the same fear of attack, a very unstable situation can develop with each side hoping to preempt the other's potential preemption.

Preventive war is a response not to imminent danger, but to long-term threat. According to one useful definition, "Preventive war is based on the concept that war is inevitable, and that it is better to fight now while costs are low rather than later when the costs are high.

---

[2] Condoleezza Rice, Wriston Lecture to the Manhattan Institute, New York, 1 October 2002.

[3] Richard F. Grimmett, "US Use of Preemptive Military Force," Congressional Research Service, 18 September 2002; Craig Gilbert, "Can US Be First to Attack Enemy?" *Milwaukee Journal Sentinel*, 31 March 2002.

It is a deliberate decision to begin a war . . . Preemption, by contrast, is nothing more than a quick draw."[4] Lawrence Freedman provides a more colorful comparison: "Prevention is cold blooded; it intends to deal with a problem before it becomes a crisis, while preemption is a more desperate strategy employed in the heat of crisis."[5] The distinguishing factors of preventive war are a degree of premeditation and a threat that is prospective rather than immediate. Loosely interpreted, such a description is applicable to all conflicts, and Freedman cautions that – in the absence of a compelling cause – claims of preventive war can easily become a cover for aggression.[6] Hegemonic powers fearful of rising rivals, neighboring states with undefined borders, or historic enemies on constant alert all could use preventive war as a universal justification depending on one's interpretation of what constitutes an inevitable threat. This elasticity explains a great deal of the reluctance of weaker states in the international system to justify any principle of anticipatory self-defense, especially preventive in nature, fearful that it will grant the United States carte blanche to wage war with the slightest provocation or even based on mere suspicion.

In truth, it is not readily apparent whether or not the Bush administration makes a clear distinction between preemptive and preventive war, as it often uses the terms interchangeably or in a similar context. Secretary of Defense Donald Rumsfeld gave a sweeping call to action in a speech to the graduating class of the Air Force Academy in May of 2002: "Prevention and preemption are the best, and indeed in most cases the only defense against terrorism. Our task is to find and destroy the enemy before they strike us. And it's a big world."[7] A few months earlier, Paul Wolfowitz, Rumsfeld's deputy, made similar remarks to a conference in Munich: "Our approach has to aim at prevention and not merely punishment. We are at war. Self-defense

---

[4] James J. Wirtz and James A. Russell, "US Policy on Preventive War and Preemption," *The Nonproliferation Review* vol. 10, no. 1 (spring 2003): 116.

[5] Lawrence Freedman, "Prevention, Not Preemption," *The Washington Quarterly* vol. 26, no. 2 (spring 2003): 107. [6] Ibid., 108.

[7] Donald H. Rumsfeld, Speech at the Air Force Commencement Ceremony, Colorado Springs, Colorado, 29 May 2002.

requires prevention and sometimes preemption."[8] In the aftermath of 11 September, one would expect the United States to make a vigorous effort to track down members of Al Qaeda. However, given that terrorists are scattered across the globe (including within the United States), a crucial issue left unanswered by these statements was the criteria or standard of threat that the US government would use to trigger preemptive or preventive action, especially against states that lack a clear connection to Al Qaeda.

President Bush's speeches justifying Iraqi Freedom provide some clue as to how his administration interprets the Bush Doctrine. Just prior to the war, Bush described Iraq as a "direct and growing threat," adding that "Acting against the danger will also contribute greatly to the long-term safety and stability of our world."[9] Yet, even putting the WMD controversy aside, there was never any evidence that Saddam Hussein was actively planning to attack the United States or its allies (either directly or through terrorists), the traditional criterion for a pre-emptive war. Bush chose to use the word "direct" rather than "imminent" apparently to highlight the perceived severe – but not proximate – nature of the Iraqi threat. In his 2003 State of the Union Address, Bush specifically denied the need to show proof of impending harm:

> Some have said we must not act until the threat is imminent. Since when have terrorists and tyrants announced their intentions, politely putting us on notice before they strike? If this threat is permitted to fully and suddenly emerge, all actions, all words, and all recriminations would come too late. Trusting in the sanity and restraint of Saddam Hussein is not a strategy, and it is not an option.[10]

Without an indication of intentions or a fully emerged or imminent threat, it is clear that the Bush Doctrine moves beyond acts of

---

[8] Paul Wolfowitz, Remarks at the 38th Munich Conference on Security Policy, Munich, 2 February 2002.

[9] George W. Bush, Speech at the American Enterprise Institute, Washington DC, 26 February 2003.

[10] George W. Bush, State of the Union Address, Washington DC, 28 January 2003.

anticipatory self-defense. Rather, it sanctions preventive war, basing security on the elimination of potential threat rather than the power of deterrence.[11]

This adoption of a preventive war policy is nothing short of revolutionary, and it remains to be seen whether it is a practical solution to today's security environment. Recent scholarship has identified the shift in American strategic thinking toward preventive war, but has not provided an integrated analysis of the principles behind the Bush Doctrine and its policy implications. In this chapter, I will first address the theoretical and legal underpinnings of preemptive and preventive war, employing historical examples as illustrations and analogies for current dilemmas. I will then examine how contemporary circumstances might alter our understanding of these concepts, requiring a redefinition of basic terms and a reconsideration of some primary assumptions. Finally, I will show how this reformulation relates to the doctrine of deterrence and how it can inform US foreign policy. I conclude that the Bush Doctrine is a modern iteration of a historic line of thought justifying anticipatory action, but one that thus far lacks a foundation of articulated standards, however imprecise. Failure to provide any genuine restraints on an offensive notion of self-defense will likely generate a backlash among targeted states. Fearful that their security depends on a favorable American assessment of their peaceful intentions, many states will probably prefer to embrace WMD for deterrence purposes, exacerbating the US security dilemma.

PREEMPTIVE WAR: SELF-DEFENSE AGAINST IMMINENT THREATS

A state's right to self-defense is clearly expressed in international law, both in treaty and in customary practice.[12] Moreover, an allowance

---

[11] This is not to say that US policy is necessarily misguided, merely that it adheres less closely to a preemptive war strategy than its rhetoric might suggest. To be fair, the lines between the two concepts will never be clearly drawn, especially since the United States is unlikely to face a foe that telegraphs its intentions by carrying out a laborious mobilization.

[12] See Anthony Clark Arend, "International Law and the Preemptive Use of Military Force," *The Washington Quarterly* vol. 26, no. 2 (spring 2003): 90.

for responding to aggression is not necessarily limited to repelling invading troops, but can expand to include carrying out limited reprisals or an incursion into enemy territory to destroy the offending military force.[13] For example, there were few objections to Kuwait's effort to defend itself against Iraq's invasion in 1990, even to the point of enlisting an international coalition that both ejected the aggressors and carried out an extensive bombing campaign inside Iraq's borders. The act of illegitimately initiating hostilities forfeits certain aspects of territorial immunity and empowers the attacked state to undertake defensive – as well as retaliatory – measures.

This retaliatory privilege has its bounds, though, as when the international community rejected US claims to have exhausted all diplomatic options before launching air strikes against Libya in 1986 after a string of terrorist atrocities linked to Muammar Gaddafi.[14] Similar recriminations of expediency and excessive force surround President Bill Clinton's 1998 selection of a reputed pharmaceutical plant in Sudan as the target of a cruise missile attack in response to the Al Qaeda bombings of two US embassies in Africa. Ambiguous evidence connecting the plant to chemical weapons production or terrorist activity undermined America's claim of a defensively motivated reprisal, amplifying suspicions that a desire to deflect attention from Clinton's escalating personal scandals was at play.[15] In the Libyan case, Reagan was careful to identify the air strikes not as retaliation, but rather as a kind of preventive self-defense: "Gaddafi was supporting terrorist attacks against the US. He was also planning further attacks and there was no way of guarding effectively all the possible

---

[13] See Myres S. McDougal and Florentino P. Feliciano, *Law and Minimum World Order* (New Haven, CT: Yale University Press, 1961), 222–23.

[14] See Stanimir A. Alexandrov, *Self-Defense against the Use of Force in International Law* (Cambridge, MA: Kluwer Law International, 1996), 185. See also George J. Church, "Targeting Gaddafi," *Time*, 21 April 1986; Seymour Hersh, "Target Gaddafi: Reagan's Secret Plot," *The Times* (London), 22 February 1987.

[15] Karl Vick, "US, Sudan Trade Claims on Factory," *Washington Post*, 25 August 1998; Michael Barletta, "Chemical Weapons in the Sudan: Allegations and Evidence," *Nonproliferation Review* vol. 6, no. 1 (fall 1998): 115–36.

targets."[16] The parallels between this quote and the Bush Doctrine are self-evident: invoking a war on terror, discounting a feasible defense, and claiming that preventive strikes are the only alternative.

Preemptive self-defense can also include anticipatory actions made prior to the initiation of hostilities by the aggressor. In the words of former Secretary of State Elihu Root, "International law does not require the threatened state to wait in using force until it is too late to protect itself."[17] Sensible in principle, it has nevertheless proved difficult to reach a consensus over what kind of preemptive actions are legitimate in practice. Jurists at Nuremberg rejected the German defense counsel's claim that the Nazi invasion of the Soviet Union was intended to forestall a Soviet attack from the East.[18] In the Tokyo war crimes trials, Japanese defense lawyers sought to invoke a similar right of self-preservation to account for Japan's military advances, positing that the sanctions imposed upon it were a form of aggression.[19] Clearly the right of self-defense requires a more sophisticated standard than perceived danger or economic harm. Otherwise, without some sense of boundaries, it is likely to excuse any and all wars, which are usually based in some part on mutual fear and suspicion.

The United Nations Charter

The United Nations can provide a sense of international standards in such matters. Article 51 of the UN Charter states:

> Nothing in the present Charter shall impair the inherent right of individual or collective self-defense if an armed attack occurs against a Member of the United Nations, until the Security Council has taken measures necessary to maintain international peace and security. Measures taken by Members in the exercise of

[16] Quoted in Timothy L.H. McCormack, *Self-Defense in International Law: The Israeli Raid on the Iraqi Nuclear Reactor* (New York: St. Martin's Press, 1996), 230.

[17] Quoted in Barry R. Schneider, *Future War and Counterproliferation: US Military Responses to NBC Proliferation Threats* (Westport, CT: Praeger, 1999), 163.

[18] Ian Brownlie, *International Law and the Use of Force by States* (Oxford: Oxford University Press, 1963), 258.   [19] Ibid., 253.

this right of self-defense shall be immediately reported to the Security Council and shall not in any way affect the authority and responsibility of the Security Council under the present Charter to take at any time such action as it deems necessary in order to maintain or restore international peace and security.[20]

Based on this passage, some international legal scholars dispute the existence of a right of preemption altogether, noting that force is valid only "if an armed attack occurs," and not before.[21] Such a reading, known as a "restrictive" view of Article 51, would exclude all claims of potential threat, imminent or otherwise, from justifying the use of military force. Opposing this perspective, those who ascribe to the so-called "permissive" view of Article 51 focus instead on the notion of an "inherent" right of self-defense.[22] Those in the permissive school contend that preexisting rights under customary law, in place before the adoption of the UN Charter, can empower states to use force prior to being the victim of armed aggression. Justification for this interpretation springs from the recognition that being forced to wait and absorb the first blow of combat confers an enormous advantage to a hard-hitting assailant. In the words of moral theorist Michael Walzer: "[A]ggression often begins without shots being fired or borders crossed. Both individuals and states can rightfully defend themselves against violence that is imminent but not actual; they can fire the first shots if they know themselves about to be attacked."[23] Just as there might not be time to alert the police of a crime about to take place, a state may need to foil another's offensive plans before they can be put into action.

[20] United Nations Charter, Article 51. Available at http://www.un.org/aboutun/charter/chapter7.htm.

[21] See, e.g., Brownlie, *International Law and the Use of Force by States*, 275; Louis Henkin, *How Nations Behave: Law and Foreign Policy*, 2nd edition (New York: Columbia University Press, 1979), 141.

[22] See, e.g., Julius Stone, *Aggression and World Order* (London: Stevens & Sons, 1958), 44; Derek W. Bowett, *Self-Defence in International Law* (Manchester: The University Press, 1958), 185; Richard G. Maxon, "Nature's Eldest Law: A Survey of a Nation's Right to Act in Self-Defense," *Parameters* vol. 25, no. 3 (autumn 1995): 55–68.

[23] Michael Walzer, *Just and Unjust Wars* (New York: Basic Books, 1977), 74.

How does this qualification square with Article 51's requirement that states act in self-defense only if an armed attack occurs? Permissive scholars note that Article 51 does not state that armed force is authorized "if and only if" an armed attack occurs.[24] This reading theoretically leaves room for alternative interpretations of when the inherent right of self-defense might apply. Moreover, Article 2(4) of the UN Charter states: "All members shall refrain in their international relations from the threat or use of force against the territorial integrity or political independence of any state . . ."[25] This section creates an inherent tension with Article 51 because it forbids a state of affairs short of armed conflict (the threat of force), but authorizes only Security Council action in response.[26] Especially since the Security Council cannot generally be expected to respond to all instances of conflict – much less threats short of war – states may need to step in and fill the gap if they are facing an imminent attack.

Restrictive scholars criticize this interpretation as distorting the "plain meaning" of Article 51, which appears to restrict state autonomy to resort to the use of force in favor of mediation and settlement by the Security Council. By seeking an exception to the rule, "permissive" thinkers may be identifying a loophole that will be difficult to regulate, enabling states to develop their own conception of what constitutes a threat of force. As Michael Glennon notes, such a position "would render chimerical the armed attack requirement . . . because an attack would then begin not with bullets and bombs but with pencils and paper, possibly deployed months or even years before actual hostilities."[27] Not only would preemptive attack be authorized, but so too would preventive war, negating the purpose of Article 51.

---

[24] Myres S. McDougal, "The Soviet–Cuban Quarantine and Self-Defense," *American Journal of International Law* vol. 57, no. 3 (July 1963): 600; Anthony Clark Arend and Robert J. Beck, *International Law and the Use of Force: Beyond the UN Charter Paradigm* (London: Routledge, 1993), 73.

[25] United Nations Charter, Article 2(4). Available at http://www.un.org/aboutun/charter/chapter1.htm.

[26] See Michael J. Glennon, "The Fog of War: Self-Defense, Inherence, and Incoherence in Article 51 of the United Nations Charter," *Harvard Journal of Law and Public Policy* vol. 25, no. 2 (spring 2002): 546.   [27] Ibid., 547.

The Caroline case

The historical touchstone legal scholars often use to justify a limited right of preemptive attack – as well as to delegitimize preventive war – is known as the *Caroline* case. In 1837 US citizens were using a steamship (the *Caroline*) to transport men and supplies across the Niagara River to Canadians rebelling against Britain.[28] Deeming the ship of piratical character, British forces elected to board the ship forcibly, set it on fire, and send it over the Niagara Falls to ensure that it could no longer provide such support. This incident set off a flurry of correspondence between diplomatic offices; the British minister in Washington claimed that since the United States was not enforcing its laws by restraining the ship, Britain had the right to destroy it in the interests of self-preservation and self-defense. Incensed at what many perceived as an unprovoked destruction of American lives and property, the US minister in London presented the British government with a demand for reparations. The dispute languished for nearly five years, until the trial of one of the British assailants led Daniel Webster, then US secretary of state, to begin an exchange of letters with his British counterpart (Lord Ashburton). After a debate over several particulars of the *Caroline* case, Webster penned his now famous judgment that to make such an attack, there must be shown a "necessity of self-defense, instant, overwhelming, leaving no choice of means and no moment for deliberation." Lord Ashburton assured Webster that the British action met these criteria, as the *Caroline* was likely to remain moored until the very moment of departure and it was extremely unlikely that the United States would prevent it from sailing, making the danger a virtual certainty. Satisfied with the concurrence on principle, though not on substance, Webster agreed to put the matter to rest.

Daniel Webster's correspondence regarding the *Caroline* case resulted in two fundamental principles regulating the use of force under

---

[28] Historical details drawn from R.Y. Jennings, "The Caroline and McLeod Cases," *American Journal of International Law* vol. 32, no. 2 (April 1938): 82–99. See also http://www.yale.edu/lawweb/avalon/diplomacy/britian/br-1842d.htm.

international law. First, the principle of *necessity* requires that the defending state must face a proximate and severe threat before it can act.[29] Only a threat that is truly imminent, leaving not a "moment for deliberation," can be legitimately preempted; distant dangers that are merely possible or probable do not suffice. Further, the threat must be "overwhelming," serious enough to merit a military response, or even the most minor threat could be used as a pretext for war. Second, while not captured in Webster's famous quotation, the principle of *proportionality* demands that self-defense not be retaliatory or punitive, only sufficient to repel the attack and provide reasonable protection against future occurrences.[30] It would be unacceptable for a state to cite a series of small raids as justification for major conflict – a charge, for example, leveled against Israel for its role in the 1956 war with Egypt.

The Six Day War

A different Israeli–Egyptian conflict, the Six Day War of 1967, provides a useful illustration of an instance of preemption more widely perceived as legitimate. This time, prior to the outbreak of hostilities, Egypt carried out a series of unilateral provocations that seriously escalated tensions with its neighbor. Nasser, the Egyptian president, decided to mass troops in the Sinai, expel the UN Emergency Force in place as peacekeepers, and impose a blockade of the Straits of Tiran that severely threatened Israeli shipping and as such was already identified as a *casus belli* by Israel.[31] Considerable controversy remains as to whether Nasser seriously intended war, or if he was merely practicing brinksmanship at the goading of the radical leadership in Syria. Regardless, from Israel's perspective these actions amounted to a situation wherein it was as though an armed attack had already taken place. Dependent on a large pool of mobilized reservists, Israel could not afford to maintain a defensive stance counterbalancing Egypt's

---

[29] McCormack, *Self-Defense in International Law*, 263.

[30] See Christine Gray, *International Law and the Use of Force* (Oxford: Oxford University Press, 2000), 106.

[31] Edward Luttwak and Dan Horowitz, *The Israeli Army* (London: Penguin, 1975), 221.

formation on the border for a long period of time.[32] Because of this, Michael Walzer argues that Israel experienced a "just fear" legitimizing the exercise of anticipatory force.[33] Especially given that Nasser had declared that if war came Egypt's goal would be the destruction of Israel, the criterion of a severe and proximate threat mandated by Webster's principle of necessity seemed to be satisfied. Less certain is answering whether the devastating Six Day War Israel launched was proportionate, given that it virtually destroyed the Egyptian air force and secured significant portions of territory in the region.

As is evident, the concept of preemptive military action has a mixed heritage, seemingly forbidden by the UN Charter but sanctioned by precedent and the principle of self-defense. Especially in the present day, when weapons of mass destruction can cause instantaneous and devastating harm, following without exception the precepts of a document drafted to respond to the lurching mobilization of mass armies could be somewhat anachronistic. As Derek Bowett argues, "No state can be expected to await an initial attack which, in the present state of armaments, may well destroy the state's capacity for further resistance and so jeopardize its very existence."[34] And yet, how much patience should we demand? The lessons of the *Caroline* case are not as clear as they may first appear: the ship was not launching an imminent attack, but was transferring troops and supplies. There was certainly time for deliberation, if not the use of alternate measures such as demanding that the United States secure its borders. In sum, the justification of self-defense is unavoidably elastic. The following section will explore attempts to expand its scope beyond that of anticipatory action.

PREVENTIVE WAR: SELF-DEFENSE AGAINST PROSPECTIVE THREATS

Unlike the preceding analysis of preemptive conflicts, until recently there has been little legal or moral debate over the potential

---

[32] Ibid., 212.   [33] Walzer, *Just and Unjust Wars*, 84–85.
[34] Bowett, *Self-Defence in International Law*, 191–92.

justification for preventive war. Even permissive interpreters of the UN Charter have been reluctant to link the self-defense clause of Article 51 to preventive war, and few thinkers have put forward principles to provide guidance as to when it might be appropriate. Perhaps this is because of its ignoble historical record: under the pretense of avoiding a more terrible conflict in the future, some states have wrought immeasurable suffering in reputedly defensively oriented wars. For instance, some scholars deem Germany's decision to plunge into World War I as preventive in nature, born of a calculation that there was a limited window of opportunity before Russia completed its railroad network during which it was preferable to implement the Schlieffen Plan for a two-front conflict in Europe.[35] Historian A.J.P. Taylor confirms that Germany's action was hardly unique, observing in his seventy-year history of European affairs: "Every war between Great Powers with which this book deals started as a preventive war, not as a war of conquest."[36]

In the years following World War II, there were multiple instances of American journalists, military commanders, and political officials advocating an atomic strike on the Soviet Union before it could respond in kind.[37] These preventive considerations continued after the end of the US nuclear monopoly, particularly when regional crises and conflicts (such as those involving Berlin, Korea, Taiwan, and Vietnam) heated up to the extent of risking an expansion into a wider war.[38] Nor was the United States alone in contemplating advance strikes on possible nuclear rivals: in the early 1960s the Soviet Union seriously considered a military attack on China's

---

[35] Hew Strachan, *The First World War, Volume I* (Oxford: Oxford University Press, 2001), 62–63; Richard Betts, "Suicide from Fear of Death?" *Foreign Affairs* vol. 82, no. 1 (January/February 2003): 43.

[36] A.J.P. Taylor, *The Struggle for Mastery in Europe, 1848–1918* (Oxford: Oxford University Press, 1954), 166.

[37] Russell D. Buhite and William Christopher Hamel, "War for Peace: The Question of an American Preventive War against the Soviet Union, 1945–1955," *Diplomatic History* vol. 14, no. 3 (summer 1990): 367–84.

[38] See Alexander L. George and Richard Smoke, *Deterrence in American Foreign Policy: Theory and Practice* (New York: Columbia University Press, 1974).

nascent nuclear program, even conferring with the United States regarding a cooperative effort.[39] Lesser known examples include India's deliberation over whether to allow Israel to attack Pakistan's nuclear facilities in the early 1980s, and Iraq's bombing of Iran's nuclear reactor in 1984.[40] Beyond atomic diplomacy, the United States also conducted preventive military operations on a smaller scale against countries such as Nicaragua, Grenada, and Panama, basing its justification partly on the future danger such states posed to international peace and security.[41] More recently, in 1996 Secretary of Defense William Perry threatened a similar kind of intervention against Libya, asserting that it "will not be allowed to begin production" at a chemical weapons facility hidden in the desert.[42]

By far the most famous example of a preventive strike was Israel's destruction of Iraq's Osiraq nuclear reactor in June of 1981. Supplied by the French, Osiraq had survived a bombing raid by Iran in 1980 and was scheduled to "go hot" and begin producing plutonium shortly after the attack took place.[43] In a sense, then, the Israeli mission was preemptive since it targeted a suspect facility immediately before it became sheltered as a result of its radioactivity. Yet, the justification for the attack was not some inherent danger of Baghdad gaining access to fissile material, but the secondary danger that Iraq

---

[39] William Burr and Jeffrey T. Richelson, "Whether to 'Strangle the Baby in the Cradle': The United States and the Chinese Nuclear Program, 1960–64," *International Security* vol. 25, no. 3 (winter 2000–01): 54–55, 68.

[40] See Barry Schneider, *Radical Responses to Radical Regimes: Evaluating Preemptive Counter-proliferation*, McNair Paper No. 41 (Washington DC: National Defense University Press, May 1995), 8.

[41] Ann Devroy and Patrick E. Tyler, "Bush Launches Strike to Seize Noriega; Fighting Widespread in Panama City," *Washington Post*, 20 December 1989; Michael R. Gordon, "US Troops Move in Panama in Effort to Seize Noriega; Gunfire is Heard in Capital," *New York Times*, 20 December 1989; Gray, *International Law and the Use of Force*, 97.

[42] Quoted in Brad Roberts, "NBC-Armed Rogues: Is There a Moral Case for Preemption?" in *Close Calls: Intervention, Terrorism, Missile Defense, and "Just War" Today*, edited by Elliott Abrams (Washington DC: Ethics and Public Policy Center, 1998), 83.

[43] Seymour M. Hersh, *The Samson Option: Israel, America and the Bomb* (London: Faber, 1991), 9.

could eventually develop nuclear weapons that would pose a profound threat to Israel's existence. Israeli prime minister Menachem Begin saw the Osiraq bombing as "a supreme act of national self-defense," since in his mind if Saddam Hussein were armed with atomic weapons, he "would not have hesitated to drop them on Israel's cities and population centers."[44] Given that Iraq's future use of a nuclear bomb was conjecture at best, the Osiraq operation was certainly more preventive than preemptive in nature.

In Israel's defense, there was little doubt based on the type of reactor and nuclear fuel Iraq sought from France that Hussein was interested in a military device and not a civilian program.[45] Moreover, given the technical specifications of Osiraq, Iraq would have acquired the necessary fuel for atomic weapons from the reactor within eighteen months of its activation. While hardly an "instant" threat leaving not a "moment for deliberation," the prospect of a nuclear neighbor hostile to its very existence was certainly close to qualifying as an overwhelming danger for Israel. The question, of course, is how likely Iraq was to act upon its prospective capability. Hussein's animosity and threatening rhetoric toward Israel were well documented, but it does not follow that he would carry out an attack likely to be suicidal (owing to Israel's assumed retaliatory capability) without considerable cause.[46]

World opinion rejected Israel's claims of self-defense. Many speakers at the subsequent Security Council deliberations invoked the *Caroline* case, arguing that while states could justify preemptive strikes under the Charter framework (thereby supporting the stance

---

[44] Quoted in Steve Weissman and Herbert Krosney, *The Islamic Bomb: The Nuclear Threat to Israel and the Middle East* (New York: Times Books, 1981), 16. See also Shai Feldman, "The Bombing of Osiraq – Revisited," *International Security* vol. 7, no. 2 (fall 1982): 122.

[45] Uri Shoham, "The Israeli Raid upon the Iraqi Nuclear Reactor and the Right to Self-Defense," *Military Law Review* vol. 109 (summer 1985): 207; Shlomo Nakdimon, *First Strike: The Exclusive Story of How Israel Foiled Iraq's Attempt to Get the Bomb* (New York: Summit Books, 1987), 74.

[46] As for Webster's criteria, whereas the principle of necessity might remain unclear, there is widespread agreement that Israel's strike was astounding for its surgical precision and therefore would likely satisfy the principle of proportionality.

of permissive theorists), the Israeli circumstance did not meet this high standard because there was no imminent threat.[47] Even the United States initially criticized Israel, miffed that American equipment was used in the attack, but later declared that Israel had indeed acted in self-defense. The United States eventually fully reversed its position, coming to view the Osiraq bombing as a virtual textbook case in successful counterproliferation. In fact, former Secretary of State Colin Powell recently remarked, "The Israelis did it in 1981. It was a clear preemptive military strike. Everyone now is quite pleased even though they got the devil criticized out of them at the time."[48] Israel stood virtually alone in the face of a UN resolution condemning its action, defending its decision by arguing that a second Holocaust could not be permitted under any circumstances. In the words of then Israeli defense minister Ariel Sharon: "Israel cannot afford the introduction of the nuclear weapon. For us, it is not a question of a balance of terror but a question of survival. We shall therefore have to prevent such a threat at its inception."[49]

The language of Israel's justification of the Osiraq strike is remarkably similar to the US *National Security Strategy* – reflecting a fundamental rejection of the reliability of deterrence and therefore a willingness to employ preventive force as necessary. In a sense, the United States now views rogue state WMD the same way that Israel saw Iraqi nuclear weapons: as an existential threat too great to live under indefinitely. For Israel, the threshold for unacceptable danger was placed at the level not of imminent attack, nor the perception of aggressive plans, nor even the possession of nuclear weapons, but at their development – truly a remarkable step from the traditional standards of preemptive war.

---

[47] Arend and Beck, *International Law and the Use of Force*, 78.
[48] Quoted in Glenn Kessler and Peter Slevin, "Preemptive Strikes Must Be Decisive, Powell Says," *Washington Post*, 15 June 2002.
[49] Quoted in Jed C. Snyder, "The Road to Osiraq: Baghdad's Quest for the Bomb," *Middle East Journal* vol. 37 (autumn 1983): 582. However, uncertainty remained over the long-term utility of such a strike since it may have led the Iraqis to hide and protect their weapons programs better.

EVOLVING STANDARDS OF SELF-DEFENSE

Acceptable defensive thresholds have certainly changed over time. Even prior to the *Caroline* incident, James Monroe articulated his eponymous doctrine in 1823 which held that the United States would consider any attempt by Europe to extend its political influence into the Western hemisphere as a threat to its security. As Elihu Root observed:

> The [Monroe] doctrine is not international law but it rests upon the right of self-protection and that right is recognized by international law. The right is a necessary corollary of independent sovereignty. It is well understood that the exercise of the right of self-protection may and frequently does extend beyond the limits of the territorial jurisdiction of the state exercising it.[50]

The Cuban Missile Crisis demonstrated yet another redefinition of the bounds of self-defense, as the United States refused to accept the introduction of nuclear weapons to a country so close to its borders. In the subsequent UN deliberations, as would occur again in the debates over Osiraq, various delegations referenced the principle of necessity and its requirement of an imminent threat as the basis for opposing the quarantine.[51] From the American perspective, the Soviet missile shipment may not have been overtly aggressive, but neither was it entirely benign in its attempt to shift the global balance of power against the United States. Even without plans for a direct attack, such weapons carried a coercive potential not easily measured and certainly not accounted for under Article 51 or Webster's principles.

President Kennedy revealed a shift in strategic thinking in his famous television and radio address at the height of the crisis:

> We no longer live in a world where only the actual firing of weapons represents a sufficient challenge to a nation's security to

---

[50] Elihu Root, "The Real Monroe Doctrine," *American Journal of International Law* vol. 8, no. 3 (July 1914): 432.

[51] Arend and Beck, *International Law and the Use of Force*, 75.

constitute maximum peril. Nuclear weapons are so destructive and ballistic missiles so swift, that any substantially increased possibility of their use or any sudden change in their deployment may well be regarded as a definite threat to peace.[52]

Regardless of its validity at the time, this outlook has taken root and found new adherents in the Bush administration, which seeks to adapt traditional notions of self-defense – and imminent threat in particular – to contemporary circumstances. Whereas the Cuban Missile Crisis dealt with ballistic missiles that could not easily be defended against, the current panoply of threat involves weapons that are equally destructive but may offer even less warning and possibly no indication of their origin. President George Bush remarked, "Terrorists and terror states do not reveal these threats with fair notice, in formal declarations – and responding to such enemies only after they have struck first is not self-defense, it is suicide."[53] Akin to the British perspective in the *Caroline* case, the Bush administration believes that there are enemies plotting and gathering strength in secret, and that there will be no warning of their design until the moment of attack.

The Bush Doctrine

The Bush administration's willingness to take action against prospective threats appears to reflect a realization that, at some point in the future, either deterrence will fail against a regional adversary or a rogue state will transfer WMD to a terrorist client, requiring the United States to have a near perfect defense to prevent catastrophe. In effect, the specter of WMD presents the equivalent of the famous Irish Republican Army assassination threat made against UK Prime Minister Margaret Thatcher, but instead directed at an entire nation: "We only have to be lucky once. You will have to be lucky always."

[52] John F. Kennedy, Address to the Nation on the Soviet Arms Buildup in Cuba, The White House, Washington DC, 22 October 1962. Available at http://www.jfklibrary.org/j102262.htm.

[53] George W. Bush, Remarks by the President in Address to the Nation, The White House, Washington DC, 17 March 2003.

In a world where one cannot take the chance that WMD will be used, the line of self-defense must be drawn not at imminent use, but at development and possession. Under this conception, the standards espoused by Webster are swept aside by the notion that capability equals culpability, and that possession is the same as use.

The NSS includes assurances that the number of cases where anticipatory action would be justified will always be small, limited to instances when the threat is very grave and the risks of waiting unacceptable.[54] Left unclear, though, is how the very uncertainty that makes anticipatory force necessary will not also obscure estimations of when a threat reaches a level that is too risky to tolerate. After all, some states may seek WMD solely for defensive purposes, and so a distinction must be drawn between the motivation to acquire and the motivation to use such weapons. Otherwise, as legal scholar Louis Henkin sharply observed, "To say that whoever sets up 'offensive weapons' justifies preemptive use of force would justify unilateral force by everyone everywhere."[55] In a sense, given that the American military has the most potent offensive weapons, this may be the implicit bargain the United States hopes to strike, building forces "strong enough to dissuade potential adversaries from pursuing a military build-up in hopes of surpassing, or equaling, the power of the United States."[56] Ideally, if the US threat of preventive war is fearsome and credible enough, it will eventually become unnecessary as states will accept the futility of developing WMD or other offensive weapons, regardless of their intent.

Critics of this strategy warn of a backlash against what may be perceived as US hegemonic impulses, seeking a pliant international system to go with its one-sided sense of security:

> At the extreme, these notions form a neoimperial vision in which the United States arrogates to itself the global role of setting

---

[54] US Government, *National Security Strategy*, 15.
[55] Henkin, *How Nations Behave*, 295.
[56] US Government, *National Security Strategy*, 30.

standards, determining threats, using force, and meting out justice. It is a vision in which sovereignty becomes more absolute for America even as it becomes more conditional for countries that challenge Washington's standards of internal and external behavior.[57]

If opponents are not cowed into forswearing WMD, aggressive American enforcement born of fear of deterrence failure will probably accelerate proliferation as states will feel compelled to turn to deterrence as their sole source of protection against US conventional power. This certainly appears to be the case in the deepening weapons crises with Iran and North Korea. Worse, a unilateralist attitude toward security may spur additional attacks against American interests, motivating new recruits in the war *for* terror. As columnist Maureen Dowd succinctly noted, "Terrorism is not, as the president seems to suggest, a finite thing."[58] Thus, a fine line exists between trying to gain universal security by eliminating WMD, and provoking universal vulnerability by taking actions that lead weaker states and their people to feel desperate and unjustly targeted.

Such concerns are raised with even greater intensity in the aftermath of Iraqi Freedom, as there is overwhelming evidence of growing popular unrest and insurgent attacks, but not of the scope or depth of threat that the Bush administration implied was present.[59] The war in Iraq represented a definitive departure from the precepts of Article 51 as well as the principle of necessity, because there was no evidence demonstrating active Iraqi plans to attack the United States or its allies. Perhaps the danger was that

[57] G. John Ikenberry, "America's Imperial Ambition," *Foreign Affairs* vol. 81, no. 5 (September/October 2002): 44.

[58] Maureen Dowd, "The Jihad All-Stars," *New York Times*, 27 August 2003. See also Dana Priest, "Iraq New Terror Breeding Ground," *Washington Post*, 14 January 2005.

[59] See US Senate, Select Committee on Intelligence, *Report on the US Intelligence Community's Prewar Intelligence Assessments on Iraq*, Washington DC: 7 July 2004.

Iraq would eventually rearm with WMD and thereby shift the balance of power in the region in its favor or divert weapons to terrorists.[60] Whether a nuclear Iraq would be strategically significant depends on one's assessment of the durability of deterrence: preventive war will become more attractive the less confidence there is in deterrence succeeding over the long run. As was the case in Osiraq, the question was over the likelihood that Hussein would act on his prospective capability. If that likelihood was high, then the standard of preventive attack was correctly drawn quite early, before the world had to discover how far Iraq would press its leverage as a nuclear power. If low, then Iraqi Freedom was a very expensive and damaging insurance policy against a risk that perhaps could have been managed in other ways.

Establishing criteria for preventive war

Where does this leave the Bush Doctrine? The critical judgment will be over where to draw the line in measuring the imminence and magnitude of a prospective threat. How elastic ought these terms to become? On the one hand, designating the mere development of WMD as sufficient to merit offensive military action may appear to be a recipe for perpetual conflict – an endless string of Osiraqs and Iraqi Freedoms. On the other hand, since WMD are uniquely capable of causing such an astounding degree of harm, some states may not find it prudent to put faith in deterrence alone to ward off a surprise attack. After all, an adversary may never overtly demonstrate the intent to injure; it could try to evade identification altogether and merely sow fear and destruction through covert operations. Further, weapons transfers might take place to terrorist groups who, even when clearly culpable, can be difficult to find and punish.

To attempt to reconcile these competing concerns, numerous analysts have proposed criteria to serve as guidelines for exercising

---

[60] See Walter B. Slocombe, "Force, Preemption and Legitimacy," *Survival* vol. 45, no. 1 (spring 2003): 127.

preventive force.[61] Despite different emphases and slight variations, these recommendations boil down to six main considerations that form a "strategic profile"[62] and can serve as the basis for policy recommendations:

1 consider the risk-tolerance and values of the target state and whether it is likely to remain fundamentally conservative, or be highly motivated to challenge the status quo and threaten the United States;

2 estimate US interests in the region to determine the overall balance of resolve in a potential conflict;

3 calculate the likelihood of success of a military strike, based on the vulnerability of the target state's forces and American offensive capabilities;

4 determine the likelihood and potential consequences of a retaliatory strike relative to US defensive assets;

5 ensure that all other nonmilitary options have been exhausted; and

6 if there are no other alternatives, be certain that the United States has clear objectives and the public support to carry the action through to completion.

Two critical issues are intertwined with these determinations: who is making them, and what information they are based upon. Flaws in American intelligence gathering have been under intense

---

[61] See, e.g., Michele A. Flournoy, "Implications for US Strategy," in *New Nuclear Nations: Consequences for US Policy*, edited by Robert D. Blackwill and Albert Carnesale (New York: Council on Foreign Relations Press, 1993), 135–61; Philip Zelikow, "Offensive Military Options," in *New Nuclear Nations*, 162–63; Schneider, *Radical Responses to Radical Regimes*, 23–26; Roberts, "NBC-Armed Rogues," 83–107; Christopher Greenwood, "International Law and the Pre-emptive Use of Force: Afghanistan, Al Qaida, and Iraq," *San Diego International Law Journal* vol. 4 (2003): 7–37; Gareth Evans, "When is it Right to Fight?" *Survival* vol. 46, no. 3 (autumn 2004): 59–82; Terrence Taylor, "The End of Imminence?" *The Washington Quarterly* vol. 27, no. 4 (autumn 2004): 57–72.

[62] See, e.g., Derek D. Smith, "North Korea and the United States: A Strategic Profile," *The Korean Journal of Defense Analysis* vol. 16, no. 1 (spring 2004): 25–47. See also Robert S. Litwak, "The New Calculus of Preemption," *Survival* vol. 44, no. 4 (winter 2002–03): 73.

scrutiny by numerous commissions,[63] and it is self-evident that confidence in strategic assessments will only flow from credible and trustworthy sources. Similarly, although President Bush has ridiculed the notion of submitting national security decisions to a "global test,"[64] there is little doubt that international support and cooperation will be crucial in combating WMD proliferation, particularly in attempting to negotiate disarmament agreements with states such as Iran and North Korea. The harsh reality is that there is an inverse relationship between how advanced a WMD program is – a well-developed program should be more likely to elicit proof of a concrete threat – and how vulnerable it will be to attack given the stronger inclination to protect it.[65] Israel is now facing very different circumstances vis-à-vis Iran than it did back in 1981 with Osiraq, and despite its recent bluster it actually has few viable military options.[66] Moreover, as a program becomes more robust, it will also pose a greater risk of retaliation, as the United States is well aware in its foreign policy toward North Korea. In these cases, without international assistance, disarmament efforts will likely be futile and the default will be a renewed reliance on deterrence against two new nuclear nations.

Does this mean that the United States should pursue an even more ambitious preventive strategy against a state such as Syria to prevent it from following Iran's lead? The prime difficulty lies in the inescapable ambiguity of target state intentions – the first factor in the "strategic profile." It may be obvious that terrorist organizations

---

[63] See, e.g., US Government, National Commission on Terrorist Attacks upon the United States, *The 9/11 Commission Report* (Washington DC: July 2004).

[64] Elisabeth Bumiller and David M. Halbfinger, "Bush and Kerry Follow Debate with Sharp Jabs," *New York Times*, 2 October 2004.

[65] Michele Flournoy and Vinca LaFleur, "Quick-Stick Doctrine," *Washington Post*, 18 June 2002. See also Philip Zelikow, "The Transformation of National Security: Five Redefinitions," *The National Interest* no. 71 (spring 2003): 26.

[66] Joshua Mitnick, "Would Israel Strike First at Iran?" *Christian Science Monitor*, 18 August 2004; Youssef M. Ibrahim, "Think Twice before Targeting Iran," *USA Today*, 24 August 2004; Anton La Guardia, "Israel Challenges Iran's Nuclear Ambitions," *Daily Telegraph* (London), 22 September 2004; Gerald Steinberg, "Iran Analysis: Israel's Options," *Jerusalem Post*, 5 October 2004.

are fair game for anticipatory attacks since they clearly intend to cause harm, but much more uncertainty surrounds states such as Iran and Syria that are reputed to be harboring Al Qaeda members and are suspected of seeking WMD. Should such allegations be grounds for an attack if they could somehow be proved? A US poll taken nine months after 11 September 2001 found that four out of five Americans favored military action against a country that is aiding terrorists who target Americans, and three out of four favored action against enemies that are developing WMD.[67] Chances are that after Iraqi Freedom, those numbers are not the same.

There are no easy answers, but given the inherent costs and dangers of preventive war it is obviously preferable to attempt to influence the factors of the "strategic profile" to make it unnecessary. A global test may be inappropriate, but a global effort at reaching an international consensus on grounds for forcible disarmament is essential. Even if the United States and other nations determine that Article 51 is an unsuitable constraint on self-defense, it is necessary to articulate a new doctrine beyond declaring that the USA will attack its adversaries before they can strike first. The United States may ultimately have to define self-defense on its own terms, but it should make every effort to come to a common understanding on nonproliferation principles. Otherwise, there will be a growing list of candidates for preventive war, and an ever-shrinking coalition to fight them. The following chapter will investigate the prospects for a robust regime of interdiction as a viable alternative to preventive war.

[67] Andrea Stone, "Americans in Survey Support First Strike," *USA Today*, 26 June 2002.

7 Establishing a global quarantine against WMD

Faced with mounting international insecurity, Franklin Delano Roosevelt gave his famous "Quarantine Speech" in 1937, likening the rise of fascism to an outbreak of world lawlessness. "When an epidemic of physical disease starts to spread," FDR remarked, "the community approves and joins in a quarantine of the patients in order to protect the health of the community against the spread of the disease."[1] Fearful of becoming embroiled in another world war, the United States was slow to shed its isolationism, only gradually increasing the provision of arms to its allies and restricting exports to the Axis powers. When war finally came at Pearl Harbor, Nazi and Japanese forces had expanded like a cancer throughout Europe and Asia, requiring far more than a quarantine to eliminate the malignancy.

Today the proliferation of WMD represents another danger that is on the brink of developing into an epidemic. With the Indian and Pakistani nuclear tests in 1998, the clandestine nuclear progress of North Korea and Iran, and over a dozen nuclear-capable states waiting indecisively on the sidelines, the world has arrived at what is fairly described as a "nuclear tipping point," where a few decisions to produce WMD could spark a cascade of proliferation.[2] Since the United States may be unwilling to rely entirely on deterrence and unable feasibly to wage preventive wars against rogue states with WMD, it should, together with the international community, lay the

---

[1] For the text and audio of FDR's speech, see http://history.sandiego.edu/gen/text/us/fdr1937.html.

[2] See *The Nuclear Tipping Point: Why States Reconsider their Nuclear Choices*, edited by Kurt M. Campbell, Robert J. Einhorn, and Mitchell B. Reiss (Washington DC: Brookings Institution Press, 2004).

foundation for a global quarantine[3] against WMD, prohibiting all forms of transfer. Toward these ends, I will analyze in this chapter how the international community can legally justify a global quarantine upon principles of self-defense, as well as explore how practically to integrate the global quarantine concept with existing institutions.

INTERNATIONAL LAW, SELF-DEFENSE, AND INTERDICTION

As discussed in chapter 6, Article 51,[4] the UN Charter provision concerning self-defense, has become highly controversial, particularly given the events surrounding the 2003 US invasion of Iraq. Some scholars claim that the specter of terrorists gaining access to WMD has undermined the central premise of Article 51, leaving states unwilling to absorb an attack before taking action.[5] That is not to say that Article 51 lacks supporters. The UN High-level Panel on Threats, Challenges and Change, a blue ribbon commission convened by Secretary-General Kofi Annan to analyze emerging security concerns and propose UN reforms, stated unequivocally in its December 2004 report that Article 51 "needs neither extension nor restriction of its long-understood scope."[6] This section will assess these clashing positions, outlining how a global quarantine is supported by the principle of self-defense.

[3] Inspiration to apply the quarantine concept to this topic is drawn partly from Ruth Wedgwood, "A Pirate is a Pirate," *Wall Street Journal*, 16 December 2002.

[4] United Nations Charter, Article 51. Available at http://www.un.org/aboutun/charter/chapter7.htm. ("Nothing in the present Charter shall impair the inherent right of individual or collective self-defence if an armed attack occurs against a Member of the United Nations, until the Security Council has taken measures necessary to maintain international peace and security. Measures taken by Members in the exercise of this right of self-defence shall be immediately reported to the Security Council and shall not in any way affect the authority and responsibility of the Security Council under the present Charter to take at any time such action as it deems necessary in order to maintain or restore international peace and security.")

[5] See, e.g., Michael J. Glennon, "The Fog of War: Self-Defense, Inherence, and Incoherence in Article 51 of the United Nations Charter," *Harvard Journal of Law and Public Policy* vol. 25, no. 2 (spring 2002): 541.

[6] United Nations, *A More Secure World: Our Shared Responsibility*, Report of the Secretary-General's High-level Panel on Threats, Challenges and Change (2004), 3. Available at http://www.un.org/secureworld/report2.

To provide a sense of perspective, it is worth noting that the drafters of the UN Charter, which celebrated its sixtieth anniversary in June 2005, faced a very different security environment from today, centered on the threat of land invasion and aerial bombardment. The terminology of Article 51 was thus enmeshed in an international context with a very conspicuous and unambiguous notion of what qualified as an armed attack.[7] Today, the prime danger to the United States is not an army charging across the border, but an individual stepping off a plane with a suitcase of plutonium. Against what columnist Thomas Friedman artfully describes as "people of mass destruction,"[8] there is likely to be little warning, limited ability to defend, and an uncertain target for retaliation.

Such changing conditions often lead states to consider whether they should adapt their existing security frameworks to meet the new threat. Professor W. Michael Reisman noted that innovations in science and technology often create a "legal gap in which authority becomes uncertain . . . When some of these factors change to the point that communities can no longer assure their defense within the ambit of inherited law, those charged with national defense inevitably demand changes in the law."[9] The unique security circumstances surrounding air travel, for instance, have required corresponding modifications in the interpretation of privacy.[10] The immense difficulties of border control, likewise, have necessitated a relaxed standard of reasonable suspicion for

---

[7] Similarly, although based on ancient maritime principles, the UN Convention on the Law of the Sea is a product of the Cold War, concerned with safeguarding innocent passage and free navigation amidst superpower tensions. See United Nations Convention on the Law of the Sea, art. 17, 87, UN Doc. A/CONF. 62/122, opened for signature 10 December 1982, 1833 UNTS 397 (1994) (hereinafter UNCLOS). For instance, today it may seem rather anachronistic for a document to authorize the boarding of a ship and prosecution of individuals if they are broadcasting illegally, but not if they are transporting a nuclear bomb. See UNCLOS, art. 109.

[8] Thomas L. Friedman, "The Suicide Supply Chain," *New York Times*, 9 December 2004.

[9] W. Michael Reisman, "Assessing Claims to Revise the Laws of War," *American Journal of International Law* vol. 97, no. 1 (January 2003): 82.

[10] See, e.g., *United States v. Edwards*, 498 F.2d 496 (2d Cir. 1984).

checkpoint searches.[11] The inherent challenge is how to ensure that such legal remedies do not extend beyond the apparent gap and begin to overreach, perhaps infringing upon civil liberties.[12] In the domestic setting, courts assist legislators in determining the proper constitutional bounds of enforcement activity.[13] Within the anarchic international system, which lacks comparable institutional authorities, guiding rules are more malleable and in the shadow of the constant resort to military force. In modern international law, Reisman continues, "[d]octrines are positioned at the interface of law and power."[14]

The United Nations Charter includes provisions meant to balance competing interests in international affairs. On the one hand, the Charter incorporates the "inherent right of individual or collective self-defense" into Article 51, acknowledging that there may be instances when a state cannot wait for the United Nations to act before defending itself.[15] On the other, the Charter protects the notion of sovereignty, based on the principle that a state should be free from interference in its domestic affairs if it has not violated the rights of another state.[16] It is not always clear what degree of deference to sovereignty is appropriate, however, given the UN Charter's parallel mandate in Article 2(4) that all member states shall refrain from the threat of force "against the territorial integrity or political independence of any state."[17] Certainly sovereignty should not act as a shield protecting a state from all foreign intervention up until the point that it attacks another state, regardless of its other actions. If a modern-day Hitler were to come to power and begin to develop nuclear weapons, FDR's quarantine notion – and perhaps yet more active

[11] See, e.g., *United States v. Martinez-Fuerte*, 428 U.S. 543 (1976).
[12] See Bruce Ackerman, "The Emergency Constitution," *Yale Law Journal* vol. 113, no. 5 (March 2004): 1029; Harold Hongju Koh, "The Spirit of the Laws," *Harvard International Law Journal* vol. 43, no. 1 (winter 2002): 34.
[13] See, e.g., *Michigan Dept. of State Police v. Sitz*, 496 U.S. 444 (1990); *City of Indianapolis v. Edmond*, 531 U.S. 32 (2000).
[14] Reisman, "Assessing Claims to Revise the Laws of War," 90.
[15] United Nations Charter, art. 51.   [16] Ibid., art. 2(7).   [17] Ibid., art. 2(4).

measures – would be sensible. Increasingly, scholars are defining sovereignty as a source of responsibility as much as a claim of immunity.[18] Under this conception, states may lose their sovereign status if they fail to protect their citizens or become a menace to the international community by trafficking in WMD. A correlated duty of other states might be forcibly to prevent such nations from carrying out genocide against their citizens or selling WMD.[19]

To provide flexibility to this bright-line rule, the UN High-level Panel on Threats, Challenges and Change urged not the abandonment of Article 51, but recourse to Article 39. Since Article 39 empowers the Security Council to recommend military measures in response to "any threat to the peace, breach of the peace, or act of aggression,"[20] a state that cannot legally pursue independent action under Article 51 can always turn to the Security Council for authorization, even for a preventive military operation.[21] The dilemma with this alternative, as the world is well aware from the wrangling at the Security Council in the months prior to the 2003 US invasion of Iraq, is the potential for Council stalemate or a veto in an authorization vote. According to the Panel, if the Security Council elects to withhold its consent for a preventive action, "there will be, by definition, time to pursue other strategies, including persuasion, negotiation, deterrence and containment – and to visit again the military option."[22] While this reasoning could be convincing in considering whether to attack and disarm a state that is gradually developing a WMD arsenal, in which case there might be time to make a subsequent request to the Security Council down the road, with interdiction missions there may be no second chance: once the weapons go they are gone and the intelligence goes stale.

[18] See, e.g., International Commission on Intervention and State Sovereignty, *The Responsibility to Protect* (2001), 13. Available at http://www.dfait-maeci.gc.ca/iciss-ciise/pdf/Commission-Report.pdf.

[19] See Lee Feinstein and Anne-Marie Slaughter, "A Duty to Prevent," *Foreign Affairs* vol. 83, no. 1 (January/February 2004): 147.

[20] United Nations Charter, art. 39.   [21] United Nations, *A More Secure World*, 62.

[22] Ibid., 63.

Article 39 alone, then, is insufficient to deal with fleeting windows of opportunity of the kind associated with interdiction. Without a more robust and streamlined process, rather than risk delay and dissension at the Security Council, the United States would probably act on its own or with its close allies, claiming a rationale of self-defense. To prevent this outcome, the United Nations should provide an avenue for multilateral interdiction efforts, adopting a bright-line rule against the transfer of WMD. Such a reform is in accord with the UN Charter because the proliferation of WMD is not defensive; rather, it is a form of aggression against world order that merits a limited form of protection in the same vein. When a state elects not merely to build but to transfer WMD, placing other states in danger, it sacrifices the sovereignty its ships and planes would traditionally enjoy in international waters and airspace. In a sense, even though there may not be a traditional state of belligerency, the United Nations should treat WMD as international contraband, permitting search and seizure when there is reasonable suspicion of their presence.[23] To be sure, the potential for an abuse of interdiction power will remain, even when carried out multilaterally. Establishing a global quarantine in principle will not eliminate the problems of proof surrounding authorization of interdiction operations in practice, but it is a step in the right direction. The next section will attempt to map out a potential path for those steps to take.

BUILDING BLOCKS OF A GLOBAL QUARANTINE

An effective global quarantine system will require an integrated framework of initiatives, supplying both the legal foundation to establish a global norm against WMD proliferation and the needed capabilities to carry out interdiction missions. There are doubtless numerous combinations of means to achieve this end, but this section will focus on those I believe are most promising: first, the

[23] See Ruth Wedgwood, "Self-Defense, Pirates, and Contraband," *Wall Street Journal*, 29 May 2003.

International Maritime Organization (IMO) can strengthen and extend its general provisions forbidding the transfer of WMD on the high seas; second, the UN Security Council can broaden its mandate against WMD proliferation to include all forms of transfers; finally, the Proliferation Security Initiative (PSI) can enforce this system, acquiring a UN mandate as needed. These three proposals are not mutually exclusive, since the PSI can always act independently as a last resort, but they would ideally operate complementarily.

International Maritime Organization

The London-based IMO, established in 1948 to promote maritime safety, has adopted about forty conventions and protocols since its inception.[24] At a December 2002 Conference on Maritime Security,[25] IMO members approved a number of amendments to the 1974 Safety at Sea Convention (SOLAS),[26] establishing a comprehensive new security regime for international shipping that entered into force in July 2004. The centerpiece of these changes is the International Ship and Port Security Code (ISPS Code), requiring all vessels and port facilities to develop security plans in order to reduce their vulnerability to terrorism.[27] Subsequent reports indicate that by August 2004 nearly 90 percent of the more than 9,000 declared port facilities had approved security plans.[28] The ISPS Code also requires a number of tracking, monitoring, and security alert systems that should be useful in WMD interdiction missions.[29]

---

[24] Andreas Persbo and Ian Davis, *Sailing into Uncharted Waters? The Proliferation Security Initiative and the Law of the Sea* (London: British American Security Information Council Research Report, June 2004), 70.

[25] International Maritime Organization, Press Release, "IMO Adopts Comprehensive Maritime Security Measures" (17 December 2002). Available at http://www.imo.org/Newsroom/mainframe.asp?topic_id=583&doc_id=2689.

[26] International Convention for the Safety of Life at Sea, 1 November 1974, 1184 UNTS 276 (entered into force 25 May 1980).

[27] Press Release, "IMO Adopts Comprehensive Maritime Security Measures."

[28] International Maritime Organization, Press Release, "Security Compliance Shows Continued Improvement" (6 August 2004). Available at http://www.imo.org/Newsroom/mainframe.asp?topic_id=892&doc_id=3760.

[29] Persbo and Davis, *Sailing into Uncharted Waters?*, 71.

Perhaps more relevant to a quarantine regime is the IMO's 1988 Convention for the Suppression of Unlawful Acts against the Safety of Maritime Navigation (SUA).[30] Originally drafted to ensure the extradition and prosecution of persons who attacked or attempted to seize ships at sea, the IMO's Legal Committee began reviewing the SUA Convention in the wake of 11 September to consider amendments that would broaden the range of covered offenses to include acts of terrorism and introduce provisions for boarding vessels suspected of being involved in terrorist activities.[31] Specifically, the United States proposed including boarding provisions that would streamline the process of gaining consent from flag states to inspect their vessels, similar to those included in its agreements with Liberia, Panama, the Marshall Islands, Croatia, Cyprus, and Belize.[32] At its October 2002 meeting, the Legal Committee also discussed seven proposed criminal offenses, two of which concerned the use of a ship to transport WMD.[33] Overall, the Legal Committee's response to the American proposals was mixed. At a meeting in April 2004, the committee "[R]ecognized that the inclusion of boarding provisions implied a substantial inroad into the fundamental principles of freedom of navigation on the high seas and the exclusive jurisdiction of flag States over their vessels."[34]

In the end the Diplomatic Conference on the Revision of the SUA Treaties adopted the proposed amendments in October 2005, incorporating protocols forbidding the transport of WMD on any ship and outlining basic boarding provisions that require flag state consent.[35] While

---

[30] Convention for the Suppression of Unlawful Acts against the Safety of Maritime Navigation, 10 March 1988, 1678 UNTS 222 (entered into force 1 March, 1992).

[31] Persbo and Davis, *Sailing into Uncharted Waters?*, 72.

[32] Mark T. Alper and Charles A. Allen, "The PSI: Taking Action against WMD Proliferation," *The Monitor* vol. 10, no. 1 (spring 2004): 5.

[33] Persbo and Davis, *Sailing into Uncharted Waters?*, 72.

[34] International Maritime Organization, Legal Committee, Press Release (19–23 April 2004). Available at http://www.imo.org/Newsroom/mainframe.asp?topic_id=280&doc_id=3352.

[35] International Maritime Organization, Legal Committee, Press Release (10–14 October 2005). Available at http://www.imo.org/Newsroom/mainframe.asp?topic_id=1018&doc_id=5334. The 2005 protocols also include exceptions for the transport of nuclear materials within the confines of the NPT or pursuant to an IAEA safeguards agreement.

unquestionably a remarkable step forward, the 2005 protocols continue to honor exclusive flag state jurisdiction, failing to take a firm stance against the abuse of flag state privileges. Such a change is probably politically unfeasible for the foreseeable future, but remains a loophole for proliferators who can secure a promise to deny consent from their flag state patron. Regardless, it is important for IMO members to ratify the new SUA protocols as soon as possible in order for them to take effect. These international standards will then form the normative substructure for building a global quarantine regime.

UN Security Council

In April 2004, the UN Security Council unanimously passed Resolution 1540, its strongest proclamation against the proliferation of WMD to date.[36] Acting under Chapter VII of the UN Charter, Resolution 1540 mandates that "all States shall refrain from providing any form of support to nonstate actors that attempt to develop, acquire, manufacture, possess, transport, transfer or use nuclear, chemical or biological weapons and their means of delivery."[37] It also requires all states to "adopt and enforce appropriate effective laws" to preclude providing assistance to nonstate actors and to "establish domestic controls to prevent the proliferation of [WMD]."[38] A special committee of the Security Council is responsible for monitoring the resolution's implementation based on reports from member states, the first of which were due in October 2004.[39] On the positive side, Resolution 1540 is a step forward because "it makes strong national controls and enforcement a requirement

---

[36] United Nations, Security Council Resolution 1540, UN Doc. S/RES/1540 (2004).

[37] Ibid., para 1.   [38] Ibid., para 2, 3.

[39] Ibid., para 4. By the October deadline, only fifty-four countries had submitted their reports, a response rate of less than one-third. See Andrew Semmel, Remarks to the Asia-Pacific Nuclear Safeguards and Security Conference, Sydney, Australia, 8 November 2004. Available at http://www.state.gov/t/np/rls/rm/38256.htm. As of March 2005, a total of 105 countries had reported to the committee. See Nuclear Threat Initiative, WMD 411, "Provisions of Resolution 1540." Available at http://www.nti.org/f_wmd411/f2n1.html.

rather than an option."[40] At the very least, it reaffirms the universal appreciation of the threat posed by WMD, and forces states to examine their own nonproliferation laws and practices. The United States ought to work together with its fellow members on the implementation committee seriously to examine the reports submitted and offer model legislation to states that fall short of compliance.[41]

At the same time, Resolution 1540 addresses only part of the WMD threat. By far the most glaring shortcoming is the specific limitation of several portions of the document to transfers to nonstate actors. It may be true that nonstate actors represent the most serious WMD threat, but this restriction clashes with Resolution 1540's unqualified opening statement that proliferation – of all forms – constitutes a threat to international peace and security.[42] Even if a WMD transfer takes place between states, it represents proliferation and is a threat to international security. Every sale, every shipment, leads to a greater supply of WMD materials and further opportunities for diversion onto the black market. A follow-on resolution could thus expand the scope of Resolution 1540 to apply to all transfers of WMD, regardless of the status of the proliferation recipient.[43] It would explicitly declare that no transportation method – by sea, land, or air – in the pursuit of WMD transfer will receive sovereign protection, being an affirmative danger to the security of all states.

Resolution 1540 is also very conservative in its enforcement procedures, merely calling upon all states, "in accordance with their national legal authorities and legislation and consistent with international law, to take cooperative action to prevent illicit trafficking

---

[40] Andrew Semmel, Remarks at Conference on Global Nonproliferation and Counterterrorism: United Nations Security Council Resolution 1540, London, 12 October 2004. Available at http://www.state.gov/t/np/rls/rm/37145.htm.

[41] See United Nations, *A More Secure World*, 45.

[42] United Nations, Security Council Resolution 1540, preamble.

[43] Alternatively, the Security Council could pass a resolution expanding interdiction authority in dealing with a specific state – a more focused quarantine. There are some indications that the United States is considering pushing for such a resolution vis-à-vis North Korea. See David E. Sanger, "White House May Go to UN over North Korean Shipments," *New York Times*, 25 April 2005.

in [WMD]."[44] Given that current international law does not allow for any form of nonconsensual interdiction on the high seas, this provision may provide little restraint to WMD suppliers and flag-state traffickers. Although it is always possible that the Security Council could authorize a one-time interdiction mission under Article 39 of the UN Charter, states will be reluctant to bring an interdiction request if the legal and institutional framework is not in place to support it, inviting stalemate in the Council.

Instead, the Security Council should either attempt to take a leading role itself in institutionalizing interdiction operations, or loosely coordinate with the PSI which can carry out its own missions, along the lines of NATO's military action in Kosovo in 1998.[45] On balance, the former route is preferable in order to ensure the Security Council's continued relevance in nonproliferation matters. By embracing Resolution 1540's implementation committee, the Security Council could institutionalize it and establish an "interdiction committee" empowered to decide cases on short notice.[46] In effect, the committee could serve to expedite interdiction requests, reviewing the supporting intelligence (which is often of a fleeting nature) and making a rapid recommendation.[47] Of course, even if the interdiction committee meets in secret, many states will be reluctant to divulge sensitive intelligence in a multinational setting. In such an event, if a state elects to pursue an interdiction mission outside the auspices of the Security Council, perhaps through the PSI (as discussed below), the committee could review the results of the interdiction, declaring an appropriate level of compensation if the search turns up nothing. Such a regime has precedent in UNCLOS itself,

---

[44] United Nations, Security Council Resolution 1540, para 10.

[45] See Persbo and Davis, *Sailing into Uncharted Waters?*, 75–76.

[46] See ibid., 91; Andrew Prosser, "The Proliferation Security Initiative in Perspective," unpublished manuscript, 16 June 2004. Available at http://www.cdi.org/pdfs/psi.pdf.

[47] Voting in the interdiction committee could perhaps parallel the Security Council itself, with veto-holding permanent members and a limited number of additional seats on a rotating basis.

which in the section that deals with exceptions to the flag state exclusivity rule requires compensation to the boarded ship "for any loss or damage that may have been sustained" if suspicions prove unfounded.[48] Setting monetary compensation for a violation of sovereignty is surely not a simple task, but the alternative of never allowing searches regardless of the level of suspicion is untenable.

Proliferation Security Initiative

A multilateral approach acquiring Security Council authorization for any interdiction mission would be ideal, particularly given that international cooperation in tasks such as freezing assets of WMD traffickers and providing access to airspace and foreign bases is likely integral to its success.[49] Especially if the Security Council integrates the SUA Convention amendments into an expanded version of Resolution 1540, partnerships like the PSI would enjoy new legal authorities to act upon as opposed to the current limitations imposed by UNCLOS. Although the PSI's gradual accumulation of bilateral boarding agreements may at some point form the basis for a universal right of interdiction based on customary law, this is unlikely for the foreseeable future.[50]

Realistically, it may be that the United States has to "go it alone" in the event that the Security Council does not authorize an interdiction mission that US leaders believe is vital to its national security. Even the UN High-level Panel acknowledged that the Security Council "may well need to be prepared to be much more proactive" on threats to international peace and security, "taking more decisive action earlier, than it has been in the past."[51] In such an event, the United States may need to explore alternative avenues to support its action. One option is to turn to regional organizations,

---

[48] UNCLOS, art. 110(3).
[49] See Michael Byers, "Preemptive Self-Defense: Hegemony, Equality and Strategies of Legal Change," *Journal of Political Philosophy* vol. 11, no. 2 (June 2003): 174.
[50] See Michael Byers, "Policing the High Seas: The Proliferation Security Initiative," *American Journal of International Law* vol. 98, no. 3 (July 2004): 532–40.
[51] United Nations, *A More Secure World*, 64.

perhaps built on the PSI framework, and invoke Article 52(1) of the UN Charter: "Nothing in the present Charter precludes the existence of regional arrangements or agencies for dealing with such matters relating to the maintenance of international peace and security as are appropriate for regional action . . ."[52] During the Cuban Missile Crisis of 1962, for example, the United States legitimized its maritime quarantine based on the provisions of the Rio Treaty of the Organization of American States, which sanctioned assistance to meet threats of aggression in the region.[53] Although some legal scholars were deeply critical of this justification,[54] a similar strategy could serve to impose an inspection zone in a troubled region, for example if intelligence indicated that North Korea was engaging in sales of WMD materials. As legal scholar Ruth Wedgwood wryly observed, "If a maritime quarantine against offensive weapons was legal enough for John Kennedy, some might say, it should be legal enough for Ari Fleischer."[55]

If even regional cooperation is not forthcoming, the United States would either assert a revised conception of self-defense or ultimately rely on what Michael Byers termed "exceptional illegality," wherein a state simply chooses to violate the law rather than seek to modify it.[56] Considering the politically sensitive nature of interdiction operations, and the need for international cooperation in such missions, it is crucial that the United States do everything it can to avoid this situation and maximize the possibility that action can be taken through the PSI and/or the Security Council.[57] A sensible starting point is to ensure that all interdiction decisions are based upon sound criteria such as those included as part of a "strategic profile" in chapter 6. Overall, these criteria should serve as a guiding

---

[52] United Nations Charter, art. 52(1).

[53] See Leonard C. Meeker, "Defense Quarantine and the Law," *American Journal of International Law* vol. 57, no. 3 (July 1963): 516.

[54] See, e.g., Thomas M. Franck, *Recourse to Force: State Action against Armed Threats and Armed Attacks* (Cambridge: Cambridge University Press, 2002), 107.

[55] Wedgwood, "A Pirate is a Pirate."   [56] See Byers, "Policing the High Seas," 543.

[57] Gareth Evans, "When is it Right to Fight?" *Survival* vol. 46, no. 3 (autumn 2004): 59, 78.

principle for any actor or institution deciding on interdiction, be it the United States, the PSI, or the Security Council interdiction committee.

Even before FDR applied the term to international affairs, states used quarantines to protect themselves from threats on the high seas, requiring the temporary detention of incoming ships and sailors to ensure that they did not pass on the plague or other infectious diseases. Today, since a local system of quarantine is impractical with the flood of international trade and travel, the quarantine must take on a global character, aiming to prevent the spread of WMD altogether. This chapter examined the legal principles behind a global quarantine, demonstrating that Article 51 of the UN Charter rests upon a notion of self-defense that may need to adapt in order to respond to catastrophic but nonimminent threats. The principle enshrined in the UN Charter of states waiting for the Security Council before taking action does not mesh well with the special characteristics of interdiction, rooted in speed and secrecy. To bring the concept of self-defense in line with present security needs, this chapter then explored the various international institutions available to serve as a framework for a global quarantine, concluding that the IMO can articulate principles which the Security Council can extend and universalize, relying on the PSI for enforcement.

This proposal does not claim to identify the sole path for achieving a global quarantine. Its main purpose is to demonstrate the urgency and sound legal basis for a quarantine, as well as offer some initial ideas for how to begin making it a reality. Some observers may contend that these proposals go too far and there is only a modest chance that they will gain widespread approval. It may be that the SUA Protocols and Resolution 1540 represent the furthest the IMO and the Security Council are willing to go in countering proliferation. However, the default alternative is ever-increasing reliance on the PSI, since the threat posed by WMD will not go away and cannot be ignored. The prospect of a more robust role for the PSI, given the

prominent position of the United States within it, may be disconcerting to much of the world. Many states are fearful of granting the
United States any greater latitude in confronting proliferation and terrorism than it already possesses, especially in light of the absence of
WMD in Iraq. However, the best way to maintain the relevance of
international institutions such as the Security Council is to frame
them so that the United States and others have an incentive to use
them. If the UN cannot expedite interdiction claims through a special
committee, there is little chance at all that PSI nations will turn to it
for authorization.

Other critics may object that these proposals do not go far
enough. As alluded to in chapter 5, since interdiction relies heavily
on intelligence capabilities and good fortune, some might conclude
that forcible disarmament is the only reliable solution. Especially if a
series of WMD terrorist attacks were to occur, I fear that victimized
states would believe they had no other choice but to eliminate all
WMD supplies beyond their allies. Given the incredible risk and
likely damage from such a course, I believe a global quarantine offers
a middle-ground approach with the best matching of ends and means.
To avoid leaving interdiction to the United States alone, and to forestall more drastic disarmament measures, the world community
should join together to draw a clear line in the sand, on the water, and
in the air forbidding all forms of WMD transfer.

8   Conclusion

Probably more than at any point in its history, the United States enjoys a commanding, and growing, military advantage over other states in the international system.[1] The troubling and counter-intuitive result is that such undisputed superiority is not making the United States safer. Rather, it is spurring an underground network of trade in unconventional technology and weapons that is both increasing American vulnerability to catastrophic acts of WMD terrorism and potentially decreasing the credibility of US commitments to resolve regional crises and conflicts in its favor.

Part I introduced this dilemma, with chapter 1 observing that there is a crisis of confidence regarding the durability of deterrence. It examined reasons why the United States may be unwilling to adopt a purely reactive posture in international affairs, including the stability–instability paradox and the possibility of states providing terrorists with sanctuary or WMD. Chapter 2 then applied a theoretical lens to the puzzle, explaining how asymmetries of interest and brinksmanship techniques can confer a strategic advantage beyond what one would expect from a pure comparison of military capability. It explained that estimations of resolve are directly linked to subjective variables such as risk-sensitivity and degree of commitment, each based on psychological factors that may not be strictly rational. Thus, even were the United States fully committed to a particular course of action, deterrence may not function as it expects, particularly in last resort situations or when dealing with millenarian regimes.

---

[1] Gregg Easterbrook, "American Power Moves beyond the Mere Super," *New York Times*, 27 April 2003.

Part II tested these theoretical principles against the historical record, observing how asymmetric regional crises and conflicts played out when WMD were involved. Chapter 3 addressed the United States and its repeated clashes with Saddam Hussein and Iraq, where the numerous deterrent and compellent threats made by both sides met with varying degrees of success. For the United States, although it was unable to persuade Iraq voluntarily to withdraw from Kuwait in 1990 or allow unrestricted arms inspections in 2003, chemical and biological weapons remained unused throughout Operation Desert Storm and appear to have been dismantled before Operation Iraqi Freedom. For Iraq, its uncertain WMD arsenal was of little protection in 2003, but may have played a partial role in leading the United States to decide against invading Baghdad in 1991. Chapter 4 uncovered similar patterns over the past dozen years in the US relationship with North Korea. North Korea's shadow nuclear capability provided it with substantial deterrent power, particularly in 2002–05 when it dispersed its supplies of plutonium and recommenced reprocessing to augment its arsenal. Unlike the situation during the 1993–94 crisis, the United States could not restrain North Korea from crossing over these red lines, as the DPRK expelled IAEA inspectors, withdrew from the NPT, and openly acknowledged its nuclear possession. These chapters demonstrated the continuing strength of deterrence, but also revealed some disturbing trends in need of new pragmatic responses.

Part III took up the challenge of thinking beyond deterrence in responding to WMD proliferation, with chapter 5 providing an overview of the various counterproliferation strategies available to the United States. Unfortunately, major doubts surround the prospects for export controls, missile defenses, homeland security measures, counterforce, and interdiction efforts alike. Chapter 6 elaborated on the moral, legal, and political difficulties inherent in any choice for preemptive or preventive war, including the immense practical barriers to carrying out a successful attack. Not only will the United States generally lack adequate intelligence to support a strike on suspected

WMD sites, but the diplomatic consequences will be overwhelmingly negative in all but the most extreme circumstances. Finally, chapter 7 developed a proposal for coordinating the Proliferation Security Initiative with various international legal authorities to create a global quarantine against all forms of WMD transfer. Since defensive measures may be unsatisfactorily passive, and direct offensive strikes may be too aggressive and costly, targeting all sales and transfers of WMD may be the best middle-ground response to the proliferation threat.

In the final analysis, it is clear that there is no uniform strategy for responding to the proliferation of WMD. The United States would be foolhardy to embark on a global crusade to rid the world of weapons and evil regimes; in fact, there is an inherent tension between striking a threat at its source, and that action eventually contributing to the very source of the threat.[2] Power alone can never change people's hearts and minds, and since the decision of whether to use WMD will ultimately always rest with the adversary, a long-term development toward peaceful relations is the best hope for security. At the same time, there are some states and organizations that pose too great a danger to adopt a "wait and see" approach. It is frightening to think of a terrorist group like Al Qaeda finding a true sanctuary behind a fully WMD-armed nation, or taking over a vulnerable nuclear state such as Pakistan. Containment can be a very effective and prudent doctrine, but only against those regimes that accept the status quo and judge that the balance of deterrence is not in their favor. Those that believe otherwise, or do not care about consequences, must be dealt with in a different manner. Secretary of Defense Rumsfeld cautions:

> I think realistically we have to face up to the fact that we live in a world where our margin for error has become quite small . . . we have to recognize that terrorist networks have relationships with

---

[2] Richard K. Betts, "The New Threat of Mass Destruction," *Foreign Affairs* vol. 77, no. 1 (January/February 1998): 40.

terrorist states that have weapons of mass destruction and that they inevitably are going to get their hands on them, and they would not hesitate one minute in using them. That's the world we live in.[3]

By way of illustration, the critical question is, if the United States determines it cannot afford to count on the adversary always swerving in these international games of "chicken," what policies – driving an armored car, disabling the other driver, avoiding the contest altogether – ought it to follow? I suggest that the United States is on the right track in refashioning deterrence to incorporate counterproliferation strategies, bolstering US defensive capabilities so that an adversary's WMD threat is drained of its coercive power. Ultimately, America's willingness to accept risks and, if necessary, to absorb or deflect costs in regional conflicts will determine whether deterrence will favor the United States or its adversaries in the age of WMD.

The spread of WMD is a common threat, and it must be met with united resolve. Yet, the United States feels a unique vulnerability stemming from its superpower status and active role in foreign affairs. The menace of terrorism is particularly salient to Americans in the wake of 11 September, and there is an understandable urge to take to the warpath, embodied in Secretary Rumsfeld's quip that "the best – and, in some cases, the only – defense is a good offense."[4] This statement resonates because, with the destructive potential of WMD and the growing reservations over deterrence, there is a feeling that "no place will be safe until *every* place is made safe."[5] There may be an underlying truth to this belief, but it does not follow that war – preemptive or otherwise – is the appropriate means toward that end.

[3] Donald H. Rumsfeld, Hearing on FY 2003 Appropriations for the Defense Department before the Appropriations Committee, US Senate, Washington DC, 21 May 2002.

[4] Donald H. Rumsfeld, Speech on 21st Century Transformation of the US Armed Forces, National Defense University, Washington DC: 31 January 2002.

[5] William E. Burrows and Robert Windrem, *Critical Mass: The Dangerous Race for Superweapons in a Fragmenting World* (London: Simon & Schuster, 1994), 21 (emphasis added).

The United States cannot conquer every state that poses a threat, and there is simply no way to uncover weapons that can be hidden even in private homes.

To return once more to the "chicken" analogy, it will be necessary, especially in the Middle East and Central Asia, for the United States to undertake nontraditional missions such as nation-building, peacekeeping, and – in the case of Israel and Palestine – peacemaking to try and minimize the number of disgruntled drivers on the road looking for a challenge.[6] The United States will need to recalibrate its diplomatic strategy toward the empowerment of moderate elements in all societies, elevating those forces to a position where they can resolve regional security dilemmas and reduce the need and desire for WMD. The challenge is to temper the increasing proficiency of the American military at destroying adversaries and breaking down governments with the ability of the United States to cultivate allies and build up friendly regimes.

In the long run, because the spread of WMD technology is inevitable, the best hope for the future lies in promoting peace since there is no surefire defense or offense against suicide bombers and the eventual prospect of suicide states. Ultimately, the United States must develop the capabilities to deter and defeat its adversaries when it really counts, but it should also work to create an international environment where it has to "roll the dice" of deterrence as few times as possible. It is a deadly game, so one must know the other players and choose opponents wisely.

---

[6] See US Government, National Commission on Terrorist Attacks upon the United States, *The 9/11 Commission Report* (Washington DC: July 2004), 361–63, 375–79.

Bibliography

GOVERNMENT DOCUMENTS

Central Intelligence Agency. *Unclassified Report to Congress on the Acquisition of Technology Relating to Weapons of Mass Destruction and Advanced Conventional Munitions,* 1 July–31 December 2003. 2004.

City of Indianapolis v. Edmond, 531 US 32 (2000).

Convention for the Suppression of Unlawful Acts against the Safety of Maritime Navigation (SUA). 10 March 1988.

Grimmett, Richard F. "US Use of Preemptive Military Force." Congressional Research Service, 18 September 2002.

International Atomic Energy Agency. *Implementation of the NPT Safeguards Agreement in the Islamic Republic of Iran,* IAEA Doc. GOV/2004/83. November 2004.

International Commission on Intervention and State Sovereignty. *The Responsibility to Protect.* 2001.

International Convention for the Safety of Life at Sea (SOLAS). 1 November 1974.

International Maritime Organization. Legal Committee, Press Release. 19–23 April 2004.

Press Release, "Security Compliance Shows Continued Improvement." 6 August 2004.

Press Release, "Amendments to Suppression of Unlawful Acts (SUA) Treaties Set for Adoption in October 2005." 2004.

Press Release, "IMO Adopts Comprehensive Maritime Security Measures." 17 December 2002.

Michigan Dept. of State Police v. Sitz, 496 US 444 (1990).

National Defense University, Center for Counterproliferation Research. *The Counterproliferation Imperative: Meeting Tomorrow's Challenges.* Washington DC: November 2001.

People's Republic of China, Ministry of Foreign Affairs, Joint Statement of the Fourth Round of the Six-Party Talks, 19 September 2005.

Permanent Court of International Justice, S.S. Lotus Case (Fr. v. Turk.). 7 September 1927.

Special Advisor to the Director of Central Intelligence. *Addendums to the Comprehensive Report*. March 2005.

Comprehensive Report on Iraq's Weapons of Mass Destruction. 30 September 2004.

Squassoni, Sharon. "Iran's Nuclear Program: Recent Developments." Congressional Research Service. March 2004.

United Nations. Charter. 1945.

Convention on the Law of the Sea (UNCLOS), UN Doc. A/CONF. 62/122, 1994.

A More Secure World: Our Shared Responsibility, Report of the Secretary-General's High-level Panel on Threats, Challenges and Change. 2004.

Security Council Resolution 1441, UN Doc. S/RES/1441. 2002.

US Department of Defense. Chemical and Biological Defense Program, *Annual Report to Congress and Performance Plan*. Washington DC: April 2003.

Nuclear Posture Review. Washington DC: 31 December 2001.

Proliferation: Threat and Response. Washington DC: January 2001.

US Department of Homeland Security. *National Response Plan*. Washington DC: December 2004.

Securing our Homeland. Washington DC: 2004.

US Department of State. Bureau of Nonproliferation, "Fact Sheet: The G8 Global Partnership against the Spread of Weapons and Materials of Mass Destruction." 24 August 2004.

Bureau of Nonproliferation, "Fact Sheet: Proliferation Security Initiative Frequently Asked Questions (FAQ)." 24 May 2004.

Bureau of Nonproliferation, Press Release, "The Proliferation Security Initiative." May 2005.

Country Reports on Terrorism, 2004. Washington DC: April 2005.

Office of the Spokesman, Media Note, "The United States and Belize Proliferation Security Initiative Ship Boarding Agreement." 4 August 2005.

US General Accounting Office. *Post-Shipment Verification Provides Limited Assurance that Dual-Use Items are Being Properly Used*, GAO-04-357. Washington DC: January 2004.

US Government. National Commission on Terrorist Attacks upon the United States, *The 9/11 Commission Report*. Washington DC: July 2004.

Apparatus of Lies. Washington DC: 2003.

Joint Resolution to Authorize the Use of United States Armed Forces against Iraq. Office of the Press Secretary, 2 October 2002.

The National Security Strategy of the United States of America. Washington DC: September 2002.

US Senate. Select Committee on Intelligence, *Report on the US Intelligence Community's Prewar Intelligence Assessments on Iraq*. Washington DC: 7 July 2004.

United States v. Edwards, 498 F.2d 496 (2d Cir. 1984).

United States v. Martinez-Fuerte, 428 U.S. 543 (1976).

White House. Office of the Press Secretary, "Fact Sheet: Proliferation Security Initiative: Statement of Interdiction Principles." 4 September 2003.

What Does Disarmament Look Like? Washington DC: January 2003.

BOOKS/ARTICLES

Abrams, Eliot, ed. *Close Calls: Intervention, Terrorism, Missile Defense, and "Just War" Today*. Washington DC: Ethics and Public Policy Center, 1998.

Aburish, Said K. *Saddam Hussein: The Politics of Revenge*. London: Bloomsbury, 2000.

Ackerman, Bruce. "The Emergency Constitution." *Yale Law Journal* vol. 113, no. 5 (March 2004): 1029–91.

Ackerman, Gary and Laura Snyder. "Would They if They Could?" *Bulletin of the Atomic Scientists* vol. 58, no. 3 (May/June 2002): 41–47.

Albright, David. "A Proliferation Primer." *The Bulletin of Atomic Scientists* vol. 49, no. 5 (June 1993): 14–23.

Alexandrov, Stanimir A. *Self-Defense against the Use of Force in International Law*. Cambridge, MA: Kluwer Law International, 1996.

Allison, Graham. *Nuclear Terrorism: The Ultimate Preventable Catastrophe*. New York: Times Books, 2004.

Alper, Mark T. and Charles A. Allen. "The PSI: Taking Action against WMD Proliferation." *The Monitor* vol. 10, no. 1 (spring 2004): 4–6.

Arend, Anthony Clark. "International Law and the Preemptive Use of Military Force." *The Washington Quarterly* vol. 26, no. 2 (spring 2003): 89–103.

Arend, Anthony Clark and Robert J. Beck. *International Law and the Use of Force: Beyond the UN Charter Paradigm*. London: Routledge, 1993.

Arkin, William M. "Calculated Ambiguity: Nuclear Weapons and the Gulf War." *The Washington Quarterly* vol. 19, no. 4 (autumn 1996): 3–18.

Arquilla, John. "Bound to Fail: Regional Deterrence after the Cold War." *Comparative Strategy* vol. 14, no. 2 (April–June 1995): 123–35.

Art, Robert J. and Patrick M. Cronin, eds. *The United States and Coercive Diplomacy*. Washington DC: United States Institute of Peace Press, 2003.

Art, Robert J. and Kenneth N. Waltz, eds. *The Use of Force: Military Power and International Relations*, 4th edition. Lanham, MD: University Press of America, 1993.

Atkinson, Rick. *Crusade: The Untold Story of the Gulf War.* London: HarperCollins, 1994.

Bailey, Kathleen C. *Doomsday Weapons in the Hands of Many: The Arms Control Challenge of the 90s.* Chicago: University of Illinois Press, 1991.

Baker, James A. III, with Thomas M. DeFrank. *The Politics of Diplomacy.* New York: G.P. Putnam's Sons, 1995.

Baram, Amatzia. "Saddam Husayn: Between his Power Base and the International Community." *Middle East Review of International Affairs* vol. 4, no. 4 (December 2000): 9–21.

Baram, Amatzia and Barry Rubin, eds. *Iraq's Road to War.* London: Macmillan, 1994.

Barletta, Michael. "Chemical Weapons in the Sudan: Allegations and Evidence." *Nonproliferation Review* vol. 6, no. 1 (fall 1998): 115–36.

Bender, Bryan. "USA Planning Warhead to Hit CB Weapons." *Jane's Defence Weekly* vol. 31, no 12 (24 March 1999).

Bengio, Ofra. *Saddam's World: Political Discourse in Iraq.* New York: Oxford University Press, 1998.

Bermudez, Joseph S. Jr. *The Armed Forces of North Korea.* New York: I.B. Tauris, 2001.

"Exposing North Korea's Secret Nuclear Infrastructure – Part Two." *Jane's Intelligence Review* vol. 11, no. 8 (August 1999): 41–45.

"The Rise and Rise of North Korea's ICBMs." *Jane's International Defence Review* vol. 32, no. 7 (1 July 1999).

Bertram, Christoph, ed. *Strategic Deterrence in a Changing Environment.* London: International Institute for Strategic Studies, 1981.

Betts, Richard. "The New Threat of Mass Destruction." *Foreign Affairs* vol. 77, no. 1 (January/February 1998): 26–41.

Nuclear Blackmail and Nuclear Balance. Washington DC: Brookings Institution Press, 1987.

"Suicide from Fear of Death?" *Foreign Affairs* vol. 82, no. 1 (January/February 2003): 34–43.

"What Will it Take to Deter the United States?" *Parameters* vol. 21, no. 4 (winter 1995–96): 70–79.

Blackwill, Robert D. and Albert Carnesale, eds. *New Nuclear Nations: Consequences for US Policy.* New York: Council on Foreign Relations Press, 1993.

Blight, James G. and David A. Welch, "Risking 'the Destruction of Nations': Lessons of the Cuban Missile Crisis for New and Aspiring Nuclear States." *Security Studies* vol. 4, no. 4 (summer 1995): 811–50.

Blum, William. *Rogue State: A Guide to the World's Only Superpower*. London: Zed Books, 2001.

Boniface, Pascal. "What Justifies Regime Change?" *The Washington Quarterly* vol. 26, no. 3 (summer 2003): 61–71.

Booth, Ken. *Strategy and Ethnocentrism*. London: Croom Helm, 1979.

Bowett, Derek W. *Self-Defence in International Law*. Manchester: The University Press, 1958.

Bracken, Paul. *Fire in the East: The Rise of Asian Military Power and the Second Nuclear Age*. New York: HarperCollins, 1999.

Bradford, William C. " 'The Duty to Defend Them': A Natural Law Justification for the Bush Doctrine of Preventive War." *Notre Dame Law Review* vol. 79 (2004): 1365–492.

Brinkley, Douglas. *The Unfinished Presidency*. New York: Penguin Putnam, 1998.

Brodie, Bernard. *The Absolute Weapon: Atomic Power and World Order*. New York: Harcourt, 1946.

Strategy in the Missile Age. Princeton, NJ: Princeton University Press, 1959.

Brownlie, Ian. *International Law and the Use of Force by States*. Oxford: Oxford University Press, 1963.

Buhite, Russell D. and William Christopher Hamel. "War for Peace: The Question of an American Preventive War against the Soviet Union, 1945–1955." *Diplomatic History* vol. 14, no. 3 (summer 1990): 367–84.

Bunn, M. Elaine. "Preemptive Action: When, How, and to What Effect?" *Strategic Forum* no. 200 (July 2003): 1–8.

Burr, William and Jeffrey T. Richelson. "Whether to 'Strangle the Baby in the Cradle': The United States and the Chinese Nuclear Program, 1960–64." *International Security* vol. 25, no. 3 (winter 2000–01): 54–99.

Burrows, William E. and Robert Windrem. *Critical Mass: The Dangerous Race for Superweapons in a Fragmenting World*. London: Simon & Schuster, 1994.

Bush, George and Brent Scowcroft. *A World Transformed*. New York: Alfred A. Knopf, 1998.

Byers, Michael. "Policing the High Seas: The Proliferation Security Initiative." *American Journal of International Law* vol. 98, no. 3 (July 2004): 526–45.

"Preemptive Self-Defense: Hegemony, Equality and Strategies of Legal Change," *Journal of Political Philosophy* vol. 11, no. 2 (June 2003): 171–90.

Byman, Daniel and Matthew Waxman. *Confronting Iraq: US Policy and the Use of Force since the Gulf War*. Santa Monica, CA: RAND, 2000.

Byman, Daniel, Kenneth Pollack, and Matthew Waxman. "Coercing Saddam Hussein: Lessons from the Past." *Survival* vol. 40, no. 3 (autumn 1998): 127–52.

Cain, Anthony C. *Iran's Strategic Culture and Weapons of Mass Destruction,*

Maxwell Paper No. 26. Maxwell Air Force Base, AL: Air War College, April 2002.

Campbell, Kurt M., Robert J. Einhorn, and Mitchell R. Reiss, eds. *The Nuclear Tipping Point: Why States Reconsider their Nuclear Choices*. Washington DC: Brookings Institution Press, 2004.

Carter, Ashton B. and William J. Perry. *Preventive Defense: A New Security Strategy for America*. Washington DC: Brookings Institution Press, 1999.

Cha, Victor D. "North Korea's Weapons of Mass Destruction: Badges, Shields, or Swords?" *Political Science Quarterly* vol. 117, no. 2 (summer 2002): 209–30.

"The Second Nuclear Age: Proliferation Pessimism Versus Sober Optimism in South Asia and East Asia." *Journal of Strategic Studies* vol. 24, no. 4 (December 2001): 79–120.

Cha, Victor D. and David C. Kang. "The Korea Crisis." *Foreign Policy* no. 136 (May/June 2003): 20–28.

Chandler, Robert W., with Ronald J. Trees. *Tomorrow's War, Today's Decisions: Iraqi Weapons of Mass Destruction and the Implications of WMD-Armed Adversaries for Future US Military Strategy*. McLean, VA: AMCODA Press, 1996.

Chol, Kim Myong. "Kim Jong Il's Military Strategy for Reunification." *Comparative Strategy* vol. 20 (2001): 303–420.

Chubin, Shahram. "Does Iran Want Nuclear Weapons?" *Survival* vol. 37, no. 1 (spring 1995): 86–104.

Whither Iran? Reform, Domestic Politics and National Security, Adelphi Paper No. 342. Oxford: Oxford University Press, International Institute for Strategic Studies, 2002.

Cimbala, Stephen J. *The Past and Future of Nuclear Deterrence*. Westport, CT: Praeger, 1998.

Cirincione, Joseph, with John B. Wolfsthal and Miriam Rajkumar. *Deadly Arsenals: Tracking Weapons of Mass Destruction*. Washington DC: Carnegie Endowment for International Peace, June 2002.

Cockburn, Andrew and Patrick Cockburn. *Out of the Ashes: The Resurrection of Saddam Hussein*. London: Verso, 2000.

Cohen, Yohanan. *Small Nations in Times of Crisis and Confrontation*. Albany, NY: State University of New York Press, 1989.

Cole, Leonard A. *The Eleventh Plague: The Politics of Biological and Chemical Warfare*. New York: W.H. Freeman, 1997.

Cordesman, Anthony H. *Iran's Military Forces in Transition: Conventional Threats and Weapons of Mass Destruction*. Westport, CT: Praeger, 1999.

Coughlin, Con. *Saddam: The Secret Life*. London: Macmillan, 2002.

Council on Foreign Relations. *America Still Unprepared – America Still in Danger.* 17 October 2002.

Craig, Gordon A. and Alexander L. George. *Force and Statecraft: Diplomatic Problems of our Time,* 3rd edition. Oxford: Oxford University Press, 1995.

Critchlow, Robert D. "Whom the Gods Would Destroy: An Information Warfare Alternative for Deterrence and Compellence." *Naval War College Review* vol. 53, no. 3 (summer 2000): 21–38.

Darwish, Adel and Gregory Alexander. *Unholy Babylon: The Secret History of Saddam's War.* London: Victor Gollancz, 1991.

Davis, Jim A. and Barry R. Schneider, eds. *The Gathering Biological Warfare Storm.* Maxwell Air Force Base, AL: USAF Counterproliferation Center, April 2002.

Doolin, Joel A. "Operational Art for the Proliferation Security Initiative." Unpublished final paper at the Naval War College, 2004.

Dougherty, James E. and J.F. Lehman Jr., eds. *Arms Control for the Late Sixties.* Princeton, NJ: D. Van Nostrand, 1967.

Dowdy, William L. and Barry R. Schneider. "On to Baghdad? Or Stop at Kuwait? A Gulf War Question Revisited." *Defense Analysis* vol. 13, no. 3 (December 1997): 319–29.

Dowler, Thomas M. and Joseph S. Howard II. "Stability in a Proliferated World." *Strategic Review* vol. 23, no. 2 (spring 1995): 26–37.

Downs, Chuck. *Over the Line: North Korea's Negotiating Strategy.* Washington DC: AEI Press, 1999.

Dror, Yehezkel. *Crazy States: A Counterconventional Strategic Problem.* Lexington, MA: Heath Lexington Books, 1971.

Dunn, Lewis A. *Containing Nuclear Proliferation,* Adelphi Paper No. 263. London: International Institute for Strategic Studies, winter 1991.

    Controlling the Bomb: Nuclear Proliferation in the 1980s. New Haven, CT: Yale University Press, 1982.

    "Rethinking the Nuclear Equation: The United States and the New Nuclear Powers." *The Washington Quarterly* vol. 17, no. 1 (winter 1994): 5–25.

Edwards, A.J.C. *Nuclear Weapons, the Balance of Terror, the Quest for Peace.* London: Macmillan, 1986.

Ellis, Jason D. "The Best Defense: Counterproliferation and US National Security." *The Washington Quarterly* vol. 26, no. 2 (spring 2003): 115–33.

Evans, Gareth. "When is it Right to Fight?" *Survival* vol. 46, no. 3 (autumn 2004): 59–82.

Falkenrath, Richard A., Robert D. Newman, and Bradley A. Thayer. *America's Achilles' Heel: Nuclear, Biological, and Chemical Terrorism and Covert Attack.* Cambridge, MA: MIT Press, 1998.

Feinstein, Lee and Anne-Marie Slaughter. "A Duty to Prevent." *Foreign Affairs* vol. 83, no. 1 (January/February 2004): 136–51.

Feldman, Shai. "The Bombing of Osiraq – Revisited." *International Security* vol. 7, no. 2 (fall 1982): 114–42.

Fest, Joachim. *Speer: The Final Verdict*. London: Phoenix Press, 1999.

Finel, Bernard I. "The Role of Aerospace Power in US Counterproliferation Strategy." *Air & Space Power Journal* vol. 13, no. 4 (winter 1999): 77–89.

Franck, Thomas M. *Recourse to Force: State Action against Armed Threats and Armed Attacks*. Cambridge: Cambridge University Press, 2002.

Frank, Jerome D. *Sanity and Survival: Psychological Aspects of War and Peace*. London: The Cresset Press, 1967.

Freedman, Lawrence. *Deterrence*. Cambridge: Polity Press, 2004.

  The Evolution of Nuclear Strategy, 2nd edition. London: Macmillan, in association with the International Institute of Strategic Studies, 1989.

  "Prevention, Not Preemption." *The Washington Quarterly* vol. 26, no. 2 (spring 2003): 105–14.

  ed. *Strategic Coercion: Concepts and Cases*. Oxford: Oxford University Press, 1998.

Freedman, Lawrence and Efraim Karsh. *The Gulf Conflict 1990–1991: Diplomacy and War in the New World Order*. London: Faber and Faber, 1993.

  "How Kuwait was Won: Strategy in the Gulf War." *International Security* vol. 16, no. 2 (fall 1991): 5–41.

Gallois, Pierre. *The Balance of Terror: Strategy for the Nuclear Age*. Boston, MA: Houghton Mifflin, 1961.

Garnham, David. *Deterrence Essentials: Keys to Controlling an Adversary's Behavior*. Abu Dhabi: Emirates Center for Strategic Studies and Research, 1995.

Garwin, Richard L. "A Defense that Will Not Defend." *The Washington Quarterly* vol. 23, no. 3 (summer 2000): 109–23.

Gelman, Harry. *The Soviet Far East Buildup and Soviet Risk-Taking against China*. Santa Monica, CA: RAND, August 1982.

George, Alexander L. and Richard Smoke. *Deterrence in American Foreign Policy: Theory and Practice*. New York: Columbia University Press, 1974.

Glaser, Charles L. and Steve Fetter. "National Missile Defense and the Future of US Nuclear Weapons Policy." *International Security* vol. 26, no. 1 (summer 2001): 40–92.

Glennon, Michael J. "The Fog of War: Self-Defense, Inherence, and Incoherence in Article 51 of the United Nations Charter." *Harvard Journal of Law and Public Policy* vol. 25, no. 2 (spring 2002): 539–58.

"Preempting Terrorism: The Case for Anticipatory Self-Defense." *The Weekly Standard* vol. 7, no. 19 (28 January 2002).

Glosson, Buster. *War with Iraq: Critical Lessons.* Charlotte, NC: Glosson Family Foundation, 2003.

Goldstein, Lyle J. "Do Nascent WMD Arsenals Deter? The Sino-Soviet Crisis of 1969." *Political Science Quarterly* vol. 118, no. 1 (spring 2003): 53–79.

Gordon, Michael R. and Bernard E. Trainor. *The General's War.* New York: Little, Brown and Company, 1995.

Gordon, Philip. "Bush, Missile Defence, and the Atlantic Alliance." *Survival* vol. 43, no. 1 (spring 2001): 17–36.

Gray, Christine. *International Law and the Use of Force.* Oxford: Oxford University Press, 2000.

Gray, Colin. *The Second Nuclear Age.* London: Lynne Rienner, 1999.

The Sheriff: America's Defense of the New World Order. Lexington, KY: University Press of Kentucky, 2004.

Greenwood, Christopher. "International Law and the Pre-emptive Use of Force: Afghanistan, Al-Qaida, and Iraq." *San Diego International Law Journal* vol. 4 (2003): 7–37.

Hadley, Stephen J. "A Call to Deploy." *The Washington Quarterly* vol. 23, no. 3 (summer 2000): 95–108.

Hagerty, Devin T. "Nuclear Deterrence in South Asia: The 1990 Indo-Pakistani Crisis." *International Security* vol. 20, no. 3 (winter 1995–96): 79–114.

Halperin, Morton. *Limited War in the Nuclear Age.* Westport, CT: Greenwood Press, 1963.

Harrison, Selig S. *Korean Endgame: A Strategy for Reunification and US Disengagement.* Princeton, NJ: Princeton University Press, 2002.

Haselkorn, Avigdor. *The Continuing Storm: Iraq, Poisonous Weapons, and Deterrence.* New Haven, CT: Yale University Press, 1999.

"Iraq's Bio-Warfare Option: Last Resort, Preemption, or a Blackmail Weapon?" *Biosecurity and Bioterrorism: Biodefense Strategy, Practice, and Science* vol. 1, no. 1 (2003): 19–26.

Henkin, Louis. *How Nations Behave: Law and Foreign Policy*, 2nd edition. New York: Columbia University Press, 1979.

Herring, Eric. "Rogue Rage: Can We Prevent Mass Destruction?" *Journal of Strategic Studies* vol. 23, no. 1 (March 2000): 188–212.

Hersh, Seymour M. *The Samson Option: Israel, America and the Bomb.* London: Faber, 1991.

Hiro, Dilip. *Desert Shield to Desert Storm: The Second Gulf War.* New York: Routledge, 1992.

The Longest War: The Iran–Iraq Military Conflict. New York: Routledge, 1991.

Huntington, Samuel. "The Lonely Superpower." *Foreign Affairs* vol. 78, no. 2 (March/April 1999): 35–49.

"Why International Primacy Matters." *International Security* vol. 17, no. 4 (spring 1993): 68–83.

Ikenberry, G. John. "America's Imperial Ambition." *Foreign Affairs* vol. 81, no. 5 (September/October 2002): 44–60.

Iklé, Fred Charles. "Can Nuclear Deterrence Last Out the Century?" *Foreign Affairs* vol. 51, no. 2 (January 1973): 267–85.

Inbar, Efraim, ed. *Regional Security Regimes.* Albany, NY: State University of New York Press, 1995.

Janis, Irving L. and Leon Mann. *Decision Making: A Psychological Analysis of Conflict.* New York: The Free Press, 1977.

Jennings, R.Y. "The Caroline and McLeod Cases." *American Journal of International Law* vol. 32, no. 2 (April 1938): 82–99.

Jervis, Robert. "Deterrence and Perception." *International Security* vol. 7, no. 3 (winter 1982–83): 3–30.

The Illogic of American Nuclear Strategy. Ithaca, NY: Cornell University Press, 1984.

Perception and Misperception in International Politics. Princeton, NJ: Princeton University Press, 1976.

"Why Nuclear Superiority Doesn't Matter." *Political Science Quarterly* vol. 94, no. 4 (winter 1979–80): 617–33.

Jervis, Robert, Richard Ned Lebow, and Janice Gross Stein, eds. *Psychology and Deterrence.* Baltimore, MD: The Johns Hopkins University Press, 1985.

Jodoin, Vincent J. and Alan R. Van Tassel, eds. *Countering the Proliferation and Use of Weapons of Mass Destruction.* New York: McGraw-Hill, 1998.

Johnson, Stuart E., ed. *The Niche Threat: Deterring the Use of Chemical and Biological Weapons.* Washington DC: National Defense University Press, 1997.

Jones, Rodney M., ed. *Small Nuclear Forces and US Security Policy.* Washington DC: Center for Strategic and International Studies, 1984.

Joseph, Jofi. "The Proliferation Security Initiative: Can Interdiction Stop Proliferation?" *Arms Control Today* vol. 34, no. 5 (June 2004): 6–13.

Joseph, Robert G. and John F. Reichart. *Deterrence and Defense in a Nuclear, Biological, and Chemical Environment.* Washington DC: National Defense University Press, 1999.

Joyner, Daniel H. "The Proliferation Security Initiative: Nonproliferation, Counterproliferation and International Law." *Yale Journal of International Law* vol. 30, no. 2 (summer 2005): 507–48.

Kagan, Donald. *On the Origins of War and the Preservation of Peace*. New York: Doubleday, 1995.

Kahn, Herman. *On Thermonuclear War*. Princeton, NJ: Princeton University Press, 1969.

Thinking about the Unthinkable. London: Weidenfeld and Nicolson, 1962.

Kaplan, Morton A. *System and Process in International Politics*. New York: John Wiley & Sons, 1957.

Karsh, Efraim and Inari Rautsi. *Saddam Hussein: A Political Biography*. London: Brassey's, 1991.

Katzman, Kenneth. *The Warriors of Islam: Iran's Revolutionary Guard*. Oxford: Westview Press, 1993.

Kay, David. "Denial and Deception Practices of WMD Proliferators: Iraq and Beyond." *The Washington Quarterly* vol. 18, no. 1 (winter 1995): 85–105.

Keeny, Spurgeon M. Jr. and Wolfgang K.H. Panofsky. "MAD Versus NUTS: Can Doctrine or Weaponry Remedy the Mutual Hostage Relationship of the Superpowers?" *Foreign Affairs* vol. 60, no. 2 (winter 1981–82): 287–304.

Khong, Yuen Foong. "Vietnam, the Gulf, and US Choices: A Comparison." *Security Studies* vol. 2, no. 1 (autumn 1992): 74–95.

Kim, Samuel S., ed. *The North Korean System in the Post-Cold War Era*. New York: Palgrave, 2001.

Kissinger, Henry. *Does America Need a Foreign Policy?* New York: Simon & Schuster, 2001.

Nuclear Weapons and Foreign Policy. New York: Harper & Brothers, 1957.

Kiziah, Rex R. *Assessment of the Emerging Biocruise Threat*, Future Warfare Series No. 6. Maxwell Air Force Base, AL: Air War College, August 2000.

Knorr, Klaus. *The Power of Nations: The Political Economy of International Relations*. New York: Basic Books, 1975.

Koch, Andrew. "Dual Delivery is Key to Buried Targets." *Jane's Defence Weekly* vol. 33, no. 10 (8 March 2000).

Koh, Harold Hongju. "The Spirit of the Laws." *Harvard International Law Journal* vol. 43, no. 1 (winter 2002): 23–39.

Krauthammer, Charles. "The Unipolar Moment." *Foreign Affairs* vol. 70, no. 1 (1990–91): 23–33.

Krepon, Michael. "Moving away from MAD." *Survival* vol. 43, no. 2 (summer 2001): 81–95.

Kristensen, Hans M. *Nuclear Futures: Proliferation of Weapons of Mass Destruction and US Nuclear Strategy*. London: British American Security Information Council, March 1998.

Laney, James T. and Jason T. Shaplen. "How to Deal with North Korea." *Foreign Affairs* vol. 82, no. 2 (March/April 2003): 16–30.

Lavoy, Peter R., Scott D. Sagan, and James J. Wirtz, eds. *Planning the Unthinkable: How New Powers will Use Nuclear, Biological, and Chemical Weapons.* Ithaca, NY: Cornell University Press, 2000.

Law, Alfred D. *The Sino-Soviet Dispute.* London: Associated University Presses, 1976.

Lebovic, James H. "The Law of Small Numbers: Deterrence and National Missile Defense." *The Journal of Conflict Resolution* vol. 46, no. 4 (August 2002): 455–83.

Lebow, Richard Ned. *Between Peace and War: The Nature of International Crisis.* Baltimore, MD: The Johns Hopkins University Press, 1981.

Lebow, Richard Ned and Janice Gross Stein. "Beyond Deterrence." *Journal of Social Issues* vol. 43, no. 4 (1987): 5–71.

Lederberg, Joshua, ed. *Biological Weapons: Limiting the Threat.* Cambridge, MA: The MIT Press, 1999.

Levi, Michael A. *Fire in the Hole: Nuclear and Non-Nuclear Options for Counterproliferation*, Working Paper No. 31. Washington DC: Carnegie Endowment for International Peace, November 2002.

Lewis, George, Lisbeth Gronlund, and David Wright. "National Missile Defense: An Indefensible System." *Foreign Policy* no. 117 (winter 1999–2000): 120–37.

Lieberman, Elli. *Deterrence Theory: Success or Failure in Arab-Israeli Wars?* McNair Paper No. 45. Washington DC: Institute for National Strategic Studies, National Defense University, October 1995.

Lindsay, James M. and Michael E. O'Hanlon. "Correspondence." *International Security* vol. 26, no. 4 (spring 2002): 190–201.

Defending America: The Case for Limited National Missile Defense. Washington DC: Brookings Institution Press, 2001.

Litwak, Robert S. "The New Calculus of Pre-emption." *Survival* vol. 44, no. 4 (winter 2002–03): 53–80.

Rogue States and US Foreign Policy: Containment after the Cold War. Baltimore, MD: The Johns Hopkins University Press, 2000.

Lodal, Jan. *The Price of Dominance: The New Weapons of Mass Destruction and their Challenge to American Leadership.* New York: Council of Foreign Relations, 2001.

Luttwak, Edward and Dan Horowitz. *The Israeli Army.* London: Penguin, 1975.

Mack, Andrew. "A Nuclear North Korea." *World Policy Journal* vol. 11, no. 2 (summer 1994): 27–35.

"Why Big Nations Lose Small Wars: The Politics of Asymmetric Conflict." *World Politics* vol. 27, no. 2 (January 1975): 175–200.

McCormack, Timothy L.H. *Self-Defense in International Law: The Israeli Raid on the Iraqi Nuclear Reactor*. New York: St. Martin's Press, 1996.

McCullough, David. *Truman*. New York: Simon & Schuster, 1992.

McDougal, Myres S. "The Soviet–Cuban Quarantine and Self-Defense." *American Journal of International Law* vol. 57, no. 3 (July 1963): 597–604.

McDougal, Myres S. and Florentino P. Feliciano. *Law and Minimum World Order*. New Haven, CT: Yale University Press, 1961.

McKinney, Cynthia. "Should the US Have a Missile Defense System?" *American Legion Magazine* vol. 148, no. 1 (January 2000): 42.

McNaugher, Thomas L. "Ballistic Missiles and Chemical Weapons: The Legacy of the Iran–Iraq War." *International Security* vol. 15, no. 2 (fall 1990): 5–34.

Mahnken, Thomas G. "America's Next War." *The Washington Quarterly* vol. 16, no. 3 (summer 1993): 171–84.

Manwaring, Max G., ed. *Deterrence in the 21st Century*. London: Frank Cass, 2001.

Maxon, Richard G. "Nature's Eldest Law: A Survey of a Nation's Right to Act in Self-Defense." *Parameters* vol. 25, no. 3 (autumn 1995): 55–68.

Maxwell, Stephen. *Rationality in Deterrence*, Adelphi Paper No. 50. London: International Institute for Strategic Studies, 1968.

May, Michael M. and Zachary Haldeman. *Effectiveness of Nuclear Weapons against Buried Biological Agents*. Stanford, CA: Center for International Security and Cooperation, June 2003.

Mazarr, Michael J. *North Korea and the Bomb: A Case Study in Nonproliferation*. London: Macmillan, 1995.

Mearsheimer, John J. and Stephen M. Walt. "An Unnecessary War." *Foreign Policy* no. 134 (January/February 2003): 50–59.

Meeker, Leonard C. "Defense Quarantine and the Law." *American Journal of International Law* vol. 57, no. 3 (July 1963): 515–24.

Miles, James. "Waiting Out North Korea." *Survival* vol. 44, no. 2 (summer 2002): 37–49.

Miller, Judith, Stephen Engleberg, and William Broad. *Germs: The Ultimate Weapon*. London: Simon & Schuster, 2001.

Millot, Marc Dean. "Facing the Emerging Reality of Regional Nuclear Adversaries." *The Washington Quarterly* vol. 17, no. 3 (summer 1994): 41–71.

Mitchell, Gordon R. *Strategic Deception: Rhetoric, Science, and Politics in Missile Defense Advocacy*. East Lansing, MI: Michigan State University Press, 2000.

Morgan, Patrick M. *Deterrence: A Conceptual Analysis*. Beverly Hills, CA: Sage, 1977.

Deterrence Now. Cambridge: Cambridge University Press, 2003.

Nakdimon, Shlomo. *First Strike: The Exclusive Story of How Israel Foiled Iraq's Attempt to Get the Bomb*. New York: Summit Books, 1987.

Nelson, Robert W. "Low-Yield Earth-Penetrating Nuclear Weapons." *Journal of the Federation of American Scientists* vol. 54, no. 1 (January/February 2001): 1–5.

Nitze, Paul H. "Deterring our Deterrent." *Foreign Policy* no. 25 (winter 1976–77): 195–210.

Noland, Marcus. *Avoiding the Apocalypse: The Future of the Two Koreas*. Washington DC: Institute for International Economics, 2000.

Norris, Robert S. and Hans M. Kristensen. "North Korea's Nuclear Program, 2005." *Bulletin of the Atomic Scientists* vol. 61, no. 3 (May/June 2005): 64–67.

Oberdorfer, Don. *The Two Koreas: A Contemporary History*. London: Warner Books, 1997.

Oh, Kongdan and Ralph C. Hassig. *North Korea: Through the Looking Glass*. Washington DC: Brookings Institution Press, 2000.

Osgood, Robert. *Limited War: The Challenge to American Security*. Chicago: University of Chicago Press, 1957.

Panofsky, Wolfgang K.H. "The Mutual-Hostage Relationship between America and Russia." *Foreign Affairs* vol. 52, no. 1 (October 1973): 109–18.

Paul, T.V. *Asymmetric Conflicts: War Initiation by Weaker Powers*. Cambridge: Cambridge University Press, 1994.

Paul, T.V., Richard J. Harknett, and James J. Wirtz, eds. *The Absolute Weapon Revisited: Nuclear Arms and the Emerging International Order*. Ann Arbor, MI: Michigan University Press, 1998.

Payne, Keith B. *Deterrence in the Second Nuclear Age*. Lexington, KY: The University Press of Kentucky, 1996.

The Fallacies of Cold War Deterrence and a New Direction. Lexington, KY: The University Press of Kentucky, 2001.

Payne, Keith B. and Lawrence R. Fink. "Deterrence without Defense: Gambling on Perfection." *Strategic Review* vol. 17, no. 1 (winter 1989): 25–40.

Perry, William J. "Preparing for the Next Attack." *Foreign Affairs* vol. 80, no. 6 (November/December 2001): 31–45.

Persbo, Andreas and Ian Davis. *Sailing into Uncharted Waters? The Proliferation Security Initiative and the Law of the Sea*. London: British American Security Information Council Research Report, June 2004.

Pollack, Kenneth M. *The Threatening Storm*. New York: Random House, 2002.

Powell, Colin L., with Joseph E. Persico. *A Soldier's Way*. London: Arrow Books, 1995.

Powell, Robert. *Nuclear Deterrence Theory*. Cambridge: Cambridge University Press, 1990.

 "Nuclear Deterrence Theory, Nuclear Proliferation, and National Missile Defense." *International Security* vol. 27, no. 4 (spring 2003): 86–118.

Prosser, Andrew. "The Proliferation Security Initiative in Perspective." Unpublished manuscript, 16 June 2004.

Quester, George. "The Future of Nuclear Deterrence." *Survival* vol. 34, no. 1 (spring 1992): 74–88.

Quinlan, Michael. *Thinking about Nuclear Weapons*. London: Royal United Services Institute for Defence Studies, 1997.

Ranger, Robin and David Wiencek. *The Devil's Brews II: Weapons of Mass Destruction and International Security*, Bailrigg Memorandum 17. Lancaster: Centre for Defence and International Security Studies, 1997.

Rathjens, G.W. "Flexible Response Options." *Orbis* vol. 18, no. 3 (fall 1974): 677–88.

Reisman, W. Michael. "Assessing Claims to Revise the Laws of War." *American Journal of International Law* vol. 97, no. 1 (January 2003): 81–90.

Reiss, Mitchell. *Bridled Ambition*. Washington DC: Woodrow Wilson Center Press, 1995.

Rhodes, Edward. *Power and MADness: The Logic of Nuclear Coercion*. New York: Columbia University Press, 1989.

Riecke, Henning. "NATO's Non-Proliferation and Deterrence Policies: Mixed Signals and the Norm of WMD Non-Use." *Journal of Strategic Studies* vol. 23, no. 1 (March 2000): 25–51.

Ritcheson, Philip L. "Proliferation and the Challenge to Deterrence." *Strategic Review* vol. 23, no. 2 (spring 1995): 38–48.

Roberts, Brad. "From Nonproliferation to Antiproliferation." *International Security* vol. 18, no. 1 (summer 1993): 139–73.

Root, Elihu. "The Real Monroe Doctrine." *American Journal of International Law* vol. 8, no. 3 (July 1914): 427–42.

Rumsfeld, Donald H. "Transforming the Military." *Foreign Affairs* vol. 81, no. 3 (May/June 2002): 20–32.

Russell, Richard L. "CIA's Strategic Intelligence in Iraq." *Political Science Quarterly* vol. 117, no. 2 (summer 2002): 191–207.

Sagan, Scott D. "The Commitment Trap: Why the United States Should not Use

Nuclear Threats to Deter Biological and Chemical Weapons Attacks." *International Security* vol. 24, no. 4 (spring 2000): 85–115.

Sagan, Scott D. and Kenneth N. Waltz. *The Spread of Nuclear Weapons: A Debate.* New York: W.W. Norton, 1995.

Sandoval, Robert R. "Consider the Porcupine: Another View of Nuclear Proliferation." *The Bulletin of the Atomic Scientists* vol. 32, no. 5 (May 1976): 17–19.

Schake, Kori N. and Judith S. Yaphe. *The Strategic Implications of a Nuclear-Armed Iran*, McNair Paper No. 64. Washington DC: Institute for National Strategic Studies, National Defense University, 2001.

Schelling, Thomas C. *Arms and Influence.* New Haven, CT: Yale University Press, 1966.

The Strategy of Conflict. Cambridge, MA: Harvard University Press, 1960.

Schneider, Barry R. *Counterforce Targeting Capabilities and Challenges*, Counterproliferation Paper No. 22. Maxwell Air Force Base, AL: Air War College, August 2004.

Future War and Counterproliferation: US Military Responses to NBC Proliferation Threats. Westport, CT: Praeger, 1999.

Radical Responses to Radical Regimes: Evaluating Preemptive Counter-proliferation, McNair Paper No. 41. Washington DC: National Defense University Press, May 1995.

"Strategies for Coping with Enemy Weapons of Mass Destruction." *Airpower Journal* (Special Edition 1996): 36–47.

Schwarzkopf, H. Norman, with Peter Petre. *It Doesn't Take a Hero.* London: Bantam Press, 1992.

Sciolino, Elaine. *The Outlaw State: Saddam Hussein's Quest for Power and the Gulf Crisis.* New York: John Wiley & Sons, 1991.

Sepp, Eric M. *Deeply Buried Facilities: Implications for Military Operations*, Occasional Paper No. 14. Maxwell Air Force Base, AL: Air War College, May 2000.

Shoham, Uri. "The Israeli Raid upon the Iraqi Nuclear Reactor and the Right to Self-Defense." *Military Law Review* vol. 109 (summer 1985): 191–223.

Sigal, Leon V. *Disarming Strangers: Nuclear Diplomacy with North Korea.* Princeton, NJ: Princeton University Press, 1998.

Slocombe, Walter B. "Force, Pre-emption and Legitimacy." *Survival* vol. 45, no. 1 (spring 2003): 117–30.

Smith, Derek D. "North Korea and the United States: A Strategic Profile." *The Korean Journal of Defense Analysis* vol. 16, no. 1 (spring 2004): 25–47.

Snyder, Jed C. "The Road to Osiraq: Baghdad's Quest for the Bomb." *Middle East Journal* vol. 37 (autumn 1983): 565–93.

Sokolski, Henry D., ed. *Prevailing in a Well-Armed World: Devising Competitive Strategies against Weapons Proliferation.* Carlisle, PA: Strategic Studies Institute, March 2000.

Spector, Leonard S., with Jacqueline R. Smith. *Nuclear Ambitions: The Spread of Nuclear Weapons 1989–1990.* Boulder, CO: Westview Press, 1990.

Speer, Albert. *Inside the Third Reich.* New York: Macmillan, 1970.

Spiers, Edward M. *Weapons of Mass Destruction: Prospects for Proliferation.* London: Macmillan, 2000.

Stein, Janice Gross. "Deterrence and Compellence in the Gulf, 1990–91: A Failed or Impossible Task?" *International Security* vol. 17, no. 2 (fall 1992): 147–79.

Stern, Jessica. *Terror in the Name of God: Why Religious Militants Kill.* New York: Ecco, 2003.

The Ultimate Terrorists. Cambridge, MA: Harvard University Press, 1999.

Sterner, Michael. "Closing the Gate: The Persian Gulf War Revisited." *Current History* vol. 96, no. 606 (January 1997): 13–19.

Stone, Julius. *Aggression and World Order.* London: Stevens & Sons, 1958.

Strachan, Hew. *The First World War, Volume I.* Oxford: Oxford University Press, 2001.

Suh, Dae-sook. *Kim Il Sung.* New York: Columbia University Press, 1988.

Taylor, A.J.P. *The Struggle for Mastery in Europe, 1848–1918.* Oxford: Oxford University Press, 1954.

Taylor, Terrence. "The End of Imminence?" *The Washington Quarterly* vol. 27, no. 4 (autumn 2004): 57–72.

Thucydides. *The Peloponnesian War*, translated by Rex Warner. London: Cassell, 1954.

Timmerman, Kenneth R. *The Death Lobby: How the West Armed Iraq.* London: Fourth Estate, 1992.

Utgoff, Victor A. "Proliferation, Missile Defence and American Ambitions." *Survival* vol. 44, no. 2 (summer 2002): 85–102.

ed. *The Coming Crisis: Nuclear Proliferation, US Interests, and World Order.* Cambridge, MA: MIT Press, 2000.

Van Creveld, Martin. *Nuclear Proliferation and the Future of Conflict.* New York: The Free Press, 1993.

Walt, Stephen M. "Beyond Bin Laden: Reshaping US Foreign Policy." *International Security* vol. 26, no. 3 (winter 2001–02): 56–78.

Waltz, Kenneth N. "A Reply." *Security Studies* vol. 4, no. 4 (summer 1995): 802–05.

The Spread of Nuclear Weapons: More May Be Better, Adelphi Paper No. 171. London: International Institute for Strategic Studies, 1981.

Walzer, Michael. *Just and Unjust Wars*. New York: Basic Books, 1977.

Watman, Kenneth and Dean Wilkening, with John Arquilla and Brian Nichiporuk. *US Regional Deterrence Strategies.* Santa Monica, CA: RAND, 1995.

Weissman, Steve and Herbert Krosney. *The Islamic Bomb: The Nuclear Threat to Israel and the Middle East*. New York: Times Books, 1981.

Wich, Richard. *Sino-Soviet Crisis Politics: A Study of Political Change and Communication*. Cambridge, MA: Harvard University Press, 1980.

Wilkening, Dean. *Ballistic-Missile Defence and Strategic Stability*, Adelphi Paper No. 334. Oxford: Oxford University Press, International Institute for Strategic Studies, 2000.

Wilkening, Dean and Kenneth Watman. *Nuclear Deterrence in a Regional Context*. Santa Monica, CA: RAND, 1995.

Wirtz, James J. "Counterproliferation, Conventional Counterforce and Nuclear War." *Journal of Strategic Studies* vol. 23, no. 1 (March 2000): 5–24.

Wirtz, James J. and Jeffrey A. Larsen. *Rockets Red Glare: Missile Defense and the Future of World Politics*. Boulder, CO: Westview Press, 2001.

Wirtz, James J. and James A. Russell. "US Policy on Preventive War and Preemption." *The Nonproliferation Review* vol. 10, no. 1 (spring 2003): 113–23.

Wit, Joel S., Daniel Poneman, and Robert Gallucci. *Going Critical: The First North Korean Nuclear Crisis*. Washington DC: Brookings Institution Press, 2004.

Wohlstetter, Albert. "The Delicate Balance of Terror." *Foreign Affairs* vol. 37, no. 2 (January 1959): 211–34.

Wolf, Barry. *When the Weak Attack the Strong: Failures of Deterrence*, RAND Note. Santa Monica, CA: RAND, 1991.

Wolfgang, Marvin E. *International Terrorism*. Beverly Hills, CA: Sage, 1982.

Yoo, John C. "Using Force." *University of Chicago Law Review* vol. 71, no. 3 (summer 2004): 729–97.

Zagare, Frank C. and D. Marc Kilgour. *Perfect Deterrence*. Cambridge: Cambridge University Press, 2000.

Zelikow, Philip. "The Transformation of National Security: Five Redefinitions." *The National Interest* no. 71 (spring 2003): 17–28.

NEWSPAPER ARTICLES

Allen, Mike. "Iraq's Weapons Could Make it a Target, Bush Says." *Washington Post*, 27 November 2001.

Apple, R.W. Jr. "Allies Destroy Iraqis' Main Force; Kuwait is Retaken after 7 Months." *New York Times*, 28 February 1991.

Arkin, William M. "Desert Fox Delivery; Precision Undermined its Purpose." *Washington Post*, 17 January 1999.

Associated Press. "Bin Laden Said to Have Sought Nuclear Arms." *Baltimore Sun*, 30 December 2002.

"Senate Approves Money for New Nuclear Weapon." *Los Angeles Times*, 2 July 2005.

Baker, Peter. "But What if the Iraqis Strike First?" *Washington Post*, 23 January 2003.

Bender, Bryan. "Regime Ordered Chemical Attack, Investigator Says." *Boston Globe*, 8 August 2003.

Beyer, Lisa. "Coping with Chemicals." *Time*, 25 February 1991.

Boettcher, Mike. "Evidence Suggests Al Qaeda Pursuit of Biological, Chemical Weapons." *CNN*, 14 November 2001.

Bone, James. "Iraq Sites for Bio-War Revealed by Defector." *The Times* (London), 12 July 2002.

de Borchgrave, Arnaud. "Commentary: Saddam Hussein's War Plan." *United Press International*, 10 July 2002.

Broad, William J. "Achilles' Heel in Missile Plan: Crude Weapons." *New York Times*, 27 August 2001.

"Call for New Breed of Nuclear Arms Faces Hurdles." *New York Times*, 11 March 2002.

"Facing a Second Nuclear Age." *New York Times*, 3 August 2003.

"The Nuclear Shield: Repelling an Attack." *New York Times*, 30 June 2000.

Broad, William J., Stephen Engelberg, and James Glanz. "Assessing Risks, Chemical, Biological, Even Nuclear." *New York Times*, 1 November 2001.

Broad, William J. and David E. Sanger. "Pakistani's Black Market May Sell Nuclear Secrets." *New York Times*, 15 April 2002.

Broad, William J., David E. Sanger, and Raymond Bonner. "A Tale of Nuclear Proliferation." *New York Times*, 12 February 2004.

Brooke, James. "North Korea Says it Has Nuclear Weapons and Rejects Talks." *New York Times*, 10 February 2005.

"North Korea Says it Plans to Expel Nuclear Monitors." *New York Times*, 28 December 2002.

"North Koreans Claim to Extract Fuel for Nuclear Weapons." *New York Times*, 12 May 2005.

Bryen, Stephen D. "Ironic Chemistry: The UN Boosts Saddam's Threat." *Wall Street Journal*, 9 December 2002.

Bumiller, Elisabeth and David M. Halbfinger. "Bush and Kerry Follow Debate with Sharp Jabs." *New York Times*, 2 October 2004.

Burns, John F., with Eric Schmitt. "US Forces Join Big Assault on Afghan Stronghold." *New York Times*, 3 March 2002.

Calabresi, Massimo. "Iran's Nuclear Threat." *Time*, 17 March 2003.

Carter, Ashton B. and William J. Perry. "Back to the Brink." *Washington Post*, 20 October 2002.

Chandrasekaran, Rajiv. "For India, Deterrence May Not Prevent War." *Washington Post*, 17 January 2002.

Choe, Sang-hun. "North Korea Rejects US Nuclear Proposal." *Philadelphia Inquirer*, 15 December 2003.

Church, George J. "Targeting Gaddafi." *Time*, 21 April 1986.

Coman, Julian. "Pentagon Wants 'Mini-Nukes' to Fight Terrorists." *Sunday Telegraph* (London), 26 October 2003.

Connolly, Ceci. "Readiness for Chemical Attack Criticized." *Washington Post*, 4 June 2003.

Cooper, Richard T. "Making Nuclear Bombs 'Usable.'" *Los Angeles Times*, 3 February 2003.

Coryell, George. "New Humvee Protects against All Chemical, Biological Warfare." *Tampa Tribune*, 11 March 2003.

Cox, Matthew and William Matthews. "The Best Protective Gear in the World?" *Air Force Times*, 24 February 2003.

Curl, Joseph. "North Korea Gets Stern Warning." *Washington Times*, 15 May 2003.

Dao, James. "Bush Urges Chinese President to Push North Korea on Arms." *New York Times*, 9 February 2003.

"Call in Congress for Full Airing of Iraq Policy." *New York Times*, 18 July 2002.

"Pentagon Optimistic about Missile Shield." *New York Times*, 15 April 2002.

"Pentagon's Worry: Iraqi Chemical Arms." *New York Times*, 19 May 2002.

"Senior Bush Defends '91 Decision on Iraq." *New York Times*, 1 March 2003.

Demick, Barbara. "N. Korea Denies it Has a Warhead." *Los Angeles Times*, 13 January 2004.

"N. Korea Says it Will Be a No-Show at Six-Party Talks." *Los Angeles Times*, 10 December 2003.

Devroy, Ann and Patrick E. Tyler. "Bush Launches Strike to Seize Noriega; Fighting Widespread in Panama City." *Washington Post*, 20 December 1989.

Dewar, Helen. "'Realistic' Missile Tests Ordered." *Washington Post*, 18 June 2004.

"Senate Passes $447 Billion Defense Bill." *Washington Post*, 24 June 2004.

DeYoung, Karen. "Baghdad Weapons Programs Dormant; Iraq's Inactivity Puzzles US Officials." *Washington Post*, 15 July 1999.

Diamond, John. "N. Korea Keeps US Intelligence Guessing." *USA Today*, 10 March 2003.

"Split over Iraq Grows More Public." *USA Today*, 19 August 2002.

Diamond, John and Tom Squitieri. "House Panel Says No to Nuke Funding." *USA Today*, 10 June 2004.

Diedrich, John. "SpaceCom Improves Ability to Dodge Scuds." *Colorado Springs Gazette*, 31 January 2003.

Divis, Dee Ann. "BioWar: Biowatch Expansion Developing." *Washington Times*, 24 February 2005.

Dobbs, Michael. "A Story of Iran's Quest for Power." *Washington Post*, 13 January 2002.

Dowd, Maureen. "The Jihad All-Stars." *New York Times*, 27 August 2003.

Doyle, Neil. "Al Qaeda Nukes are Reality, Intelligence Says." *Washington Times*, 28 October 2002.

Drogin, Bob. " '91 Iraq Toxics Plan Reported." *Los Angeles Times*, 10 March 2003.

"The Other Weapons Threat in Iraq." *Los Angeles Times*, 10 October 2004.

Drummond, James and Edward Alden. "Rumsfeld Orders Extra Forces to Mideast." *Financial Times* (London), 13 January 2003.

Duffy, Michael. "Weapons of Mass Disappearance." *Time*, 9 June 2003.

Easterbrook, Gregg. "American Power Moves beyond the Mere Super." *New York Times*, 27 April 2003.

Eckholm, Erik. "Experts Try to Make Missile Shield Plan Palatable to China." *New York Times*, 28 January 2001.

Efron, Sonni. "US Said to be Resigned to a Nuclear Korea." *Los Angeles Times*, 5 March 2003.

Evans, Michael. "Secret Files on Baghdad's Weapons Plans." *The Times* (London), 29 August 2002.

Faiola, Anthony. "N. Korea Deploying New Missiles with Longer Range, South Says." *Washington Post*, 9 July 2004.

Fischer, Ian. "Iraqi Aide Threatens Suicide Attacks." *New York Times*, 2 February 2003.

Flournoy, Michele and Vinca LaFleur. "Quick-Stick Doctrine." *Washington Post*, 18 June 2002.

Ford, Peter. "Europe Persuades Iran to Cool Nuclear Program – For Now." *Christian Science Monitor*, 16 November 2004.

Frantz, Douglas. "Iran Closes in on Ability to Build a Nuclear Bomb." *Los Angeles Times*, 4 August 2003.

"Iran Moving Methodically toward Nuclear Capability." *Los Angeles Times*, 21 October 2004.

"N. Korea's Nuclear Success is Doubted." *Los Angeles Times*, 9 December 2003.

French, Howard W. "North Korea Clarifies Statement on A-Bomb." *New York Times*, 19 November 2002.

"North Korea Restarts Reactor with Ability to Fuel Arms." *New York Times*, 6 February 2003.

"North Korea Warns the US to Negotiate or Risk 'Catastrophe.'" *New York Times*, 24 December 2002.

"North Korean Radio Asserts Country Has Nuclear Arms." *New York Times*, 18 November 2002.

"Official Says US Will Reposition its Troops in South Korea." *New York Times*, 3 June 2003.

"US Gets Warning from North Korea." *New York Times*, 25 December 2002.

Friedman, Thomas L. "Envoy to Iraq, Faulted in Crisis, Says She Warned Hussein Sternly." *New York Times*, 21 March 1991.

"The Suicide Supply Chain." *New York Times*, 9 December 2004.

"Who's Crazy Here?" *New York Times*, 15 May 2001.

Fulghum, David A. "Iraq's Hidden Weapons 'Are Likely Underground.'" *Aviation Week & Space Technology*, 16 December 2002.

"Microwave Weapons May Be Ready for Iraq." *Aviation Week & Space Technology*, 5 August 2002.

Fuller, Thomas. "Iraq Vows 'Unconventional' Tactics to Defend Capital." *New York Times*, 4 April 2003.

Gaffney, Frank J. Jr. "Go Navy Missile Defense." *Washington Times*, 1 March 2005.

Gargill, David. "The Libya Fallacy: The Iraq War is Not What Disarmed Qaddafi." *Harper's Magazine*, November 2004.

Gellman, Barton. "Fears Prompt US to Beef up Nuclear Terror Detection." *Washington Post*, 3 March 2002.

"Iraq's Arsenal Was Only on Paper." *Washington Post*, 7 January 2004.

"Frustrated, US Arms Team to Leave Iraq." *Washington Post*, 11 May 2003.

Gertz, Bill. "2nd N. Korean Nuclear Site Not Likely." *Washington Times*, 22 July 2003.

"British Report Links Al Qaeda, Baghdad." *Washington Times*, 15 July 2004.

"China Ships North Korea Ingredient for Nuclear Arms." *Washington Times*, 17 December 2002.

"CIA Says Al-Qaeda Ready to Use Nukes." *Washington Times*, 3 June 2003.

"Coalition Still Wary of Chemical Weapons." *Washington Times*, 5 April 2003.

"Iraqi Weapons Pipeline Probed." *Washington Times*, 25 May 2004.

"N. Korea Ship Gets Arms in and out." *Washington Times*, 18 February 2003.

"North Korea Can Build Nukes Right Now." *Washington Times*, 22 November 2002.

"Photos Point to Removal of Weapons." *Washington Times*, 29 October 2004.

"US Commander Fears N. Korea Would Sell Nukes." *Washington Times*, 18 November 2003.

"US Says Tehran is Pursuing Nuke Arms," *Washington Times*, 25 November 2005.

Gertz, Bill and Nicholas Kralev. "Pyongyang Takes a Hard-Line at Six-Way Talks." *Washington Times*, 26 June 2004.

Gilbert, Craig. "Can US Be First to Attack Enemy?" *Milwaukee Journal Sentinel*, 31 March 2002.

Gonzalez, David. "At Cuba Conference, Old Foes Exchange Notes on 1962 Missile Crisis." *New York Times*, 14 October 2002.

Goodman, Peter S. "N. Korea Moves to Activate Complex." *Washington Post*, 27 December 2002.

"N. Korean Official Threatens 'Fight to the End' with US." *Washington Post*, 25 December 2002.

Gordon, Michael R. "Iraq Said to Plan Strategy of Delay and Urban Battle." *New York Times*, 16 February 2003.

"Iraq Said to Plan Tangling the US in Street Fighting." *New York Times*, 26 August 2002.

"US Troops Move in Panama in Effort to Seize Noriega; Gunfire is Heard in Capital." *New York Times*, 20 December 1989.

Gosden, Christine. "Why I Went, What I Saw." *Washington Post*, 11 March 1998.

Gottemoeller, Rose. "On Nukes, We Need to Talk." *Washington Post*, 2 April 2002.

Graham, Bradley. "General Says Missile Defense Could Be Ready Soon." *Washington Post*, 28 April 2004.

"Scientists Raise Doubts about Missile Defense." *Washington Post*, 16 July 2003.

"'Scorched Earth' Plans in Iraq Cited." *Washington Post*, 19 December 2002.

"As US Girds for Worst in Iraq, Retaliation isn't Clear-Cut Issue." *Washington Post*, 29 January 2003.

Grant, Thomas D. "For an Iraq Amnesty." *Washington Post*, 20 August 2002.

Greenhouse, Steven. "Perry Says US Considered Bombing North Korean Reactor." *The Houston Chronicle*, 25 January 1995.

Guynn, Jessica. "As Coalition Nears Baghdad, Chemical Arms a Question Mark." *The Mercury News*, 3 April 2003.

Hendren, John. "Pentagon Battles Unknown Preparing for a Toxic War." *Los Angeles Times*, 29 September 2002.

"US Studies Foam Bombs among Options to Isolate Chemicals." *Los Angeles Times*, 18 July 2002.

Hersh, Seymour. "Target Gadaffi: Reagan's Secret Plot." *The Times* (London), 22 February 1987.

Hosenball, Mark and Evan Thomas. "High-Seas Hunting." *Newsweek*, 23 December 2003.

Hsu, Spencer S. "Anthrax Alarm Uncovers Response Flaws." *Washington Post*, 17 March 2005.

"Sensors May Track Terror's Fallout." *Washington Post*, 2 June 2003.

Hulse, Carl. "Senate Votes to Lift Ban on Producing Nuclear Arms." *New York Times*, 21 May 2003.

Ibrahim, Youssef M. "Iran Reports New Iraqi Gas Raids, and Says Cities May be Hit Next." *New York Times*, 2 April 1988.

"Think Twice before Targeting Iran." *USA Today*, 24 August 2004.

Ignatius, David. "Dubious Iraqi Link." *Washington Post*, 15 March 2002.

Jaffe, Greg. "Intelligence Suggests Hussein Allowed Chemical-Weapon Use." *Wall Street Journal*, 20 March 2003.

Jehl, Douglas. "Iraq Removed Arms Material, Aide Says." *New York Times*, 29 October 2003.

"Report Warned Bush Team about Intelligence Doubts," *New York Times*, 6 November 2005.

Kahn, Joseph. "Diplomats See Modest Progress in North Korea Nuclear Talks." *New York Times*, 28 February 2004.

"North Korea Says it is against More Talks." *New York Times*, 30 August 2003.

Kaplan, Fred. "Strikes Didn't Finish Job US Set out to Do." *Boston Globe*, 21 December 1998.

Kelley, Matt. "Iraq Can Make Chemical Weapons that Penetrate US Protective Gear." *Associated Press*, 17 November 2002.

Kemper, Vicki. "Senate Approves $5.6 Billion for 10-Year 'Bioshield' Project." *Los Angeles Times*, 20 May 2004.

"Vaccine Program Going Well, Military Reports." *Los Angeles Times*, 14 February 2003.

Kessler, Glenn. "More N. Korean Bombs Likely, US Official Says." *Washington Post*, 16 July 2004.

"N. Korea Continues Criticism of Bush." *New York Times*, 25 August 2004.

"US Agrees to Statement on North Korea Talks." *Washington Post*, 8 December 2003.

"US Rejects North Korean Conditions for Dismantling Nuclear Programs." *New York Times*, 23 October 2004.

Kessler, Glenn and Walter Pincus. "N. Korea Stymied on Plutonium Work." *Washington Post*, 20 March 2003.

Kessler, Glenn and Peter Slevin. "Preemptive Strikes Must Be Decisive, Powell Says." *Washington Post*, 15 June 2002.

Kessler, Glenn and Robin Wright. "US, Allies Agree on Iran Move." *Washington Post*, 25 November 2003.

Kimery, Anthony L. "Searching for 'Dirty Bombs.'" *Insight Magazine*, 21 January 2003.

Kirk, Donald. "N. Korea Flirts with 'Red Line.'" *Christian Science Monitor*, 28 May 2004.

Knickerbocker, Brad. "Risk of Terrorism to Nation's Food Supply." *Christian Science Monitor*, 24 December 2002.

Kralev, Nicholas. "North Korea Offers Nigeria Missile Deal." *Washington Times*, 29 January 2004.

Krauthammer, Charles. "Calling Iraq's Bluff." *Washington Post*, 30 January 2004.

"Get Ready for War." *Washington Post*, 3 June 1994.

La Guardia, Anton. "Israel Challenges Iran's Nuclear Ambitions." *Daily Telegraph* (London), 22 September 2004.

Lakely, James G. "Libya Will Dismantle its Weapons." *Washington Times*, 20 December 2003.

Lee, Soo-Jeong. "Bush Rejects N. Korea's Offer of Nuclear Programs Freeze for Energy." *Washington Post*, 10 December 2003.

Levi, Michael. "Uncontainable: North Korea's Loose Nukes." *New Republic*, 26 May 2003.

Linzer, Dafna. "Iran is Judged 10 Years from Nuclear Bomb." *Washington Post*, 2 August 2005.

"US Misled Allies about Nuclear Export." *Washington Post*, 20 March 2005.

Lumpkin, John J. "US Sees Limit to Iraqi Chemical Threat." *Philadelphia Inquirer*, 14 July 2002.

Lynch, Colum. "Bin Laden Sought Uranium, Jury Told." *Washington Post*, 8 February 2001.

"Iraqi Defector Claimed Arms Were Destroyed by 1995." *Washington Post*, 1 March 2003.

McAllister, J.F.O. "Pyongyang's Dangerous Game." *Time*, 4 April 1994.

McGeary, Johanna. "What Does Saddam Have?" *Time*, 16 September 2002.

Magnier, Mark. "Rice Puts Pressure on N. Korea." *Los Angeles Times*, 21 March 2005.

Masland, Tom with Douglas Waller. "Are We Ready for Chemical War?" *Newsweek*, 4 March 1991.

Mazzetti, Mark and Kevin Whitelaw. "Six Deadly Fears." *US World and News Report*, 17 February 2003.

Meyer, Josh. "Al Qaeda Feared to Have 'Dirty Bombs.'" *Los Angeles Times*, 8 February 2003.

Milbank, Dana and Mike Allen. "US Will Take Action against Iraq, Bush Says." *Washington Post*, 14 March 2002.

Miller, Bill. "Denver Stages Mock Terror Attack." *Washington Post*, 23 February 2002.

Miller, Greg. "Analysis of Iraqi Weapons 'Wrong.'" *Los Angeles Times*, 31 May 2003.

"US Claims 90% Hit Rate in Missile Plan." *Los Angeles Times*, 19 March 2003.

Miller, Judith. "An Iraqi Defector Tells of Work on at Least 20 Hidden Weapons Sites." *New York Times*, 20 December 2001.

"Qaeda Videos Seem to Show Chemical Tests." *New York Times*, 19 August 2002.

"US is Deploying a Monitor System for Germ Attacks." *New York Times*, 22 January 2003.

Mitnick, Joshua. "Would Israel Strike First at Iran?" *Christian Science Monitor*, 18 August 2004.

Myers, Steven Lee. "The Targets: Jets Said to Avoid Poison Gas Sites." *New York Times*, 18 December 1998.

New York Times. "In Defense of Deterrence." 10 September 2002.

Nunn, Sam and Michele Flournoy. "A Test of Leadership on Sea Island." *Washington Post*, 8 June 2004.

Ottaway, David B. "In Mideast, Warfare with a New Nature." *Washington Post*, 5 April 1988.

Pan, Philip P. "N. Korea Says it Can 'Show Flexibility.'" *Washington Post*, 26 June 2004.

"Nuclear Talks Clouded by N. Korea's Denial of Enrichment Effort." *Washington Post*, 25 February 2004.

Perry, William J. and Ashton B. Carter. "The Crisis Last Time." *New York Times*, 19 January 2003.

Peterson, Scott. "Behind Diplomacy, Iran Sees a Fight Coming." *Christian Science Monitor*, 31 March 2005.

"Iran's Nuclear Challenge: Deter, not Antagonize." *Christian Science Monitor*, 21 February 2002.

Pincus, Walter. "Future of US Nuclear Arsenal Debated." *Washington Post*, 4 May 2003.

"Hussein Tries to Mend Fences with Neighbors." *Washington Post*, 19 July 2002.

"Military Study Mulled Deterrence of 'Fear.'" *Washington Post*, 5 July 2001.

"No Link between Hijacker, Iraq Found, US Says." *Washington Post*, 1 May 2002.

"Nuclear Strike on Bunkers Assessed." *Washington Post*, 20 December 2001.

"US Effort Aimed at Iraqi Officers." *Washington Post*, 30 September 2002.

"US Explores Developing Low-Yield Nuclear Weapons." *Washington Post*, 20 February 2003.

"US Has Still Not Found Iraqi Arms." *Washington Post*, 26 April 2003.

"US Nuclear Arms Stance Modified by Policy Study." *Washington Post*, 23 March 2002.

Pincus, Walter and Dana Priest, "Hussein's Weapons May Have Been Bluff." *Washington Post*, 1 October 2003.

Pollack, Kenneth. "Why Iraq Can't Be Deterred." *New York Times*, 26 September 2002.

Preston, Julia. "North Korea Demands US Agree to Nonaggression Pact." *New York Times*, 25 October 2002.

"Security Council Votes, 15–0, for Tough Iraq Resolution." *New York Times*, 9 November 2002.

Price, Joyce Howard. "US Reprisal to be 'Annihilation.'" *Washington Times*, 9 September 2002.

Priest, Dana. "Al Qaeda–Iraq Link Recanted." *Washington Post*, 1 August 2004.

"Iraq New Terror Breeding Ground." *Washington Post*, 14 January 2005.

Raspberry, William. "Our Insane Focus on Iraq." *Washington Post*, 9 September 2002.

Ratnesar, Romesh. "Can They Strike Back?" *Time*, 3 February 2003.

Reid, T.R. "North Korea Warns of 'Brink of War.'" *Washington Post*, 23 March 1994.

Revkin, Andre C. "Advanced Armaments." *New York Times*, 3 December 2001.

Rice, Condoleezza. "Why We Know Iraq is Lying." *New York Times*, 23 January 2003.

Richter, Paul. "Missile Defense System Doubts." *Los Angeles Times*, 22 January 2004.

"US Works up Plan for Using Nuclear Arms." *Los Angeles Times*, 9 March 2002.

Riordan, Teresa. "Plastic Pods for Biological Attacks." *New York Times*, 30 September 2002.

Risen, James. "CIA Held Back Iraqi Arms Data, US Officials Say." *New York Times*, 6 July 2004.

Robbins, Carla Anne and Jeanne Cummings. "How Bush Decided that Hussein Must Be Ousted from Atop Iraq." *Wall Street Journal*, 14 June 2002.

Safire, William. "Clear Ties of Terror." *New York Times*, 27 January 2003.

Sakamaki, Sachiko and Doug Struck. "Japan Cracks down on Firms Tied to N. Korea." *Washington Post*, 22 May 2003.

Sanchez, Rene. "Robot Race is Giant Step for Unmanned Kind." *Washington Post*, 10 March 2004.

Sands, David R. "Israeli General Says Saudis Seek to Buy Pakistan Nukes." *Washington Times*, 23 October 2003.

Sanger, David E. "Bush Shifts Focus to Nuclear Sales by North Korea." *New York Times*, 5 May 2003.

"In North Korea and Pakistan, Deep Roots of Nuclear Barter." *New York Times*, 24 November 2002.

"North Korea Says it Has Made Fuel for Atom Bombs." *New York Times*, 15 July 2003.

"North Korea Says it Now Possesses Nuclear Arsenal." *New York Times*, 25 April 2003.

"North Korea Seems to Reject Butter-for-Guns Proposal From US." *New York Times*, 25 July 2004.

"Steps at Reactor in North Korea Worry the US." *New York Times*, 18 April 2005.

"US to Offer North Korea Incentives in Nuclear Talks." *New York Times*, 23 June 2004.

"US Officials Fear Iraqis Plan to Use Gas on GIs." *New York Times*, 25 March 2003.

"US Sees Quick Start of North Korean Nuclear Site." *New York Times*, 1 March 2003.

"US vs. a Nuclear Iran." *New York Times*, 12 December 2004.

"White House May Go to UN over North Korean Shipments." *New York Times*, 25 April 2005.

Sanger, David E. and William J. Broad. "Evidence is Cited Linking Koreans to Libya Uranium." *New York Times*, 23 May 2004.

"North Korea Said to Expand Arms Program." *New York Times*, 6 December 2004.

"From Rogue Nuclear Programs, Web of Trails Leads to Pakistan." *New York Times*, 3 January 2004.

Sanger, David E. and James Dao. "North Korea Says it Regains Access to its Plutonium." *New York Times*, 23 December 2002.

Sanger, David E. and Howard W. French. "North Korea Prompts US to Investigate Nuclear Boast." *New York Times*, 1 May 2003.

Sanger, David E. and Eric Schmitt. "Satellites Said to See Activity at North Korean Nuclear Site." *New York Times*, 31 January 2003.

Sanger, David E. and Thom Shanker. "North Korea Hides New Nuclear Site, Evidence Suggests." *New York Times*, 20 July 2003.

Savage, David G. "Nuclear Plan Meant to Deter." *Los Angeles Times*, 11 March 2002.

Scarborough, Rowan. "CIA Can't Rule out WMD Move to Syria." *Washington Times*, 27 April 2005.

"Saddam Agents on Syria Border Helped Move Banned Materials." *Washington Times*, 16 August 2004.

"Saddam Ready to Kill Iraqis, Blame US." *Washington Times*, 12 March 2003.

"Saddam Would Hit Buildup of Troops." *Washington Times*, 17 June 2002.

Schmitt, Eric and David E. Sanger. "Admiral Seeks Deterrent Force in Korea Crisis." *New York Times*, 1 February 2003.

Schneider, Howard. "Iraqi Leader Says Invaders will be 'Buried.'" *Washington Post*, 9 August 2002.

Sciolino, Elaine. "Europe Gets Iran to Extend Freeze in Nuclear Work." *New York Times*, 26 May 2005.

Scowcroft, Brent. "Don't Attack Saddam." *Wall Street Journal*, 15 August 2002.

Shanker, Thom. "North Korean Missile Said to Advance; US is Unworried." *New York Times*, 5 August 2004.

"Threats and Responses: Arms Smuggling; Scud Missiles Found on Ship of North Korea." *New York Times*, 11 December 2002.

Shanker, Thom and David Johnston. "US Lists Iraqis to Punish, or to Work with." *New York Times*, 26 February 2003.

Shenon, Philip. "Border Inspectors to Look for Radioactive Material." *New York Times*, 1 March 2003.

Slavin, Barbara. "Iran's Nuke Plans May Be Unstoppable." *USA Today*, 30 August 2004.

Smith, Michael. "Saddam to be Target of Britain's 'E-Bomb.'" *Daily Telegraph* (London), 26 August 2002.

Smith, R. Jeffrey. "Perry Sharply Warns North Korea." *Washington Post*, 31 March 1994.

"US Warns of Retaliation if Iraq Uses Poison Gas." *Washington Post*, 9 August 1990.

Smith, Stephen. "US Farms Called Vulnerable to Terrorism." *Boston Globe*, 22 November 2002.

Smucker, Philip. "Iraq Flexes its Military Trump Card." *Christian Science Monitor*, 19 March 2003.

Steinberg, Gerald. "Iran Analysis: Israel's Options." *Jerusalem Post*, 5 October 2004.

Sterngold, James. "US Alters Nuclear Weapons Policy." *San Francisco Chronicle*, 28 November 2005.

Stober, Dan. "Nuclear 'Bunker Busters' Sought." *San Jose Mercury News*, 23 April 2003.

Stone, Andrea. "Americans in Survey Support First Strike." *USA Today*, 26 June 2002.

Stout, David. "Bush Again Accuses Iran and Syria of Harboring Terrorists." *New York Times*, 21 July 2003.

"Bush and Seoul Call North Korea Nuclear Plan 'Unacceptable.'" *New York Times*, 13 December 2002.

"Rumsfeld Says, if Necessary, US Can Fight 2 Wars at Once." *New York Times*, 23 December 2002.

Stout, David and John H. Cushman. "Defense Missile for US System Fails to Launch." *New York Times*, 16 December 2004.

Struck, Doug. "Crisis Could Push N. Korea to Expel Nuclear Inspectors." *Washington Post*, 14 November 2002.

"For North Korea, US is Violator of Accords." *Washington Post*, 21 October 2002.

Struck, Doug and Glenn Kessler. "Foes Giving in to N. Korea's Nuclear Aims." *Washington Post*, 5 March 2003.

Swain, John and James Adams. "Saddam Gives Local Commanders Go-Ahead for Chemical Attacks." *Sunday Times* (London), 3 February 1991.

Thompson, Mark. "Going Door to Door." *Time*, 16 September 2002.

"Well, Maybe a Nuke or Two." *Time*, 11 April 1994.

Tiboni, Frank. "War Game Stuns US Strategists." *Defense News*, 12 May 2003.

Torchia, Christopher. "N. Korea Warns US Risking Nuclear War." *Washington Post*, 24 December 2002.

Toth, Robert. "American Support Grows for Use of Nuclear Arms." *Los Angeles Times*, 3 February 1991.

Tyler, Patrick E. "Both Iraq and Iran Gassed Kurds in War, US Analysis Finds." *Washington Post*, 3 May 1990.

"As China Threatens Taiwan, It Makes Sure US Listens." *New York Times*, 24 January 1996.

"Officers Say US Aided Iraq in War Despite Use of Gas." *New York Times*, 18 August 2002.

"Stirring the Iraqi Pot." *New York Times*, 21 March 1991.

Tyson, Ann Scott. "For Army, a New Primer in Chemical War." *Christian Science Monitor*, 21 October 2002.

"Nuclear Plan Changes Calculus of Deterrence." *Christian Science Monitor*, 14 March 2002.

Vick, Karl. "Iran's Leader Backs Deal on Inspections." *Washington Post*, 4 November 2003.

"US, Sudan Trade Claims on Factory." *Washington Post*, 25 August 1998.

Viorst, Milton. "Imagining the Worst-Case Scenario in Iraq." *New York Times*, 12 September 2002.

Wald, Matthew L. and Judith Miller. "Energy Department Plans a Push to Retrieve Nuclear Materials." *New York Times*, 26 May 2004.

Warrick, Joby. "Bush to Seek Funds for Fighting 'Dirty Bombs.'" *Washington Post*, 30 January 2003.

"Iran Admits Foreign Help on Nuclear Facility." *Washington Post*, 27 August 2003.

"Uncertain Ability to Deliver a Blow." *Washington Post*, 5 September 2002.

Warrick, Joby and Glenn Kessler. "Iran's Nuclear Program Speeds Ahead." *Washington Post*, 10 March 2003.

Wedgwood, Ruth. "A Pirate is a Pirate." *Wall Street Journal*, 16 December 2002.

"Self-Defense, Pirates, and Contraband." *Wall Street Journal*, 29 May 2003.

Weinraub, Bernard. "Army Reports Iraq is Moving Toxic Arms to its Troops." *New York Times*, 28 March 2003.

Weisman, Steven R. "US to Send Signal to North Koreans in Naval Exercise." *New York Times*, 18 August 2003.

Willman, David and Alan C. Miller. "Nuclear Threat is Real, Experts Warn." *Los Angeles Times*, 11 November 2001.

Woodward, Bob. "A Course of 'Confident Action.'" *Washington Post*, 19 November 2002.

"President Bush Broadens Anti-Hussein Order." *Washington Post*, 16 June 2002.

Woodward, Bob, Robert G. Kaiser, and David B. Ottaway. "US Fears Bin Laden Made Nuclear Strides." *Washington Post*, 4 December 2001.

Wright, Robin. "An Iraqi Campaign Faces Many Hurdles." *Los Angeles Times*, 10 March 2002.

"Ship Incident May Have Swayed Libya." *Washington Post*, 1 January 2004.

SPEECHES

Berger, Samuel, Caspar Weinberger, and Senator Joseph Biden. Hearing on Iraq before the Foreign Relations Committee, US Senate. Washington DC, 1 August 2002.

Bush, George W. Graduation Speech. West Point, New York, 1 June 2002.

Remarks on Iraq. Cincinnati, Ohio, 7 October 2002.

Remarks by the President in Address to the Nation. The White House, Washington DC, 17 March 2003.

Remarks on Weapons of Mass Destruction Proliferation. Fort Lesley J. McNair, National Defense University, Washington DC, 11 February 2004.

Speech at the American Enterprise Institute. Washington DC, 26 February 2003.

State of the Union Address. Washington DC, 28 January 2003.

"Taking Action to Strengthen Small Business." St. Louis, Missouri, 22 January 2003.

Clinton, William. Statement by the President, Office of the Press Secretary, 16 December 1998.

Cohen, William S. Department of Defense News Briefing, 21 December 1998.

Kadish, Robert T. Speech at the Military Appreciation Banquet. Fairbanks, Alaska, 2 March 2001.

Kennedy, John F. Address to the Nation on the Soviet Arms Buildup in Cuba. The White House, Washington DC, 22 October 1962.

LaPorte, Leon. *This Week with George Stephanopoulos*, ABC News Transcripts. 27 July 2003.

Perry, William. Hearing on Security Implications of the Nuclear Agreement with North Korea before the Senate Armed Services Committee, US Senate. Washington DC, 26 January 1995.

Powell, Colin. Address to the UN Security Council. New York, 5 February 2003.

Rice, Condoleezza. Wriston Lecture to the Manhattan Institute. New York, 1 October 2002.

Roosevelt, Franklin Delano. Quarantine Speech. Chicago, 5 October 1937.

Rumsfeld, Donald H. Hearing on FY 2003 Appropriations for the Defense Department before the Appropriations Committee, US Senate. Washington DC, 21 May 2002.

Speech on 21st Century Transformation of the US Armed Forces. National Defense University, Washington DC, 31 January 2002.

Speech at the Air Force Commencement Ceremony. Colorado Springs, Colorado, 29 May 2002.

Semmel, Andrew. Remarks to the Asia-Pacific Nuclear Safeguards and Security Conference. Sydney, Australia, 8 November 2004.

Remarks at Conference on Global Nonproliferation and Counterterrorism: United Nations Security Council Resolution 1540. London, 12 October 2004.

Wolfowitz, Paul. Remarks at the 38th Munich Conference on Security Policy. Munich, 2 February 2002.

INTERVIEWS

Baker, James. Phone interview with author, 20 November 2003.

Gallucci, Robert. Phone interview with author, 22 August 2003.

Glosson, Buster. Phone interview with author, 26 August 2003.

Perry, William. Phone interview with author, 21 August 2003.

Roach, Ashley. Interview with author, 25 October 2004.

Scowcroft, Brent. Phone interview with author, 28 August 2003.

Wit, Joel. Interview with author, 18 August 2003.

INTERNET RESOURCES

Capaccio, Tony. "Iraq Probably Can't Mount Major Chemical Attack, General Says." *Bloomberg.com*, 4 March 2003.

Crawley, Vince. "US to Iraq: Using Weapons of Mass Destruction Would Be a Mistake." *ArmyTimes.com*, 13 August 2002.

DPRK Ministry of Foreign Affairs Statement. 10 February 2005. Available at http://news.bbc.co.uk/2/hi/asia-pacific/4252515.stm.

Federation of American Scientists. Al Hussein Missile Webpage. Available at http://www.fas.org/nuke/guide/iraq/missile/al_hussein.htm.

Johnson, Steven. "Stopping Loose Nukes." *Wired* vol. 10, no. 11 (November 2002). Available at http://www.wired.com/wired/archive/10.11/nukes.html.

Leventhal, Paul and Steven Dolley. "The North Korean Nuclear Crisis." Nuclear Control Institute, 16 June 1994. Available at http://www.nci.org/n/nkib2.htm.

Limbacher, Carl. "Clinton: I Threatened to Attack North Korea." *NewsMax.com*, 24 November 2002.

Nuclear Threat Initiative. "Interdicting Nuclear Smuggling." Available at http://www.nti.org/e_research/cnwm/interdicting/index.asp.

WMD 411, "Provisions of Resolution 1540." Available at http://www.nti.org/f_wmd411/f2n1.html.

US Department of State. State Ship Boarding Agreements. Available at http://www.state.gov/t/np/c12386.htm.

Yale Law School. Avalon Project, The Caroline Case. Available at http://www.yale.edu/lawweb/avalon/diplomacy/britian/br-1842d.htm.

Index